Rethinking Urban Development

Rethinking Urban Development

Exploring Cosmopolitanism and Regionalism in Post-Industrial Cities

(Case of Hyderabad)

Vinita Pandey

RAWAT PUBLICATIONS

Jaipur • New Delhi • Bangalore • Hyderabad • Guwahati • Kolkata

ISBN 978-81-316-0653-7

Published by
Prem Rawat for **Rawat Publications**
Satyam Apts, Sector 3, Jawahar Nagar, Jaipur 302 004 (India)
Phone: 0141 265 1748 / 7006 Fax: 0141 265 1748
E-mail: info@rawatbooks.com
Website: www.rawatbooks.com

New Delhi Office
4858/24, Ansari Road, Daryaganj, New Delhi 110 002
Phone: 011 2326 3290

Also at *Bangalore, Hyderabad, Guwahati* and *Kolkata*

Typeset by Rawat Computers, Jaipur
Printed at Chaman Enterprises, New Delhi

For

Ajay, Yash and **Harsh** – the colours of my life

Contents

Preface

According to 2011 census, about 377 million Indians comprising of about 31 per cent of the country's population, live in urban areas. This is a smaller proportion compared to other large developing countries. This proportion is 45 per cent in China, 54 per cent in Indonesia, 78 per cent in Mexico and 87 per cent in Brazil. With the more rapid growth of the Indian economy in recent years, which is expected to continue, the rate of urbanization is bound to increase. Projections are that by 2031, about 600 million Indians will reside in urban areas, an increase of over 200 million in just 20 years. The accelerated pace of urbanization is leading to steady yet gradual formation of more and more post-industrial cities with a prominent base of service sector which is one of the major contributors to economy and urban development. These cities have quite intense cosmopolitan outlook with people from diverse cultures and backgrounds making these cities their home. However, these cities are geographically part of a region with high passions for regional identity and culture.

In this background of cosmopolitan outlook and rigid (and sometimes obsessed) regional identity in post-industrial cities, urban development assumes significance. Most of the times, urban development is analyzed and assessed in terms of physical and social infrastructure. Interestingly and significantly, social and cultural processes also strongly influence the pace and direction of urban development. In past two decades, globalization had a strong bearing on urban development. It has facilitated relatively easy trans-border movement of people, thus leading to diffusion of material and non-material culture.

With specific reference to Hyderabad, the diffusion of various cultures in Hyderabad has led to a unique way of life in the city which has contributed to further consolidation and development of cosmopolitanism. On the other hand, globalization indirectly has threatened the regional identities of people and places. This has resulted in the people associating with their regional specific identities in a very rigid manner, resulting in increase in regional conflicts world over. There is thus a serious need to rethink the parameters, facilitators and hindrances to urban development. The present work presents the contrasts of cosmopolitanism and regionalism; their influence on urban development and how regionalism in its extreme form leads to regional conflicts.

Cosmopolitanism as a process and philosophy refers to whole world (cosmos) to be one territory. It reflects distinct lifestyle and culture too. Cosmopolitanism has emerged as an important theoretical approach in the social sciences in recent years. Originally, a development within moral and political philosophy concerning a universal orientation towards world principles, it has become increasingly relevant and significant to social science especially in the context of issues relating to globalization and transnational movements of all kinds. Cosmopolitanism suggests a critical attitude as opposed to an exclusively interpretative or descriptive approach to the social world. In many respects, the true inaugurator of modern cosmopolitanism is Immanuel Kant. Kant retained the idea of membership to humanity as a whole by insisting on the importance of 'knowledge of man as a citizen of the world', in his writings on pragmatic anthropology and universal history. Cosmopolitanism in contemporary times is associated with distinct style of living.

A region is a nucleus of social aggregation for a variety of purposes. A particular territory is set apart, over a period of time, when different variables operate in different degrees. These variables may be geography, topography, religion, language, usages and customs, socio-economic and political stages of development, common historical traditions and experiences, a common way of living, and, more than anything else, a widely prevalent sentiment of "togetherness." This togetherness leads to development of regionalism. At the core of regionalism is a profound sense of identity, which is as real, and as dear, to people than their feeling of identity with a state or a nation or a religious group, or a linguistic group.

Regionalism may start in an area which has experienced a rapid growth of educational opportunities for the lower, middle classes, enhancing their aspirations and expectations, but there is a high level of unemployment among the indigenous middle classes, and a substantial proportion of middle class jobs are held by culturally alien migrants. Regionalism in the Indian context, as perhaps elsewhere also, is a nebulous concept. It has both – a positive and a negative dimension. Speaking in positive terms, it embodies a quest for self-fulfillment on the part of the people of an area. It is worthwhile to emphasize that the positive thrust of regionalism has, more often been ignored by political analysis of the Indian situation. Every regional movement thus becomes suspect and is taken as an earnest of the balkanization of the country. Regionalism is a multi-dimensional phenomenon in terms of its components – geographical, historic-cultural, economic, caste and religion, politico-administrative, language and psychic. Regional movements emerge not only for achieving cultural identity, but also for having equal share in nation's economic resources. In India's highly complex regional structure, the national strategy of development with allocation of the cost and benefits of progress must emerge from the coordination and rational cumulation of the needs and goals of different regional units. The phase of development until now has been unavoidably lop-sided. Some parts of the country have become more developed because of industrialization, urbanization, communication, etc. during the plan periods, but other parts of the country have remained neglected and economically poor.

The globalization of economies, migration, culture and communications, combined with a worldwide reassertion of diverse cultural affiliations, are producing intense pressures on the co-existence of different national, ethnic, religious, racial, and linguistic groups who share the same cities. This has its implications on the development process of urban areas.

In cities throughout the world, social tensions and open conflict over region, culture and identity are overwhelming all other aspects of normal urban life thus impacting urban development. The post-industrial cities suffer different degrees of social disintegration and physical destruction, sometimes so severe that the future possibilities for peace, security and sustained urban development cannot be foreseen. The book aims to understand how cosmopolitanism is related with regionalism. Further, it also tries to understand how negatives of extreme regionalism lead to regional conflicts. It is significant to understand whether the cosmopolitanism helps in reducing or exaggerating regional conflicts. Moreover the notions of cosmopolitanism and regionalism are associated with the process of urban development. The study aims to understand the nature of their association and its implications in general and for Hyderabad in particular.

The research study has long-lasting implications. From policy perspective, the research reflects upon the issues of extreme regionalism and its ill-effects on urban development so that efforts can be made to contain it. The urban centres are centres of economic activities and extreme regionalism has the threat of leading to regional conflicts which hampers the development prospects of urban centres. Secondly, from theoretical point of view, this study proposes to present a continuum of cosmopolitanism and regionalism.

The research very clearly proves that regionalism has both positive and negative effects. The negative effects of regionalism can be curtailed only by balanced regional development. As the forces of globalization are becoming prominent, simultaneously cosmopolitanism and regionalism are reflected very prominently in day-to-day living. For instance, when globalization is affecting the regional identities there is greater assertion for the same. On the other hand, globalization has facilitated greater in-migration and out-migration and thus greater exposure to multiple cultures and lifestyles and in turn leading to cosmopolitanism. Interestingly, the study also proves that both forces of cosmopolitanism and regionalism are strongly associated with urban development.

There are six chapters in the book. The first chapter provides an overview of cosmopolitanism and regionalism. It elaborates on various facets of these two concepts. The second chapter talks about Hyderabad and its culture (*tehzeeb*). Since Hyderabad was home to prominent dynasties like Qutub Shahis and Asaf Jahis and impact of French and British is quite visible, this part of Deccan is truly cosmopolitan with multiple threads of cultural diversity. The second part of this chapter deals with methodology and profile of the respondents. The third chapter is on cosmopolitanism in Hyderabad. Hyderabad and Secunderabad, the twin cities fused into one, is a city where north meets south, Islam meets Hinduism and consent meets cosmopolitanism. All the cultures that reigned, left indelible marks and resulted in a unique cultural amalgam, a social blend to which modernism has added its might. The fourth chapter is on cosmopolitanism and urban development. It is vital to note that cosmopolitanism is not merely a philosophy, attitude of universalism, cultural amalgamation but also a catalyst of change and development. With specific reference to Hyderabad, the respondents' views have been sought whether cosmopolitanism has brought about urban development in Hyderabad. The fifth chapter is regionalism and urban development. Regionalism is a multi-dimensional phenomenon, a feeling or sentiment backed by objective factors like language, culture, economic development, etc. The regional movements, especially if separatist in nature, cause economic losses which influences the rate of urban development. The concluding chapter focusses on the major findings and policy implications of the study.

Cosmopolitanism and regionalism are two of the multiple shades and processes of urban development. Since there is no denial of the fact that urban centres are engines of socio-economic growth, it becomes imperative to rethink urban development in post-industrial cities in terms of the process of cosmopolitanism and regionalism.

The book, apart from the primary data, has also attempted to bring detail review of literature to facilitate the readers of diversified viewpoints pertaining to cosmopolitanism and regionalism. When the research was going on, Hyderabad was witnessing the peak of Telangana agitation for a separate Telangana state. Interestingly, when the preface is being written, Hyderabad has been declared the capital of 29th state of India – Telangana which as per the Government of India declaration is being formed on 2 June 2014.

This transition is not only critical but also provides the social scientists with a dynamic socio-economic milieu to explore further the various facets of social reality.

It is very clear from the research that if regionalism is vital to bring people of soil together, cosmopolitanism is critical for the development of that soil. It has been a global experience that urban development greatly depends on investments which are done if there is diversified economy and culture. As homogeneity and heterogeneity are significant in social discussions and milieu despite being contrasting yet complimenting, so are cosmopolitanism and regionalism – the critical weaves of urban development. These processes need further exploration in terms of its grassroot existence, continuity and growth. Thus it would not be an exaggeration to state that there is a need to rethink urban development in terms of these distinct weaves and further explore cosmopolitanism and regionalism.

Acknowledgements

The work 'Rethinking Urban Development: Exploring Cosmopolitanism and Regionalism in Post-Industrial Cities' has been possible primarily due to faith bestowed in me by Indian Council of Social Science Research (ICSSR), New Delhi. This book is the result of my first major research project. The confidence of ICSSR and selection committee gave me the courage to go ahead with the project. I shall remain indebted to every personnel from ICSSR who encouraged me for the project and later on for its publication.

I am extremely thankful to Mr Ajay Kumar Pandey for his continuous association with the project. He has been the foundation support right from its inception to submission and to its publication. The work done by Mr Krishna Murthy and Mr.Sadhak Navdeep Bharat is highly appreciable. Ms Sarita and Mr Mahesh were very much instrumental in data collection. My gratitude to Mr Ashwin Kumar, who helped me with data entry and analysis. I miss Kiran Tadepalli who was very excited about this project, but today he is not amidst us. My gratitude to all the faculty members of Department of Sociology, Nizam College and University College of Arts and Social Sciences, Osmania University.

Further, I sincerely express my gratitude to all the respondents who cooperated immensely in data collection. To understand the ethos of Hyderabad, the insights put forward by the respondents have been instrumental. This work would not have been possible without constant support from my family and blessings of my beloved grandparents. My thanks are also due to Mr Pranit Rawat for taking interest in the manuscript and encouraging its publication. Above all, I shall always remain indebted to divinity whose divine interventions has kept me going despite all hurdles.

Vinita Pandey

1 Cosmopolitanism and Regionalism

Concept and Overview

Human settlements form a pattern which is to a large extent the consequence of the social, economic and technological level of development at a point in time in the long process of the evolution of settlements. Thus, human settlements have undergone a long process of change, both structural and functional, from the primitive distribution based on food gathering, to the complex service-based facilities. New industry formations, the 'new' service economy and post-industrial urban landscapes – these now-familiar coinages – suggest a break from the past both in terms of employment, production and spatial practices, urban policy, cultural patterns and social living.

In the aftermath of globalization, with relatively easy trans-border movement of people, there is diffusion of material and non-material culture. With specific reference to Hyderabad, the diffusion of various cultures in Hyderabad has led to a unique way of life in cities which has contributed to further *consolidation and development of cosmopolitanism*. On the other hand, globalization indirectly has threatened the regional identities of people and places. This has resulted in the people associating with their regional specific identities in a very rigid manner resulting in increase in regional conflicts world over. The present research study tries to present the contrasts between cosmopolitanism and regionalism: their influence on urban development and how regionalism in its extreme form leads to regional conflicts.

Cosmopolitanism

Cosmopolitanism as a process and philosophy refers to whole world (cosmos) to be one territory. It reflects distinct lifestyle and culture too. Cosmopolitanism has emerged as an important theoretical approach in the social sciences in recent years. Originally, a development within moral and political philosophy concerning a universal orientation towards world principles, it has become increasingly relevant and significant to social science especially in the context of issues relating to globalization and transnational movements of all kinds. Cosmopolitanism suggests a critical attitude as opposed to an exclusively interpretative or descriptive approach to the social world.

d'Alembert's entry in the *Encyclopédie* notes that 'cosmopolitan' derives from the Greek words for 'world' (*cosmos*) and 'city' (*polis*) and that it refers to '*un homme qui n'a point de demeure fixe, ou bien un homme qui n'est étranger nulle part* (a man without a fixed abode, or better, a man who is nowhere a stranger)' (Diderot and d'Alembert, 1751–65: 4, 297). The term's philosophical usage to indicate a 'citizen of the universe', however, emphasizes that this intellectual ethos or spirit is not one of rootlessness. Instead, what is imagined is a universal circle of belonging that involves the transcendence of the particularistic and blindly given ties of kinship and country. The cosmopolitan, therefore, embodies and is inclusive of the universality and power of transcending the particular and contingent. Hence, the popular view of cosmopolitanism as an elite form of rootlessness and a state of detachment and nomadic non-belonging is mistaken. The cosmopolitan's universal circle of belonging embraces the whole of humanity.

Rousseau lamented that in relations between different societies, the law of nature, or natural piety, the original root of social virtues such as clemency and humanity, has lost almost all the force it had in the relations between one man and another, (and) lives on only in the few great cosmopolitan souls (*grandes âmes cosmopolites*) who cross the imaginary boundaries that separate people and, following the example of the sovereign being that created them, embrace the whole of mankind in their benevolence (1766: 174).

Cosmopolitanism has been equated to transnationalism by many experts. However, cosmopolitanism is not simply reducible to transnationalism, although transnationalism is an important precondition of cosmopolitan orientations. To speak of cosmopolitanism is to refer to a transformation in self-understanding as a result of the engagement with others over issues of global significance. It is concerned with identifying processes of self-transformation arising out of the encounter with others in the context of global concerns.

When we speak of 'others', a major challenge today is the development of dialogue across different (other) cultural groups. When different national interests come into play, difficulties in developing cooperation and dialogue increases. Overcoming major political and cultural divisions is one of the most challenging tasks of the present day.

Cosmopolitanism is not a European or universal western condition but occurs in a variety of societal forms. There are European and Asian expressions of cosmopolitanism, a term that can be taken to be a concern with global principles of justice and the need to take into account the perspective of the other. Until now, the dominant conceptions of cosmopolitan have focused on universal justice, identifying cosmopolitanism with a universal normative order.

Immanuel Kant (1724–1804) on Cosmopolitanism

In many respects, the true inaugurator of modern cosmopolitanism is Immanuel Kant. Kant retained the idea of membership to humanity as a whole by insisting on the importance of 'knowledge of man as a citizen of the world' in his writings on pragmatic anthropology and universal history (1968a: 400).

The history of cosmopolitanism is categorized into two major phases: that of Stoical reflection on the city of the universe (*cosmo-polis*) in distinction to the Athenian and Roman empires and, after the demise of Christendom and natural law theory, the re-emergence of cosmopolitanism in the Enlightenment thought of Immanuel Kant. Particular to the cosmopolitan outlook are the subordination of politics to morality, the moral contingency of borders and, after Kant, the foregrounding of the dignity of the moral person. The cosmopolitan tradition leads to a spectrum of cosmopolitan reflection in contemporary thought. At one end, *moral cosmopolitanism* stresses the contingency of political borders, foregrounds moral action in the name of humanity, and focuses on education and culture as the sites of cosmopolitan evolution and reform.

Kant is of the opinion that moral cosmopolitanism becomes *normative* and *institutional* when the ethical principles of human equality are recast as the normative, regulative horizon of political action, and institutional implementation of these principles is looked for at the supranational level. Forming part of institutional cosmopolitanism, *legal cosmopolitanism* focuses specifically on the legal mediation between morality. Finally, at the far end of the spectrum, *political cosmopolitanism* focuses on the democratic deficit in post-national relations, arguing that current international political institutions need to be embedded within sites of global democratic accountability.

However, Kant was primarily concerned with man as a practical being and actor in history, someone who not only knows the world as a spectator of a play but knows his way about the world as a participant (ibid.). A world-citizen acts from the pluralistic standpoint of humanity as a collective actor, as opposed to that of an egoistic individual (ibid.: 411). Accordingly, Kant articulated at least four different modalities of cosmopolitanism that would become the main topic of contemporary discussions of the concept in normative international relations theory (including accounts of global civil society and the international public sphere), liberal political economy and theories of globalization. These different modalities, which are part of a systemic whole, are: (1) a world federation as the legal and political institutional basis for cosmopolitanism as a form of right; (2) the historical basis of cosmopolitanism in world trade; (3) the idea of a global public sphere; and (4) the importance of cosmopolitan culture in instilling a sense of belonging to humanity.

What Kant calls 'a universal *cosmopolitan existence*' is nothing less than the *regulative idea* of 'a perfect civil union of mankind' (1968b: 47). It is a constitutional global federation of all existing states that is based on *cosmopolitan right*, in so far as individuals and states, coexisting in an external relationship of mutual influences, may be regarded as citizens of a universal state of mankind (1968e: 203). Although it would not possess the coercive means of enforcement available to a world-state, it would nevertheless be a legitimately institutionalized world community, able to make rightful claims on its constituent states regarding their treatment of individuals and other states. Individual states would retain their sovereignty, but would be held accountable by a universal citizenry – humanity – with regard to issues such as disarmament and imperialist expansion.

In Kant's view, world trade provided the historical basis of cosmopolitan unity. As the spirit of commerce spreads throughout the world, states find that it is in their self-interest to enter into a world federation to prevent war and violence because these deplete their financial power (ibid.: 226). Moreover, the unity brought about by trade and other forms of encounter between countries creates something like a global public sphere that will safeguard cosmopolitan right by protesting any violations of it in the same manner that a critical national public sphere safeguards the rights of citizens, vis-à-vis the territorial state: the peoples of the earth have thus entered in varying degrees into a universal community, and it has developed to the point where a violation of rights in *one* part of the world is felt *everywhere*. The idea of a cosmopolitan right is therefore not fantastic or overstrained; it is a necessary complement to the unwritten code of political and international right, transforming it into a public right of humanity (ibid.: 216–17).

In addition, forms of culture also instil a deeper subjective sense of cosmopolitan solidarity or the feeling of belonging to humanity by encouraging universal social communication and sympathy. The fine arts and the sciences play a crucial role in developing our humanity because they involve 'a universally communicable pleasure' (1968c: 83, 321). The humanities cultivate our mental powers by instilling in us the universal feeling of sympathy, and the ability to engage universally in very intimate communication. When these two qualities are combined, they constitute the sociability that befits humanity and distinguishes it from the limitation of animals (ibid.: 60, 300).

For Kant, the people are defined by the state. 'It is absurd', he suggests, 'to speak of the majesty of a people as a reason for war'. It is the majesty of a state that leads a ruler 'to order thousands of people to immolate themselves for a cause that does not truly concern them' (ibid.: 209). This means that Kant's cosmopolitanism is not opposed to nationalism but to absolutist statism. His vision is formulated prior to the spread of popular nationalism in

Europe; the period between 1825 and 1831 where nationality, in search of statehood, emerges for the first time as the primary basis of revolution. This period saw the rise of Greek, Belgian and Polish nationalist movements, first aroused by the Napoleonic invasion, and now rebelling against their Ottoman, Dutch, and Russian governments for the primary reason that these were foreign regimes. Formulated too early to take into account the role of nationalism in the transition between the age of absolutism and the age of liberalism, Kant's cosmopolitanism is more a philosophical republicanism and federalism designed to reform the absolutist dynastic state than a theory opposing the modern theory of nationality. Indeed, because Kant writes at a time when the phenomenon and concept of 'the nation' is still at an embryonic stage, he points out that the Right of Peoples or Nations is a misnomer since it actually refers to the lawful relation of states to one another. (1968d: 53, 466).

Karl Marx (1818–1883) on Cosmopolitanism

In the history of ideas, the notorious tensions between nationalism and cosmopolitanism becomes more apparent from Marx onwards. Marx, while categorizing the history of mankind into four main epochs, writes extensively about capitalist stage which he divides in to two main classes – Bourgeoisie and Proletariat. For Marx, proletarian cosmopolitanism is no longer just a normative horizon of world history or a matter of right growing out of international commerce. It is a necessary and existing form of solidarity grounded in the global exploitation that has resulted from the global development of forces of production. According to Cheah (2006a), in stark contrast to Kant's vision of cosmopolitanism, Marx's characterization of the nation and its appendages – national economy, industry, and culture – in naturalistic and primordial terms in the *Manifesto of the Communist Party* (1848) indicates that a significant sense of national belonging had already developed (Marx and Engels, 1932). But the nation is a false natural community, an ideological construction that masks the class interests of less developed bourgeois states such as the various German states and obscures the truly cosmopolitan essence of economic activity and civil society. Because economic activity transcends territorial borders, modern civil society is inherently cosmopolitan. The modern civil society embraces the whole commercial and industrial life of a given stage and, insofar, transcends the state and the nation. On the other hand again, it must assert itself in its external relations as nationality and internally must organise itself as a state (ibid.: 1932: 25–26).

The proletarian revolution must be directed against the national state because it contradicts the unbounded nature of civil society qua medium and form of economic activity. Because universal exploitation creates a universal class in advanced countries that has been dispossessed and freed of any illusions by utter poverty, the bourgeois ideology of 'humanity' will be demystified and bourgeois cosmopolitanism will be sublated (assimilated into a bigger entity) and replaced by the cosmopolitan solidarity of the proletariat. Marx's proletarian cosmopolitanism is thus different from Kant's pre-nationalist cosmopolitanism.

Marx's socialist cosmopolitanism is an anti- and post-nationalism that reduces the nation to an ideological instrument of the state. He dismissed nationalism although he witnessed its rise. Identifying the nation too hastily with the bourgeois state, Marx reduced the nation to an ideological instrument of the state and saw nationalism as a tendentious (promote a particular cause) invocation of anachronistic quasi feudal forms of belonging in modernity. However, this antagonistic relation between socialist cosmopolitanism and nationalism has almost never been maintained from a historical-practical standpoint. The uneven character of capitalism as an actually existing global system implies an irreducible disparity between the working class in different parts of the world. This has repeatedly posed obstacles for the formation of a global proletarian consciousness or world community based on labour. The national question was most notably raised in response to anti-colonialist struggles in Asia and Africa. In the historical scene of decolonization, it is not only the material economic wealth that workers have produced that needs to be reappropriated. The nation's spiritual or cultural personality has been taken away by territorial imperialism and continues to be expropriated (seized) by neo-colonial forces (Cheah, 2006b).

To remove the *nation* from the global circuit of property and commodification so that its people can have access to the products of their labour, the people must first achieve or regain their rightful cultural *personality*, which imperialism has violently usurped.

Theories of new cosmopolitanism are essentially syntheses of three different arguments, which can be found in different combinations. First, it is suggested that cultural and political solidarity and political agency can no longer be restricted to the sovereign nation-state as a unified spatio-temporal container because globalization has undermined many of the key functions from which the nation-state derives its legitimacy. Second, the various material networks of globalization are said to have formed a world that is interconnected enough to generate political institutions and non-governmental organizations that have a global reach in their regulatory functions as well as global forms of mass-based political consciousness or popular feelings of belonging to a shared world. Third, this new cosmopolitan consciousness is characterized as a more expansive form of solidarity that is attuned to democratic principles and human interests without the restriction of territorial borders. In some cases, it is also suggested that the new cosmopolitan consciousness is in a relation of mutual feedback with emerging global institutions, taking root and finding sustenance from these institutions and influencing their functioning in turn.

Cosmopolitanism and Globalization

There are several implications of a cosmopolitanism arising from the social experience of globalization and global cities – a cosmopolitan corporate work culture, the sophisticated consumption patterns of this high-income bracket, and the global culture of its growing immigrant population from the Third World. The cosmopolitanism of corporate workers is essentially the cosmopolitanism of a new technocratic professional class whose primary aim in life are making a profit and conspicuous consumption. The only feelings of solidarity that manifest here are to the global firm as a terrain for professional self-interest and advancement. This type of attachment is gradually disseminated throughout the world by the global outsourcing of white-collar jobs, which in turn establishes more bridges for higher-end migration. This also facilitates greater interaction and assimilation of multiple cultures which contribute to cosmopolitanism.

What is missing from interpretations of new cosmopolitanism in the softer social sciences and cultural studies is a thorough discussion of the normative implications of globalization, or more precisely the relationship between universality or weaker normative forms of wide inclusivity and the global extensiveness of economic, political, and cultural processes. There are, however, more recent arguments that suggest that contemporary post-Cold War human rights regimes, other emergent transnational legal and political institutions, and the international civil society of NGOs constitute a contemporary revival and updated affirmation of Kant's vision of cosmopolitanism. Among these arguments, that of the German philosopher, Jürgen Habermas, is the most sophisticated. For Habermas, the curse of globalization turns out to be a blessing in disguise. In his view, globalization is not reducible to global capitalism, but has relatively autonomous cultural and political aspects that create the conditions for transcendence/sublation, whereby the earlier national shell that imprisoned democratic republicanism will be destroyed and its kernel or truth-content, preserved in the form of deliberative democratic procedures, will rise up, phoenix-like, to a higher supranational state of existence (Cheah, 2006b).

Habermas's cosmopolitan vision consists of a dynamic complex of interconnected public spheres at both the national and transnational level rather than a world organization. Nussbaum admits that being a citizen of the world is 'a kind of exile – from the comfort of local truths, from the warm, nestling feeling of patriotism, from the absorbing drama of pride in oneself and one's own' (1996: 15). Barber (1996: 24) seizes on this weakness of the cosmopolitan imagination by emphasizing that people tend to develop attachments and a sense of belonging to specific and tangible rather than abstract things: 'we live in this particular neighbourhood of the world, that block, this valley, that seashore, this family. Our attachments start parochially (with narrow outlook) and only then grow outward'. For Barber, our capacity to develop immediacy-transcending values must not be severed from our capacity to feel comfortable in a particular place. Barber's position echoes Hannerz's (1990: 239) claim that 'there can be no cosmopolitans without locals'.

When Cheah discusses d'Alembert's entry on 'cosmopolitan' in the *Encyclopédie* he maintains that the reference to universality does not necessarily imply rootlessness. Instead, cosmopolitanism entails 'a universal circle of belonging that involves the transcendence of the particularistic and blindly given ties of kinship and country' (Cheah, 2006b: 478).

Cosmopolitanism and Nation-State with Reference to Durkheim, Weber and Simmel

Several opinions have been expressed with reference to cosmopolitanism and nation-state. Bryan S. Turner (2006) suggests that the concern of classical sociology was never simply national societies, but 'the social' more generally, always understood by the classical sociologists as a transnational phenomenon. Turner (2006: 137) shows, for example, how Parsons' work on the social was never conducted simply through the lens of national societies, but ranged through dyadic relationships, (e.g., doctor and patient), social groups and their leadership, and the sociology of international relations (Parsons, 1937, 1971). Parsons is interested in how the social ranges across various 'social systems', and was alive to the idea that these social systems might have a variety of salient 'boundaries' (so, for example, the business firms that he analysed as part of the 'adaptation' functions were understood as operating globally rather than nationally.

In particular, Durkheim's (1992) detailed account of the struggle between the nationalist-patriotic and the world-patriotic moral viewpoints is one in which Durkheim's cosmopolitan inclinations and receptiveness are on display, and in which it is evident that Durkheim's notion of society is not one limited by the container of the (French or any other) nation-state (Beck, 1992). The two excerpts from his *Professional Ethics and Civic Morals* suggest that, societies are becoming ever greater in scale and ever more complex: they are made up of circles of increasing diversity, and of manyfold agencies, and these already possess in themselves a value to be reckoned. Therefore, if it is to fulfil its function, the State, too, must branch out and evolve to the same degree (Durkheim, 1992: 65–66).

The classical sociologists like Parsons and Durkheim attempted an analysis of the social, and this social was never understood as simply contained by the practices of the nation-state. Parsons' work, as Turner (2006: 139) says is a contribution to the analysis of civilizational processes, and the 'systems'. Parsons analysis was never simply national in character. Durkheim's plea for cosmopolitanism – a desire for new forms of universal moral individualism which could be substituted for dangerous forms of national patriotism – emerged from his understanding of the social as so much more than simply a series of outcrops of national processes. Durkheim's proposed cosmopolitan solution connected to forms of 'universal moral consciousness' – a phrase that we might use as a rough definition of what he meant by the social.

Even Max Weber's work might reasonably be understood as a contribution to the emergence of culture and cultural values, and, even though the term 'cosmopolitanism' is not directly used by Weber, his work analyses the constant interconnection between cultures. In *The Protestant Ethic and Spirit of Capitalism,* Max Weber writes 'The rationalization of private law was achieved in the highest hitherto known degree in the Roman Law of late antiquity. But it remained most backward in some of the countries with the highest degree of economic rationalization, notably in England, where the Renaissance of Roman Law was overcome by the power of the great legal corporations, while it has always retained its supremacy in the Catholic countries of Southern Europe … . (I)f under practical rationalism is understood the type of attitude which sees and judges the world consciously in terms of the worldly interests of the individual ego, then this view of life was and is the special peculiarity of the peoples of the liberum arbitrium, such as the Italians and French are in very flesh and blood' (2001: 37–38).

In this short section, Weber does not shun a discussion of national characteristics and the forms of cultural, political and legal life peculiar to England and southern Europe. In doing so, he does not lose sight how elements of the phenomenon of rationalization might be repeated in different geographical locations. Weber highlights the transnational phenomenon of Roman Law as well as the role played by sub- and inter-national actors such as legal corporations, and the very localized influence of the Augustinian concept of free will. For Weber, the nation-state was the limit of his thinking about society.

George Simmel, another of the major classical sociologists, who contributed to our understanding of how culture circulates around the social, characterized as a complex interweaving of cosmopolitan entities. Two of the many themes that he developed are extraordinarily redolent of contemporary cosmopolitan scholarship. First, Simmel often dwells on the theme of the social as a variety of associations; like Durkheim, Simmel was appalled (dismayed) by the growth of egoistic and individualistic culture, and saw some higher purpose in the various associations individuals enter into (Simmel, 1949). Second, and relatedly, he develops the theme of exchange as fundamental to modern forms of the social. Simmel (2004) says money is analysed as an exchange mechanism. This exchange mechanism simultaneously erodes some of the forms of individuality of the pre-modern world and fosters a kind of cosmopolitan culture in which every individual's world becomes 'networked' with more, and further-flung, people and objects. The money economy makes possible a specific kind of mutual dependence, which affords room for a maximum of liberty. It creates a series of previously unknown obligations. Dependency upon third persons has spread into completely new areas. Essentially the evolution and consolidation of cosmopolitanism is owing to greater dependence on technology. Dependence on technology also leads to greater dependence on others.

The general tendency, however, undoubtedly moves in the direction of making the individual more and more dependent upon the achievements of people, but less and less dependent upon the personalities that lie behind them. Compared with modern man, the member of a traditional or primitive economy is dependent only upon a minimum of other persons (Simmel, 2004: 295–98). Here, Simmel recalls Durkheim's emphasis upon the modern division of labour, but his emphasis is on interconnection and exchange, as well as the more Durkheimian anomie.

Nussbaum is of the opinion that there are moral bases for politics and each individual should feel primary loyalty to humanity rather than localness (Calhoun, 2003: 538–39). Nussbaum implies a moral and logical necessity of cosmopolitan transcendence. This necessity is logically contingent on a normative framework but it is also non-sociological. Nussbaum says the formation of judgments and the politics of practice are inevitably burdened by the nature of a particular individual's location in the context of groups and institutions, but they are also dependent on identities that are performed by, or attributed to, this person. One does not become cosmopolitan in a vacuum.

Cosmopolitanism and Nationalism

Given that nationalism and cosmopolitanism are often seen as natural enemies, it may seem surprising to try to develop a conciliatory position between the two. The mutually incompatible nature of cosmopolitanism and nationalism has been referred to, following Turner (2000: 27–29), as a distinction between cold and hot loyalty to a community (Nash, 2003). Nationalism's association with hot emotions is well attested. In contrast, cosmopolitanism is seen as suitably dry, cool, ironic and largely deprived of any capacity to emotionalize and lead people into action. Clearly, the key issue in terms of the relationship between nationalism and cosmopolitanism is not the things that separate them but the various continuities that can be drawn between them. Habermas's project of constitutional cosmopolitanism is useful precisely because of its underlying ambition simultaneously to harmonize cosmopolitan institutions and reaffirm national identity (cf. Fine, 2003: 462). On the other hand, it is important to emphasize the changing nature of the state as a social institution.

Cosmopolitan Sociology

While defining 'Cosmopolitan Sociology', Ulrich Beck says: 'Let me start by attempting to nail a pudding to the wall, that is, defining the key terms "globalization" and "cosmopolitanization"'. At the beginning of the 21st century the human condition cannot be understood nationally or locally but only globally. 'Globalization' is a non-linear, dialectic process in which the global and the local do not exist as cultural polarities but as combined and mutually implicating principles. These processes involve not only interconnections across boundaries, but transform the quality of the social and the political *inside* nation-state societies. This is what Beck defines as 'cosmopolitanization': Cosmopolitanization means *internal* globalization, globalization *from within* the national societies. This transforms everyday consciousness and identities significantly. Issues of global concern are becoming part of the everyday local experiences and the 'moral life-worlds' of the people. They introduce significant conflicts all over the world.

For Ulrich Beck (2002c) the 'cosmopolitanization thesis' is a methodological concept which helps to overcome methodological nationalism and to build a frame of reference to analyse the new social conflicts, dynamics and structures. The central defining characteristic of a cosmopolitan perspective is the '*dialogic* imagination'. By this Beck means the clash of cultures and rationalities within one's own life, the '*internalized* other'. The dialogic imagination corresponds to the coexistence of rival ways of life in the individual experience, which makes it a matter of fate to compare, reflect, criticize, understand and combine contradictory certainties. It was Friedrich Nietzsche who spoke in this sense of 'the Age of Comparison'. He meant not only that the individual was free to pick and choose among competing traditions and heritages but even more significant was that the various cultures of the world were beginning to interpenetrate each other. And he foresaw this process continuing, until ideas of every culture would be side by side, in combination, comparison, contradiction and competition in every place and all the time.

'Cosmopolitanism' means – as Immanuel Kant argued 200 years ago – being a citizen of two worlds – 'cosmos' and 'polis'. There are five different dimensions to this, distinguishing between external and internal otherness. Externally it means:

(a) Including the otherness of *nature*;
(b) Including the otherness of *other civilizations and modernities*; and
(c) Including the otherness of the *future*;
Internally it means:
(d) Including the otherness of the *object*; and
(e) Overcoming the (state) mastery of (scientific, linear) rationalization.

Cosmopolitanism is a large, ancient, rich and controversial set of political ideas, philosophies and ideologies. It remains in part an ideological construct, and as such it has the abstract, even artificial atmosphere that Heinrich Heine described as the 'kingdom of the air'. Cosmopolitanization, on the other hand, is a frame of reference for empirical exploration for globalization *from within*, globalization *internalized*. It is a kind of class analysis, which takes on board globalization. Like class analysis, as Marx proposed it, it combines a descriptive analysis of social structure with the assumption that this analysis gives us a key to understand the political dynamics and conflicts of globalized social worlds.

A cosmopolitan sociology imposes fundamental questions of redefinition, reinvention and reorganization. The challenges are related to two fundamental processes: globalization and individualization. The globalization debate took up the territorial bias; the individualization debate has probed and criticized the collective bias of the social sciences (Beck and Beck-Gernsheim, 2002). For a cosmopolitan sociology Beck says '... a tiny question remains to be answered: how to research the global? Isn't the total global, let's say, a bit too global? And would a sociology of the global not necessarily transform sociology into philosophy and metaphysics *without* any systematic empirical reference for falsification? So the question has to be positioned and answered: how is an empirical sociology of the global becoming possible?'

The answers are becoming imminent especially with globalization making its presence more prominent. According to Beck there is a simple answer to this question, but this answer is blocked by common images and misunderstandings of globalization. They are paradoxes of globalization. The first is that globalization is about globalization. This isn't true. Globalization is about localization as well. Globalization should also be referred in connection to specific locations and places. One of the important consequences of the globalization is the recovering of the concept of place. It is global-local dialectics which Robert Robertson has in mind when he talks about 'glocalization'. The implication for empirical sociology is that glocalization happens not out there, but in here. Therefore Sociology can investigate the global locally. As Saskia Sassen's (2000) work shows, this has significant implications for the analysis and theorization of cities: not the city as a bounded territorialized unit, but the city as a node in a grid of cross-boundary processes. Further, this type of globalized city cannot be located simply in a hierarchical scale that places it beneath the national, regional and global. It is one of the spaces of the global, and it engages the global *directly*, often bypassing the national. This work becomes clearer if we pick up a second misunderstanding of globalization, which sees it as an additive and not substitutive aspect of nation-state society and sociological imagination. In the globalization discourse it is often assumed that globalization only changes the relation between and beyond national states and societies (interconnectedness), but not the inner quality of the social and political itself (cosmopolitanization).

But globalization includes globalization *from within*, globalization *internalized*, or, as Beck prefers to say, 'cosmopolitanization of nation-state societies'. The national has to be rediscovered as the *internalized global*. As Saskia Sassen puts it: 'Of particular interest here is the implied correspondence of national territory to the national, and the associated implication that the national and the non-national are two mutually exclusive conditions'.

Sassen argues that one of the features of the current face of globalization is the fact that a process, which happens within a territory of sovereign state, does not necessarily mean that it is a national process. Conversely, the national (such as firms, capital, culture) may increasingly be located outside the national territory, for instance, in a foreign country or digital spaces. This localization of the global, or of the non-national, in national territories, and of the national outside national territories, undermined a key duality running through many of the methods and conceptual frameworks prevalent in social sciences, that the national and the non-national are mutually exclusive (Sassen, 2000: 145ff.). If we want to distinguish between a methodological nationalism and a methodological cosmopolitanism we not only have to solve the new problem of beginning – there is also the problem of redefining the sociological frame of reference. If we want to do this for the purpose of empirical research, there are two concepts in the making: *Interconnectedness*: beautifully explained and empirically rich, as expressed in the work of David Held and his colleagues, especially their latest book, *Global Transformations* (1999). But this idea of interconnectedness somehow still presupposes the territorial unit of states and state societies, that are becoming more and more interconnected and networked. And, keeping in mind global inequalities, 'interconnectedness' is a semantic euphemism.

The new metaphor of the *fluid* that flows, neither boundaries nor relations mark the difference between one place and another. Instead, sometimes boundaries come and go, while relations transform themselves without fracture. Then, social space behaves like a fluid (Mol and Law, 1994: 643). But the very suggestiveness of the powerful metaphor of the 'fluid' begs the question of whether 'networks' and 'flows' as social processes can be so independent of national, transnational and political-economic structures that enable, channel and control the flows of people, things and ideas. In other words: there is a lack of institutional (power) structures, sometimes even an anti-institutionalism involved in the powerful cultural research and theory about 'fluids' and 'mobility' (Urry, 2000).

Dilemmas of Cosmopolitanism

Beck puts forward the dilemmas of cosmopolitanism (Beck, 2002a).

Universalist-pluralist dilemma: This is the crunch question: is there a *single* cosmopolitanism or *several* cosmopolitanisms? Universalist cosmopolitanism, that dream of 'a worldwide community of humankind', as Immanuel Kant, but also Karl Popper and many others dreamed of, is open – like all other universalisms – to the indictment of imperialism (Hacohen, 1999). There is not one language of cosmopolitanism, but many languages, tongues, grammars. The emerging significance of cosmopolitanism is about a plurality of antagonisms and differences. Cosmopolitanism, indeed, is another word for disputing about cosmopolitanisms.

Ulrich Beck suggests three characteristics – *globality, plurality* and *civility*, that is, the awareness of a global sphere of responsibility, the acknowledgement of the otherness of others and non-violence – as defining features of a 'de-territorialized' concept of cosmopolitanism. The concept stands for openness to the world and for plurality.

Ethnic dilemma: All attempts to open up the ethnic ghetto, to play down or extinguish ethnicity and racism, only appear to reinforce them. Indeed, to feel oneself as part of a cosmopolitan community and to declare one's position publicly can be turned into its opposite by others' violent ethnic definitions of what is alien.

Global-local dilemma: Cosmopolitanisms throw up the diasporas question – how being-at-home without being at home, be possible? This question has often been misunderstood in such a way that social tension and division arise between *cosmopolitans* and *locals*. The former are rooted in *no* place, the latter in *one* place. But as John Tomlinson (1999) argues, the cosmopolitan cannot be opposed to the local in terms of ideal types. Cosmopolitan forms of life and identities are ones that are ethically and culturally *simultaneously* global and local. They symbolize an 'ethical glocalism' or, as I call it, a rooted cosmopolitanism (Beck, 2002b). The difference between purely local and cosmopolitan forms of life is that cosmopolitans experience and – if necessary – defend their place as one open to the world.

The multicultural dilemma: What distinguishes the world of ideas of cosmopolitanism from that of 'multiculturalism'? Multiculturalism attempts – as Mario Vargas Llosa writes – to make permanent that miracle in which dog, cat and mouse eat from the same plate. Multiculturalism, for all its assertion of a world of variety and of the principle of plurality, fosters a collective image of humanity in which the individual remains dependent on his cultural sphere. He (or she) is the product of the language, the traditions, the convictions, the customs and landscapes in which he came into the world and in which he grew up, so that this 'homeland' is regarded as a closed, self-sufficient and sacrosanct unity, which must be protected against every possible threat against imperialism and also against those forces, such as miscegenation, internationalization and cosmopolitanism, undermining the national spirit. In this sense, multiculturalism is at loggerheads with individualization. According to the multicultural premise, the individual does not exist. He is a mere epiphenomenon of his culture.

The constructivism-realism dilemma: The 'cosmopolitan perspective' is an anti-essentialist perspective. The conception of cultures as homogeneous unities of language, origin and political identity, as maintained by methodological nationalism, is the exact opposite of the cosmopolitan self-conception. Characteristic of the latter are concepts like *transnational*, *transcultural*, *hybrid*, *diaspora*, etc. In other words, the fundamental conviction of constructivism – the idea, that collective identities are historically invented and constructed *imagined communities* – is central.

International law – human rights dilemma: Human rights, which are also asserted in international law, that is, against the sovereignty of individual states, are a kind of civil religion of modern cosmopolitanism. On the other hand, this transnational humanism can easily turn into a *military humanism*, which – as in the Kosovo War – also provides the Western nations and Allied states with a kind of 'cosmopolitan mission', but also with legitimation for military crusades under the banner of human rights. This dilemma can, ultimately, only be resolved in the spirit of Kant by a transnational legal order, which, among other things, excludes the possibility of interventions being decided and carried out unilaterally by the hegemonic military power and its allies.

Ulrich Beck speaks about three hostile forces to cosmopolitanism: first of all nationalism, second, globalism and third, democratic authoritarianism.

Nationalism

Beck says nationalism has taken shape as the remaining real danger to the culture of political freedom at the beginning of the 21st century. It is a revived anti-cosmopolitan nationalism which could give the sectarian acts of violence and eccentricities of extremists a terrible legitimation. If the nation-state paradigm of societies is breaking up from the inside, then that leaves a space for the renaissance and renewal of all kinds of cultural, political and religious movements. What has to be understood, above all, is the *ethnic globalization contradictions*. At a time when the world is growing closer together and becoming more cosmopolitan, in which, therefore, the borders and barriers between nations and ethnic groups are being lifted, ethnic identities and divisions are becoming stronger once again.

In every corner of the world, ethnic groups are fighting for recognition of the 'right to self-determination'. It must also be added that globophobia, whatever the specific motivation, is ultimately grist to the mill of ethnic reaction. And, although there are undoubtedly very diverse manifestations of nationalism, of varying significance, in different parts of the world, there are, nevertheless, common basic features, in particular that *metaphysical essentialism of the 'nation'*. These features inevitably give rise to those consequences which made the 20th century one of modernized barbarism.

Globalism

According to the *Oxford American Dictionary,* globalism is the advocacy of 'the interpretation or planning of economic and foreign policy in relation to events and developments throughout the world'. In its most extreme forms it is sometimes expressed using terms such as 'one world,' support for a single world government, and/or terms such as 'world citizen' or 'global citizen.' Some globalist groups such as the World Federalist Movement, and some non-Christian religions such as Bahai, actively campaign for world government. 'Global' is a currently fashionable term in business, where the term 'international' would be more appropriate usage; the term 'international' implies business operations between a few countries, while 'global' implies worldwide business, making it an adequate term for some forms of business that do operate across the world. Many aspects of globalism fall under the umbrella of globalization, which refers to how local phenomena can become global phenomena.

Democratic Authoritarianism

It would be a serious mistake to underestimate the degree to which the modern state has been weakened with respect to its material room for manoeuvre and its democratic qualities, but at the same time has been newly empowered with respect to authoritarian possibilities of action. The potential for achieving consensus in a democratic manner is diminishing. However, the state's capacity to enforce decisions – the combined operation of force, law and information technological control *internally* – is being modernized and increased. In other words, it has become possible to compensate for the loss of democratic power by authoritarian means – while preserving the democratic facade. That is what is meant by democratic authoritarianism. The Communist Manifesto was published 150 years ago. Today, at the beginning of a new millennium, it is time for a Cosmopolitan Manifesto (Beck, 1998). The key idea for a *Cosmopolitan Manifesto* is that we live in an age that is at once global, individualistic and more moral than we suppose. Now we must unite to create an effective cosmopolitan world politics. There is a new dialectic of global and local questions, which do not fit into national politics. These questions are already part of the political agenda – in the localities and regions, in governments and public spheres both national and international. But only in a transnational framework can they be properly posed, debated and resolved. For this there has to be reinvention of politics, a founding and grounding of the new political subject: that is – cosmopolitan parties. These represent transnational interests transnationally, but also work within the arenas of national politics. They thus become possible, both pragmatically and organizationally, only as national–global movements and cosmopolitan parties. How can cosmopolitan parties become possible and powerful? In the end this question can be answered only where people ask and listen to it – in the space of political experimentation.

With globalization making its presence stronger, the cities world over are witnessing cosmopolitanism especially the cultural cosmopolitanism. Cosmopolitan cities are multicultural in nature with greater economic interdependence. It shows assimilation of various cultures leading to a distinct lifestyle of the people. Cosmopolitanism seems to be a contrasting concept to Regionalism. Let us discuss about region and regionalism and how it manifests in the Indian context.

Regionalism

A region is a nucleus of social aggregation for a variety of purposes. A particular territory is set apart, over a period of time, when different variables operate in different degrees. These variables may be geography, topography, religion, language, usages and customs, socio-economic and political stages of development, common historical traditions and experiences, a common way of living, and, more than anything else, a widely prevalent sentiment of togetherness. This togetherness leads to development of regionalism. At the core of regionalism is a profound sense of identity, which is as real, and as dear, to a people than their feeling of identity with a state or a nation or a religious group, or a linguistic group. These are cultural realities and one cannot wish them away (Shriram, 1973: 442).

Regional autonomy demands treating regions as coherent units politically, having a right to reflect the constituents' aspirations to manage their internal affairs, while making claims on national resources, in competition with other regions. In this competition for resources, language, culture, religion, economic advancement and administrative coherence are used as the basis of identity. In India, despite occasional and remote indications of potential secessionism, regional movements do not usually go beyond claiming resource sharing within the broader national context. Regionalism in this sense, can politically be understood as 'a search for an intermediate control system between the centre and the periphery of competitive advantage in the national arena' (Das Gupta, 1997: 132).

In this relation between the state and periphery, regionalism is the outcome of the real or perceived sense of 'internal colonialism'. The essence of this argument is that the relationship between the core community and the peripheral communities in a state is characterized by exploitation. The core community acquires an advantage over the outlying communities in the period of state building or during the early periods of modernization, and then this political and economic power is used to maintain and enhance its superior position. Cultural and ethnic differences then form the basis of separatist movements by the peripheral communities.

Almost all the societies in the modern world contain subsystems which are distinct, in a positive degree, from the rest of the population. To clarify the meaning of the subsystem, or a minority, it is good to look at the dimensions of both the size and power that determine its usage. We may categorize a fourfold typology of groups to explain this phenomenon (Schermerhorn, 1978: 15).

If we define ethnic group in a larger society, it follows that an overwhelming majority of ethnic groups are in a subordinate position. An ethnic group may be geographically dispersed (Scheduled Castes in India, Muhajirs in Pakistan) or may have its own political territory (Sikhs and Tamilians in India, and Bengalies in pre-1971 Pakistan). It is the latter which may seek economic and political gains by demanding greater regional autonomy. Even if a group is numerically strong in a territory (as Maharashtrians in Mumbai) and lacks political control over that territory, greater regional autonomy would only adversely affect the group's position. Regional autonomy demands may be accompanied by or may be a sequel to preferential treatment, as in the case of Telangana in Andhra Pradesh. But where greater regional autonomy is not a variable strategy, demand for preferential treatment is only the viable technique, as in the case of Shiv Sena's demand in Mumbai.

Cultural differences, thus, may not be the causes of natives hostility against the migrants but they certainly are present in such conflicts. In fact, magnifying of cultural differences becomes a political technique, by way of defining cultural (and consequently, political) identity. The strategy is to convert cultural differences into cultural conflicts. Participants in regional movements always emphasize differences, however trivial, between their own culture and that of the migrant. Because, cultural identity has to be defined for a group to make it distinguishable, it must be different from that of the other. The cultural differences and consequent cultural conflicts are, in fact, effects of regionalism; what then, are the determinants?

Determinants of Regionalism

An aggressive regionalism may develop from varying apprehensions and threats, real or perceived. To start, there may be economic competitions leading to fears about possible shrinking of job market. This is especially true on the part of working class and the lower middle class. We may cite the example of Telangana people apprehensions against the Andhra-migrant. Then there may be status-threats posed by the migrants to the social status of the middle classes as was the case of Maharashtrians fears against the south Indians in Bombay (now Mumbai). There may be political fears of some social classes to the threat of migrants to their long-term interests. The whole Bengali influx into the Assam, over a long period, may also explain the demographic reasons of regionalism, where natives have some level of tolerance but at a given time the rate and the volume of migrants passes this level, giving rise to native apprehensions and opposition. Then, psychologically the frustration of social life may be aggressively displayed against the migrant, if the latter is easily distinguishable and can be easily made a scapegoat for self-failure. Further, regionalism develops if the native population is likely to be immobile relative to other groups in the population; in other words, if the rate of in-migration is higher than that of out-migration.

Regionalism may start in an area which has experienced a rapid growth of educational opportunities for the lower, middle classes, enhancing their aspirations and expectations, but there is a high level of unemployment among the indigenous middle classes, and a substantial proportion of middle class jobs are held by culturally alien migrants (Weiner, 1978: 285).

In this way, the factors responsible for regionalism in India may be summarized as:

1. A locale which has a large number of middle class migrants who are actually distinct from the indigenous population.
2. An indigenous middle class which is growing rapidly through expanded educational opportunities.
3. A very competitive labour market where the indigenous middle class is a disadvantage in gaining jobs vis-à-vis migrants from outside the territory.
4. An indigenous population which itself is non-mobile and there are few opportunities outside the state to seek employment.
5. An indigenous working class which can be mobilized by the politics of cultural nationalism (Levandowski, 1980: 204).

Keeping in view the above factors, taking the case of Calcutta (now Kolkata), it is easy to understand the reasons why this city has not witnessed the growth of regional movement. To start with, the Bengalis have been economically a very mobile people, giving quick response to job opportunities within the linguistic region. Taking advantage of the establishment of colleges by the British in the 19th century, they moved into civil service and professional employment. Because the overwhelming Bengali middle class has a clear preference for the white collar jobs, non-Bengalis are mostly factory workers and merchants. The preponderant majority of the 20th century migrants to Calcutta (from Bihar, Orissa (now Odisha), UP, Rajasthan, Punjab) was of the working class employed as labourers in the industrial and business tracts of the city. Because the indigenous population holds the majority of the middle class jobs, one of the largest cities in India has been free from ethnic conflicts.

Regionalism, and the concept of 'sons-of-soil' raises certain basic questions with regard to relationship between the claims of individual citizens to equal access and the collective claims of ethnic groups to equality. This concept implies that the people belonging to a particular territory have a special and the first, if not exclusive claim, to all the welfare facilities within the territory. This implies a sort of ownership by a specific group of territory it occupies. This also implies a special collective territorial right of an ethnic group. It means that the indigenous has a first claim on everything and the newcomers (migrants are outsiders) are entitled to benefits only after these have been adequately distributed to the indigenous population.

The reason behind the demands regarding 'sons-of-soil' is maldevelopment, and the rationale is the fear of being left out. Because of the uneven process of development, some ethnic groups move ahead more rapidly than others. Under the modernization process, a nation as such does not develop but only certain sections and groups do, creating islands of prosperity in oceans of underdevelopment. One consequence of such modernizations or maldevelopment is the emergence of subregionalism. A subregion is meant to be a small area within a region which, for economic, geographical, linguistic and social reasons, is aware of possessing a distinct identity. During linguistic-regional movements, the claims and significance of subregional problems are produced by historical and economical factors which encourage the growth of political subcultures in conflict with the longer unity of language, culture and caste represented by linguistic state. The national leadership has never appreciated the socio-economic and historical evolution of imbalances between historically defined subregions because of a slurred pseudo-romantic understanding of Indian historical ethos and the fact (understandable, though regrettable) that power does not always like to divide itself voluntarily (Majeed, 1978: 206).

Indigenous ethnic groups try to use political power to overcome the fears of economic defeat and cultural subordination by more enterprising and skilled migrant communities. Because competition is not viewed as a stimulus for change, but as a force for growing inequality among ethnic groups, it underscores the political argument for a protected labour market for the indigenous worker. Generally, the systematic disadvantaging of certain groups is the common feature of multi-ethnic societies. Such disadvantages may be the result of asymmetrical development or they result, as some opine, intentional or otherwise from policies and actions of the government. In the face of multi-ethnic social formations and big inter-regional disparities, masses support regional formations because of their expectation of material security and combined with their expectation of political security and advancement. Regional movements reflect not only socially formulated demands but, in fact, help formulate such demands, both at the elite and at the mass level. Because such movements make regional units more coherent and comprehensible for the masses, they prepare the ground for more intense mass demands. Some of these demands take the form of subregional claims of autonomy as a way out for redressing grievances and disadvantages.

In India, when the constitutional process started, the process of regionalism also commenced, inspired not merely by primordial sentiments but also by the existing economic conditions of the various regional ethnic groups. This regionalism may be traced to the British period, and the centralization of power and its subsequent delegation to regional middle classes. The linguistic/regional middle classes were well aligned as the result of the extension of administration to the once remote areas and the consequent induction of masses into administrative infrastructure. Just like the all-India forces, the regional forces also implied a broader participation by the masses, which till then were untouched by this development. The horizontal force of this process led to the national movement of freedom from the rule of the alien from abroad, and the vertical force of the same process led to the subnational movement of freedom from the rules of alien from outside the region or subregion. This had resulted because of an 'attitudinal integration' of the growing subregional middle classes. This coincided, in time, with the growing dissatisfaction among the working class with the political authority, with the worsening of their economic conditions, the widening of the inequality and the consolidating of the monopolies, etc. Conflicts within the all-India business class developed, between its developed monopolistic strata on the one hand, and the numerically wider lower groups of the middle class. The conflicts arose over attempts to subordinate the state-capitalist mechanism. Many of the lower levels of the business community at the state level, demanded a certain reorientation of the national economic policy, and of the state-sector of the national economy, to dislodge it from predominating positions.

Though territorial identity was recognized by the federal political formula, this recognition was of a legal nature, whose main purpose was to contain and condition the regional identity within the confines of the political formula; consequently, regionalism has been regarded as antisystem and an anti-integrated policy. This has led to negative thinking in the context of the ambition and assertion of centripetal forces for the capture of executive authority (Reddy and Sharma, 1979: 3). Rather than immerse India into a disintegrative process, as the above logic would have us believe, the reorganization of states opened the way to the emergence of new levels of elites. With the replacement of the multilingual states, the position of English as the link language was replaced and the vernacular elite assumed an advantage. In this way, those who had enjoyed power in rural areas but were denied representation were brought into the political and administrative infrastructures and given experience, a voice and a stake in the political affairs of the nation.

In the Indian context, the territorial basis is symbolic in nature. This symbolism gets reinforced by way of cultural heritage and historical myths, as in the case of DMK in Tamil Nadu and Shiv Sena in Maharashtra. Similarly, caste and religion affect regionalism when they get combined with dominance, as in the case of Punjab and anti-Brahmanism in Tamil Nadu. The economic component is the crux of the problem of regionalism. Demands of distributive justice, in the face of scarcity and regional economic imbalances, assume the form of regional and subregional movements. This is especially so in the case of the working class and the lower middle class. We may cite the example of Telangana sentiment against the Andhra migrant. Because of the uneven process of development, some ethnic groups move ahead more rapidly than others, and the latter (mostly indigenous population of an area) feeling outpaced against the migrants and outsiders, are compelled to put a firm clamp on local resources and benefits.

In Andhra Pradesh, there was a clear impression of the stagnation of Telangana region amidst the general development of Andhra Pradesh. In Telangana, the middle class believed that open jobs, with merit being the criteria, would mean that outsiders would get the overwhelming number of jobs in Telangana. The psychological need to find differences between Telangana and the rest of Andhra Pradesh led to the assertion of a distinctive cultural heritage for Telangana, with the political identity as the ultimate goal. No doubt Telangana movement originated from certain real economic disparities. It has been asserted by the experts that Telangana movement emerged through politicization of an economic problem by the political elite of the region. The even development of Andhra Pradesh as a whole depended upon the political insight and wisdom of the leaders and also the realization that disparities taking shape over decades could not be removed in a few years. The result was that the erosion of factors like caste, language, culture, etc., in the modernization process did not affect the political development in a 'modernized' way. Consequently, with the start of welfare and developmental activities, regionalism in Andhra Pradesh shook off its only language character and became primarily economic.

Political elite exploit situations of regional deprivation and unrest and convert them into movements to forge and strengthen their individual and factional support bases. Regionalism thrives on real or fancied charges of political discrimination which has, in fact, become an important facet of politics of regionalism itself. A 'we-they' distinction is asserted by the regional elite, transforming the latent emotions into regional or subregional ideology to serve certain political ends. Through examples from the Samyuktha Maharashtra movement, the Vidarbha movement, the Marathwada agitation, and the rise of Shiv Sena, Mudholkar Vora argues that such subregionalism is a movement by subregional elite for the assertion of subregional identity based on common history and grievances emanating from an underdeveloped economy of that subregion, cutting across the cultural and linguistic loyalties (Majeed, 1984).

The quest of a regional identity is not necessarily antithetical to the urge for a national identity and the two can coexist in a situation of mutually rewarding partnership, if the politico-bureaucratic and educational elite work for and bring about the delicate but certainly conceivable balance between the competing but reconcilable claims of the two. The challenge of reconciliation is at heart and essentially a managerial challenge (Iqbal Narain in Majeed, 1984).

Regionalism in the Indian context, as perhaps elsewhere also, is a nebulous concept. It has both a positive and a negative dimension. Speaking in positive terms, it embodies a quest for self-fulfillment on the part of the people of an area. It is worthwhile to emphasize that the positive thrust of regionalism has, more often than not, been ignored by political analysis of the Indian situation. Every regional movement thus becomes suspect and is taken as an earnest of the Balkanization of the country. This can vitiate the managerial approach also. It is, therefore, well to remember what the report of the State's Re-organization Commission (1955) had to say in this regard:

> It is obviously an advantage that constituent units of a federation should have a minimum measure of internal cohesion. Likewise, a regional consciousness, not merely in the sense of a negative awareness of absence of repression or exploitation but also in the sense of scope for positive expression of the collective personality of a people in habiting a state or a region may be conducive to the contentment and well-being of the community. Common language may not only promote the growth of such regional consciousness but also make for administrative convenience. Indeed, in a democracy, the people can legitimately claim and the government has a duty ensure that the administration is conducted in a language which the people can understand (Report of the State's Reorganization Commission, 1955: 255).

Regionalism also reflects a psyche of relative deprivation on the part of a people. More often than not, it is also believed, whether correctly or not, that deprivation it deliberately infected by the powers that be and this leads to acuteness of feeling on the part of those who carry the psyche of deprivation. The belief is easily cultivated in a milieu characterized by politics of scarcity as in India. The redeeming feature, however, is that to the extent the psyche of deprivation is the consequence of specific grievance, its growth could be halted and even the process reversed if the grievances are remedied. Regionalism is a multidimensional phenomenon in terms of its components – geographical, historic-cultural, economic, politico-administrative and psychic.

Geographical Components of Regionalism

The factor of geographical boundaries to which the people of an area usually relate their quest of a regional identity also differentiates, at least in degree, if not in kind, the phenomenon of minority nationalist movements from regionalism. The point of differentiation is that minority nationalist movements may have a somewhat diffused geographical underpinning in comparison to regionalism, where it is rather concrete, though only in a relative sense. It will be worthwhile to recall in the specific Indian context that the integration of the princely states after independence resulted in the merger of relatively small territorial entities into new and bigger entities. The new states which were thus brought into being came to develop split personalities, at least for the time being, with the loyalties of their citizens (and even of their political elites and the civil servants) being torn between old territorial boundaries and new territorial structures. The split in state personalities had one of its significant manifestations in the regional sentiment which fed on loyalties to old territorial units. Even at the risk of digression it may be pointed out here that this was the primary factor behind the success of princes in elections. The princes would often receive overwhelming support in their former territories in the newly created states and relatively much less in other parts of the same state.

Regional consciousness gets buttressed by geography also. People tend to relate their identity to a particular geographical area and take pride in their being sons of that particular soil. Phrases like 'Amar Sonar Bengal' or 'Deshan Bich Desh Punjab Da' (Punjab is the best among all countries) are reminiscent of peoples loyalties towards a geographical area. But 'geographical boundaries, though still clung to, are, historically speaking, symbolic, at least in the Indian context, of overlapping and vanishing footprints on the sands of time, which need economic and political props for their retrieval from time to time in the increasingly hazy memories of succeeding generations. For example, memories of old geographical boundaries of princely states still haunt and are exploited but it can hardly be denied that they are yielding place to new and bigger territorial identities, e.g., Rajasthan, Madhya Pradesh or Orissa'.

Historic-Cultural Components

It will be just emphasizing the obvious that the historic-cultural component constitute the bedrock of the phenomenon of regionalism in India. The several components in this category are not only important individually but also in conjunction with each other. To begin with, there is the factor of history which buttresses regionalism by way of cultural heritage, folk lore, myths symbolism. Nothing perhaps illustrates this better than the story of the rise of

Dravida Kazhagam (DK) and the Dravida Munnetra Kazhagam (DMK) in Tamil Nadu (Hardgrave, 1965).

Caste and Religion

Caste and religion only play a marginal role in the context of regionalism. For example, caste per se is not so important except when combined with dominance (as in Maharashtra) or when working in conjunction with linguistic preponderance (as, again, in Maharashtra or Tamil Nadu) or a religion (as, negatively speaking, in terms of anti-Brahmanism in Tamil Nadu (Irschick, 1969). Similarly, religion is not significant except when it is combined with domestic/linguistic homogeneity or fed on a sense of religious orthodoxy and economic deprivation (as in Jammu). Altogether it can even be argued that regionalism is a secular phenomenon in a relative sense because it tends to encompass caste faiths and varied caste affiliations to work together for a common cause (Rao, 1973).

Religion too, by itself, is not very important but when it is coupled with dominance as in Jammu and Kashmir and Lakshadweep Islands, where the Muslims preponderate or in Nagaland, Meghalaya and Mizoram where Christianity is the dominant religion or Punjab where the Sikhs dominate, it can create a very vocal and militant type of regionalism resting upon fundamentalism, and carrying with it, politically the most inflammable material.

Every state has some depressed pockets inhabited by people of various castes and religions. By itself, caste may carry a pejorative connotation with it but the moment it gets identified with an areal segment, it acquires ascendance and dominance. By raising the bogey of caste discrimination, it can unite people of one caste. Caste, when it is coupled with dominance as in Maharashtra (Marathas), Tamil Nadu (Nadars or Vanniyars), Kerala (Ezhavas) or Haryana (Jats) can be a factor of major reckoning and may lead to caste-based regionalism.

Language

It is fairly well known that language is perhaps the most important mark of group identification; it is more precisely discriminating than either colour or race. The latter may get overridden by other forces and as such, these may cease to refer to any distinct interacting community, while the former usually survives the wear and tear of time and continues to serve as a cohesive means of communication. Linguistic homogeneity strengthens regionalism both in the positive and negative sense; in the former, in terms of strength in unity and in the latter, through emotional frenzy. Language as an expression of shared life, thought structure and value pattern has the potential to unite people emotionally and make them work to improve their common density as also to add to their bargaining strength. Robert Dave (1958) has dealt with the advantages of remapping of states on the basis of language in the terms of better elite-mass communication, resulting in better socialization of people in democratic values; attention to social problems peculiar to linguistic groups; and sharing of membership of a regional society and possession of a distinctive culture, literary and historical tradition.

Nothing perhaps illustrates this better than the Telangana issue where economic grievances and demands would triumph over consideration of linguistic homogeneity. The very fact that language helps a group to forge an emotional identity also tends to make it highly inflammable, as shown by the language riots in Assam or in Tamil Nadu. As Rasheeduddin Khan has correctly pointed out:

Let it be remembered that, even as it is, the states are not constituted, despite popular misgivings, entirely on the basis of linguistic homogeneity. A closer scrutiny will reveal that together like ethnic-cum-economic considerations (Nagaland, Meghalaya, Manipur and Tripura); religion, script and sentiments(Haryana and Punjab); language-cum-culture (Maharashtra and Gujarat); historical and political factor (UP and Bihar); integration of princely states and the need for visible groupings (MP and Rajasthan);and, of course, language-cum-social distinctiveness (Tamil Nadu, Kerala, Mysore, Bengal and Orissa) have played a decisive role in the composition of the Indian federation. In fact, Rasheeduddin Khan argues that "the process of infrastructuring of Indian federation is not yet over" and he makes plea for further restructuring in terms of smaller and medium sized states, as "the problem is really not of numbers but of the recomposition of the

Indian federation based of objective criteria of socio-economic homogeneity and fellow group identity in order to provide a more responsive infrastructure for an industrial breakthrough and modernization" (Majeed, 1984).

The term of reference of the states' Reorganization Commission had ensured it to take note of four broad principles: (i) the preservation of the unity and security of Indians; (ii) linguistic and cultural homogeneity; (iii) financial, economic and administrative considerations and (iv) the successful working of the national plan. It cannot be denied, however, that language has been the critical factor in the reorganization of states, which became a force to be reckoned with in the context of regionalism, gained currency in the literature.

It is yet another variable which carries with it a power-keg of pent-up emotions and is a very distinctive mark of identity affiliation. According to Morris Jones, "it is perhaps the most important mark of group identification. But it is more precisely discriminating than colour or race, for whereas the latter may be overridden by other forces so that they cease to refer to any real interacting community of persons, language it used is a working link". Without contesting the overall impact of language as a factor buttressing regionalism, it is difficult to agree with Morris Jones in the Indian context because despite being a working link, language has been overridden by other factors.

In 1947, Assamese speaking Sylhet went in a referendum to East Pakistan for religious reasons. So also religion proved stronger in the case of Punjab and Bengal both, and they were partitioned in the name of religion. The people of Vidarbha region of Maharashtra are demanding the formation of new state for economic reasons. So are some of the Telugu speaking people of Andhra Pradesh demanding the formation of a separate state of Telangana for economic benefits. The demand of tribals of Chota Nagpur region of Bihar for the formation of a separate state of Jharkhand was rooted in ethnicity, and language is not a very dominating factor. It is, therefore, wrong to assume that language is the most potent factor behind any regional demand. Nevertheless, language has its own role in arousing regional feelings. Negatively, it creates linguistic fanaticism and emotional frenzy culminating in linguistic riots as happened to the composite states of Bombay in 1956, where

Gujaratis and Marathas fought pitched battles in the streets. The role of Shiv Sena in Maharashtra against South Indians is equally illustrative of linguistic hysteria being fanned systematically by vested interests. But it also has a positive side. It is also an expression of shared life, thought structure and values of a distinctive group. By uniting people of a language emotionally, it increases their bargaining powers. If intrastate regionalism divides people speaking the same language, militant linguism also unites them and equips them to wage a dour struggle for the welfare of their followers. Language is like a double-edged weapon which can be used for offence as well as for defence.

But linguistic regionalism creates manyfold problems for its adherents. Firstly, there are people who are a majority in some states but a minority elsewhere. The Bengalis are dominant in West Bengal and Tripura but are the second largest group in Assam aspiring for a majority status there. Secondly, there are some people who are in a majority now but are likely to lose their status in dim remote future. The Assamese xenophobia against the Bengali and the Sikh susceptibility against the Hindu in Punjab may be due to this reason. Thirdly, there are people who were once a majority in their habitat and are now reduced to a minority as in Tripura where unchecked Bengali immigration has reduced the Tripura tribe to an abysmal minority. Finally, there are some, whose language is recognized by the Constitution of India but who do not constitute a majority anywhere such as the Sindhis. Such minorities, whether linguistic or otherwise would resist assimilation into a broader regional cultural frame. To borrow a wise observation from Myron Weiner, "Whether the minority group is a tribe of a religious or linguistic group, it is often concerned with preserving its cultural identity and resisting assimilation into a larger regional culture. Regionalism, like its earlier counterpart, nationalism, has become a powerful loyalty within most of the states and has resulted in a degree of assimilation of related social groups but minorities are more protective of their status in the midst of growing regional sentiments" (Haqqi, 1984).

Economic Component

Indeed, economic component is the crux of regionalism. It is common knowledge that India is underdeveloped economically, in spite of the many achievements registered since independence. The resources are scarce and demands disproportionately heavy and ever growing on account of continued population explosion. There is thus acute competition among individuals, groups and regions within a state. Harrison Selig has thus described the process: As the population mounts, densely populated regions cry Lebensraum (territory which a state believes is needed for its natural development; living space) at their neighbour's. Bihari labourers flock to jobs in the mining and industrial towns, bordering Bengal, and the overcrowded Bengal protests in return that the towns should be the preserve of its own jobless. The tea plantations of Assam became a battleground between rival groups of Assamese and Bengali unemployed. Tamil Nadu demands the border plantation lands of Malayalam-speaking Travancore-Cochin to protect Tamil coolies from Malayalee competition.

To this, one could add the story of regional economic imbalances to which the political elite in general and the ruling elite in particular have contributed in no small measure. Demands for distributive justice thus get generated and assume the form of a movement. It may be recalled here that most of the demands for constituting new states were primarily based on allegedly unfair and unequal distribution of development benefits and expenditures in the multilingual states (Report of the State's Re-organization Commission, 1955: 225.) The Telangana movement is a classical instance in point. The simmerings of discontent in the depressed regions of Bihar, Orissa, Madhya Pradesh, Maharashtra, Gujarat, UP, and Rajasthan further illustrate the point. The scramble for the location of steel plants and the other heavy industries and charges of partisanship levied against the Centre in this regard is another instance in point. The tensions between migrants and 'sons of the soil' are still another manifestation of the economic component. The conflict between Assamese and the Bengalis in Assam and the Shiv Sena's slogan of 'Maharashtra for Maharashtrians' have similar genesis.

Politico-Administrative Component

The political component of regionalism is also important even though politics does not so much create as it accentuates it. Politicians, in their not always so enlightened self-interest, exploit situations of regional deprivations and unrest and convert them into movements to forge and strengthen their individual and factional support bases.

The relational pattern between regionalism and politics while being a bit nebulous continues to be very powerful. Politics may be regionalized or regionalism may give rise to acute political controversies. Both assist and aggravate each other. One can fuel the other and the relationship being entirely reciprocal, it is difficult to conceive of a dividing line. At what point of time politicians would exploit purely regional issues or when regional consciousness would permeate political parties, it is difficult to predict and hence both can be studied in their complementarities and not in their separation. More important, however, is the impact of regionalization of political parties. Whereas, certain political parties are regional in their outlook such as National Conference of Kashmir, Akali Dal of Punjab, Mizo National Front of Mizoram, Assam Gana Parishad of Assam, Naga National Council of Nagaland, the Jharkhand Party of Bihar, All Peoples Hill Leaders Conference of Meghalaya, Plains Tribal Council of Assam, DMK and AIADMK of Tamil Nadu and Telugu Desam Party of Andhra Pradesh, there are other political parties which are national in appellation but regional in character such as the CPI(M) which is dominant only in West Bengal, Tripura and Kerala and has acquired a distinct regional colouration in these states. Even well established older political identities such as the Congress cannot survive in certain states without championing regional issues. For example, the Congress in Punjab supported the demand for Chandigarh being given to Punjab, whereas in Haryana it took the opposite stand. So was the case of BJP in these two states. This is true of several other national political parties that either openly espouse regional issues or connive with them covertly.

Psychic Component

Finally, regionalism in India, as elsewhere, is a psychic phenomenon, and in the ultimate analysis its roots lie in the minds of men. Each individual, by and large, carries a split personality: he is in part rationalistic and in part nationalistic. There is always a natural tendency towards the primacy of the rationalistic over the nationalistic, though one does not usually pose the two as an either/or situation. To be an Indian it is not necessary not to be a Maharashtrian. The situation is best brought out in an observation of Lokenath Mishra (1955).

"My first ambition is the glory of mother India. I know it in my heart of hearts that I am Indian first and an Indian last. But when you say you are a Bihari, I say I am an Oriya. When you say you are Bengali, I say I am Oriya. Otherwise, I am an Indian".

Indian regionalism is also a psychic phenomenon. Despite the unitarian approach of the Indian Constitution makers owing to which only single citizenship is granted, the Indian people retain their state loyalties. Despite single citizenship the pan-Indian sentiment has not grown strong enough to subsume sectarian loyalties and people continue to remain emotionally committed to their states. People make no secret of their being Kashmiri, Punjabi, Bihari, Rajasthani, Gujarati, Marathi, Tamil or Malayalee when asked to specify their place of domicile. But this is no reason to feel dependent. To be an Indian it is not necessary to be a non-Rajasthani or a non-Bengali. In fact, it can be understood in a different way. If a Bengali visits Delhi and people ask him who he is, he would be perfectly within his right to say that he is a Bengali. But if the same question is addressed to him in London or Washington, his answer would be that he is an Indian. That is the spirit of which one's state identity should be understood.

There is no obvious dichotomy between national and state identity so long as one does not raise secessionist slogans. As long as one believes in national unity and integrity, regionalism will not create any horizontal split. Only when people tend to take a secessionist stand in the name of regional aspiration, regionalism becomes a dreaded word. A simple hankering after ones state identity without in any way compromising one's larger commitment to national identity is not bad at all. The two can be best understood complementarily. They complement and supplement each other and do not divide or split people. Most people who rail at regionalism do so owing to some misconceived notion of an overarching nationalism, which leaves no scope for the evolution and fruition of state identities. Regionalism, in other aspects, negative or positive is not bad. Negatively, it expresses a psyche of relative deprivation in economic field whereas, speaking positively, it connotes a desire for an equal share in development and progress. Which aspect is stronger and better is not a debatable issue? Which element is decisive and which as a booster is not at all relevant? The best way to understand regionalism is to comprehend it in a conjunctional perspective, keeping in view the fact that it is a resultant of an amalgam of several complex factors. To understand this factor, the approach has to be multidimensional and not unilinear. Urge for regional justice is not a demand for destroying national unity.

Major Types of Regionalism

Like the components, the types of regionalism also seem to overlap. Though regionalism is not always coterminous with present-day state boundaries, a state can still be treated as a unit for evolving types of regionalism. One can now attempt a broader taxonomy of regionalism. A plural society like India would create institutional plurality and hence Indian regionalism cannot afford to be a mono-model. It is multi-model in essence and can be classified as under:

Transcendental Regionalism: It is wrong to equate regionalism with a specific region. Sometimes it transcends national boundaries and leaps ahead of and above the ties that bound a person to a particular region and becomes mega-regional. The Sikhs of Punjab are regional in the sense of being Punjabis but they are sympathetic to the Punjabis living across the border. A Pakistani cricket team touring India played a cricket match in Amritsar and Pakistani visitors from across the Wagah border came in large numbers to watch that particular fixture. They were given an emotional welcome by the Sikhs of Punjab and were greeted "as our brothers from across the border". It was mega-Punjabi regionalism resting on fraternal links and relationship with people who once belonged to the same region but were divided now by religion and political boundary differentiation. In the same way, one can say that Indian Sikhs have their fraternal links with the Sikhs of UK, USA and Canada, though it is rooted more in religious fundamentalism than strictly regional consciousness of any sort. In a similar vein one can argue that Bengali speaking people of West Bengal and Bangladesh do maintain cultural and linguistic relationships and in 1971, this spirit manifested itself in a mega-regional consciousness that transcended national frontiers.

Transitory Regionalism: This is a temporary sort of regional urge which is issue specific and is witnessed in sporadic manifestation of temporary issues having a specific regional colouration. On the issue of division of composite state of Bombay in 1958, Maharashtra and Gujarati regions witnessed unprecedented regional unrest and people of these two states formed Samyuktha Maharashtra Samiti and Mahagujarat Janata Parishad to press their regional demand of bifurcating the state of Bombay. After a prolonged agitation, their demand was conceded and these organizations ceased to exist after formation of separate states of Maharashtra and Gujarat. Thus, regionalism can be transitory and issue-specific also where it comes to solving a particular problem. The moment the particularistic demand is fulfilled, regional bodies stop agitational politics and revert back to the task of consolidating the gains achieved.

Supra-State Regionalism: This is yet another variant of regional consciousness and it expresses itself in the unity of a group of states, who are differentiated linguistically and culturally but they come together to give birth to a larger formation to resist or espouse a particular demand. Mostly, such unity is forged for a negative purpose. The states of Kerala, Karnataka, Andhra Pradesh and Tamil Nadu together forged a non-formal union resting on multiple identity of these culturally and linguistically different and territorially identifiable units for the purpose of resisting the imposition of Hindi on them. A union like this too is non-formal and issue-specific but when one region is confronting another region, the problem also becomes intra-specific between them. The union that southern states forge rests on Dravidian ethnicity, language and culture. It is a queer case of states speaking different languages and having other dissimilarities coming closer and taking a common stand on it. The states that form group identity are not the one who have a dispute-free record and one often witnesses intra-group rivalries and tensions among them but some common issue brings them together on one platform and they develop a negative consensus among them to oppose some issue.

Inter-State Regionalism: This is a very common form of regionalism which juxtaposes one state against another on a specific matter. The distribution of river waters and territorial disputes fall in this category. To which state Chandigarh should belong whether to Haryana or Punjab, creates inter-state discord. So also the city of Belgaum in Karnataka has become a bone of contention between Maharashtra and Karnataka and rival claims to its accession to either state continue to be made for decades on and with no prospects of an early amicable solution. The issue of construction of Sutlej-Yamuna link canal has embittered relations between Punjab and Haryana. The distribution of river waters of Punjab brought the people of states of Rajasthan, Haryana, Punjab and Himachal Pradesh into a loggerhead and caused avoidable tensions. So did the questions of distribution of Narmada waters between Madhya Pradesh, Gujarat and Rajasthan. Such instances are many.

Intra-State Regionalism: Finally, it is matter of common knowledge that every state has its own depressed pockets and the affected people do voice their protest against such discrimination, economic neglect and deprivation. Several examples can be given to draw home the point of intra-state regional feuds. Demand for further vivisection of many unilingual states illustrates this. People of Vidarbha region in Maharashtra, of Saurashtra region in Gujarat and Telangana region in Andhra Pradesh are demanding separation from their parent states because of intra-state disputes.

The development is no doubt, not always smooth nor it is following the model of any other political system, but it is indigenous and unique in the face of peculiar challenges the system is facing. Sometimes, the system is able to develop with the challenges, understanding their nature, dimension, depth and direction and the development becomes easy and congenial to system-maintenance. Sometimes, the system fails to appreciate the nature and magnitude of the challenges and adopts hasty and faulty approaches in evolving the right type of responses. This has produced negative impact on development and has led to regional imbalances, recession in economic growth, occurrences of terrorists violence developing in the direction of threats of disintegration and secession, and lurking fear of foreign aggression at any moment. In context to the development of Indian political system, regionalism has appeared as one of the major challenges.

Elaborating on regionalism and politics of separatism in India, Professor Bhawani Singh begins with the uniqueness of India. India is unique in the diversities that she represents. She has been characterized as one of the greatest geographical museums in the world, where cultural pluralities are manifested in all dimensions, where political behaviour is strongly coloured by consideration of communal identification, and where there is a lack of integration among the masses all over the country because of the absence of a unified communication system. These pluralities create diversities and diversities are more concentrated in one or the other part of the country to create regionalization in India. India is not a unilingual country, there are two highly developed linguistic families: Sanskrit and Dravidian and both are concentrated geographically in such a way as to divide India further into two main regions North and South. Again, within the main division, there are a number of major languages spoken by millions of people and each language needs to get territorial as well as national identity. Like language, religion has become a dominating factor in national politics and creates regional movements as Sikhs in Punjab. Within the Hindu community, again caste distinctions separate India's people into caste group and sub-caste groups and when a particular ethnic group becomes concentrated in particular area and demands their identity, there is the emergence of regional movement like the Jharkhand movement in the borders of Orissa, Bihar and West Bengal, Bodo movement in Assam or Gorkha movement in West Bengal. This implies a special collective territorial right of an ethnic group. Moreover, in India there is uneven economic development which leads to regional movement. Some regions are more industrialized and economically developed than others.

Some parts of the country are highly westernized than other parts and there is the growth of a progressive conservative dichotomy. Economically, some parts of the country are very poor and they create regional movement and that was the main reason behind the movement in Assam as well as in Darjeeling. Administratively and politically some regions are ruled by the Opposition and regional parties which demand self-identity, more autonomy and more powers for the regions leading to regional movement. In India, a peculiar problem like geographical border because of inter-state river water, trade and commerce, electricity, road transport along with cultural diversities lead to regional movement, particularly demanding redrawing of territorial border of the state. Thus, regionalism can be economic regionalism, political administrative regionalism and territorial regionalism. These dimensions create three forms of regionalism in India as Iqbal Narain (1976) has described, namely, supra-regionalism, inter-state regionalism and intra-state regionalism. The first one is an expression of group identity of several states which join hands to take a common stand on an issue of mutual interest vis-à-vis another group of states or even the Union. In the second case, regionalism has been coextensive with state boundaries. In both these two cases regionalism has appeared as a movement against the Union. But intra-state regionalism is directed against the state governments rather than the Union of India and such regional demands are like the creation of new and separate political and administrative units within the existing state structure and of some regions within a state for equitable and fair treatment.

These forms of regionalism have produced a number of demands on the national polity, such as to give identity to particular language, religion and ethnic factors of the region, more regional autonomy and power, constitutional status of the region, separate statehood within the nation and in extreme case secession from the nation. To achieve these regional demands, sometimes, recourse have been taken to put forth the claims in the forum of state legislatures and Parliament or to make agitations and in worst cases to indulge in terrorist violence.

Development results when the existing structure and culture on the political system is unable to cope with the problem or challenge which confronts it without further structural differentiation and cultural secularization. These challenges may come in the words of Almond and Powell for state-building, nation-building, participation and distribution which are parts of the process of political development.

From a long time the regional forces have their impact on the development at the level of organization of political system in India. When the Britishers entered India, they could feel the regional variations and established 'divide and rule' policy to suit their administration as well as to be fitted to the regional demands and peculiarities. An objective study of freedom struggle reveals that it was not a process free of contradictions or variations over regions and time. But the national issue, namely, to establish a free, democratic and strong India superseded all the parochial claims of the regions and precipitated the establishment of a free democratic 'one India' even at the cost of local demands and interests. Though, regional consciousness, in its devotion to the greater cause of freedom was considerably subdued during the days of India's struggle for freedom, but off and on it found an expression through an articulated demand for regional autonomy as a necessary means of preserving regional particularism. This demand was one of the important features of programme of India's national movement.

Development, Regionalism and Performance

Performance can be visualized at the level of policy-making and policy-implementation by the government and the administrative system which will lead to the development of the system instead of breaking it up. Performance refers to the efficiency and effectiveness of the system and it can be measured from political and economic points of view. So far as performance at political level is concerned Professor Bhawani Singh highlights two issues, namely, language and race into consideration to exhibit the interaction between regionalism and development.

Language is an effective means of communication among people of a nation and there is the need for evolving a common language system for a free democratic nation. But the prevalence of a common Indian language in the face of different regional linguistic forces posed a challenge to the Indian political system. At the time of Constitution-making, Nehru himself expressed his view that the time had not yet come to find out a solution to the question of all-India language in an atmosphere of amity and cooperation. This led to the incorporation of Articles 343 and 344 of the Indian Constitution which declare that the official language of the Union shall be Hindi and the President shall by order constitute a commission and committee of Parliament on official language which would look into the matter that Hindi would not be imposed on any state. Articles 345, 346 and 347 of the Constitution provide for use of the regional language as official language within the state for the time being. The whole country was divided on the issue of official language and once English was granted associated language status, the South was happy and regional agitation there subsided.

In the early years of the federal republic, language proved to be a very forceful rallying point for regionalism. The demand for the formation of Vishal Andhra by uniting all Telugu speaking tracts into one state was an important expression of regionalism. The emergence of a chain of demands for linguistic states resulted in setting up of States Reorganization Commission to enquire into the regional demands and make recommendations for the formulation of policy that would strengthen the national polity rather than breaking it up.

The consequences of state boundaries in India in 1956 appear, in the words of D.B. Forrester (1970), to have been 'an indigenization and democratization of provincial polities, which gave a strong impetus to the development of political cultures, enhancing the political significance of case and educated regional elites'. Again Srinivas writes: 'The creation of linguistic states on 1 November 1956 in most parts of the country has strengthened the barriers between them. This is the first time in Indian history when cultural frontiers were converted into political frontiers' (Srinivas, 1962). The issue of regionalism on linguistic force, subsided for the time being because of the creation of Andhra State but this development led to further similar issues like the creation of more states or changing the boundaries of existing states not only on linguistic basis but also on tribal or racial variations. As a result, movement at sub-state levels started when a particular region within a linguistic state wanted to be separated from its own state. Examples are Telangana Movement in Andhra Pradesh, Saurashtra Movement in Gujarat, Mahavidarbha Movement in Maharashtra, Bodo Movement in Assam and Gorkhaland Movement in West Bengal.

Regional movements emerge not only for achieving cultural identity, but also for having equal share in nation's economic resources. In India's highly complex regional structure, the national strategy of development with allocation of the cost and benefits of progress must emerge from the coordination and rational cumulation of the needs and goals of different regional units. The phase of development until now has been unavoidably lopsided. Some parts of the country have become more developed because of industrialization, urbanization, communication, etc., during the plan periods, but other parts of the country till now have remained neglected and economically poor. In a developing economy, attention is always given to the growth of the total national income for which the infrastructure of the area is taken into consideration ignoring the equitable distribution system. Under such a development process, some ethnic groups move ahead more efficiently and rapidly than others. Because of the historical and cultural factors, this creates apprehensions among other ethnic groups about their prospects in the fields of education, employment, industrial development, political control and even the continuance of their culture within their historical homeland in a region. For instance the Gorkha movement was also a reflection of the discontentment of the Hill people for the neglect of social, economic, educational and cultural advancement of the people of the hill areas of the Darjeeling district. Such type of regionalism has led to the advocacy of decentralization of production, distribution and grass-root planning in India.

The other side of argument is that development creates regional consciousness among the people. No doubt, development and planning have raised to some extent the standard of living of the people and at the same time created new aspirations among the people. At the same time there has emerged a widening gap between aspirations and development. The governmental policies of economic development lag behind the new emerging aspirations of the people and thus create discontentment among them. In such case, the identity crisis is not the result of underdevelopment but of development itself. As Bhawani Singh says, the primitive Lodhas do not ask for autonomy. The underdeveloped Santhals do not raise the demand for Jharkhand. Only the developed Nepalese had started a movement for a separate state, and the developed Sikhs demand an independent Khalistan.

Regionalism, Development and People

The interaction between regionalism and development has got far-reaching effects on the people of the country as a whole. Why the cultural and economic variations exist is not important. The real issue is how people respond to such differences, variations and crisis of identity; and to the apprehensions and consequent demands that accompany such variations; and how upon that, development of the system takes place. The regional movements have created new types of elites in India. These elites have become more in number, diffused at all regions of the country as well as more active in articulating and aggregating regional demands. They are brought into the political and administrative infrastructures and given experience, a voice and a stake in the political affairs of the nation. Thus, political leadership is more concentrated only at the Centre. It is not that the political elites only at the Centre are strong. The elites at regional level are also strong to raise their legitimate claims within the fabric of national political system and this leads to the effective working of democratic system in India. It is noteworthy to point out that elites at both levels have become tolerant and of compromising nature to create an atmosphere of harmony and cooperation to make the national political system healthy.

The regional movements not only help formulate such demands at the elite level but also at the mass level. Because such movements make regional units more coherent and significant for the masses, they prepare the ground for more intense mass demands. The mass become more politically conscious for achieving identity and there is more scope for participation and mobilization of people in the political process. The elite and mass come close and the gap between them gets bridged up when there is the need for consolidating and putting forth particular and parochial demands of the region with an object of achieving them. Thus, there is a development of parochial-participant political culture in the country. However, the growth of political consciousness among the people enables them to make their regional demands – legitimate or illegitimate – intense and sometimes they want their demands to be fulfilled even at the cost of national goals and objectives. In such cases, regional movements become violent, leading to terrorism which has got an adverse effect on the political system as the case was in Punjab in 1975.

Understanding Regionalism Today

Paul Brass, a well-known political scientist and long-term student of India's political history, notes that regional groups are pushing for greater access to political power and control over Government purse, not cultural or linguistic separation (Brass, 1994). Regionalism or subregionalism should thus be seen as the desire for greater democracy and empowerment within a political unit. In fact, subregionalism is a movement which is not based on more fundamental primordial identities such as caste or language but is essentially modern – in the direction of a balanced and equitable modernization. Our analysis will show that cutting across caste, religion, gender and other divisions, the Telangana Movement brings a focus on the development of the region as a whole, a focus on rights and access to regional resources and further, it pitches for a rights-based development perspective whereby, groups and communities put forth their agendas within a larger vision of equitable development.

Contemporary regional movements should thus be interpreted in the context of 'rights based development'. This by no means should be taken to imply that people wish to monopolize regional resources and go back to autarkic economies. It does, however, mean that local people wish to assert 'first right' on decisions over resources in their region, exercise a say in their exploitation and debate the impact of particular modes of resource exploitation on their well-being. In this context, it would be germane to remember that even the Chipko Movement was first a movement for local rights over regional resources and only subsequently did it turn into an environmental movement (Guha, 1989). It was no different in the case of the Sardar Sarovar Dam on the Narmada, where the crucial issue was the need to respect the rights of native tribal and other communities and ensure their proper rehabilitation, resettlement and future livelihood. Thus various kinds of assertions, whether caste-based or environment-based have had the merit of drawing attention to various inequities and setting society on a corrective path. As M.N. Srinivas, the respected sociologist said, much of the churning in contemporary India is part of a silent revolution brought about by the very nature of democracy which willy-nilly places power through the vote in the hands of people.

It would thus be a mistake to interpret regional movements merely as a 'sons of the soil' policy or what the SRC called the 'homeland' concept. These are surely not very democratic or liberal constructs and go against the Constitutional rights of individuals in a nation-state. In the case of Andhra Pradesh, the zonal system, ushered in by the Presidential Order of 1975 may indeed have strengthened such a 'homeland' policy by reserving rights to education and jobs on a regional basis. The demand for greater equity, in our view, has to be separated from the demand for further parochial reservations.

The field of development studies shows us that there is no magic formula for rapidly reducing socio-economic disparities which prevail within both large and small political units or within cultural regions; the redressing of such disparities is through a process of local struggles, state policy responses and many fortuitous circumstances. Telangana as a region, notwithstanding some genuine grievances, is showing rapid development along most parameters; the regional sentiment for a separate state should thus be seen as a demand for greater political space, power and a stronger say in the affairs of the region and of the state. As the political space has expanded at various levels of governance, the aspiration for higher offices has grown. At a pragmatic level, a new state can often provide the fastest route to high political offices. In the following sections, an attempt is made to highlight the small and large struggles and grievances of residents of the state in the context of the current demand for separate statehood by Telangana region.

An Overview

Regionalism in India is a complex amalgam of geographical, historic-cultural, economic, politico-administrative and psychic factors. It is difficult to indicate which component has ascendancy, though it will not be surprising if the economic factor has an edge over the others in the ultimate analysis. It is also interesting to note that regionalism in India seems to manifest itself in overlapping circles in terms of its major types which, as such, are not immune fusing into each other and also being diffused, if an overreaching national loyalty structure emerges to transcend them. The basic issue is not of regionalism vs. nationalism but one of right ordering of loyalties between the regional and the national identities. This is the crux of the problem of management of regionalism in India, to the resolution of which the political elite, administrators and educationists have to join hands and work. The goal is plausible and yet it cannot be denied that the country has to go a long way even to approximate it. Will obsession with the political elite, administration and educationists in the country permit them to address themselves to the basic issue? Today it seems to be an open question, though future alone will give the final answer.

Regionalism and subregionalism pose a question for those who think in terms of nation-building. In fact, one finds that there is a kind of contradiction between two connotations or aspects of the term and process of political development. If one follows the meaning of political development in terms of nation-building he would point out that the regional movements challenge the various process of integration; and if one thinks of political development in terms of increasing political participation he would welcome the growth of regionalism because thereby, the elite in the region ask for more meaningful participation in politics and share in power or make a demand that they should be allowed to run their own affairs. This contradiction can probably be solved by creating small states, by responding to regional demands in a more positive manner or by finding out a framework whereby, powers are divided between the state and sub-state.

Referring to intra-regionalism in Andhra Pradesh, M. Subrahmanyam (Majeed, 1984) says that the problem of 'regional' identity was first started in the presidency of Madras which was a composite state, consisting of Tamil, Telugu, Kannada, Malayalam, and Oria speaking areas. The dispatch of Government of India dated 25 August 1911, visualized India as a union of autonomous provinces. The contents of the dispatch were not known immediately. But when they became known, they gave a great impetus to the consolidation of ideas on linguistic provinces. People living in the composite provinces became particularly language conscious. They thought that unless the provincial boundaries were redrawn and provinces were organized on a linguistic basis, it would not be possible for many people to profit to any appreciable extent by provincial autonomy (Roy, Mehta and Aiyar, 1965). The development of regional languages and literature had been greatly encouraged by the freedom movement, and the members of the western educated elite had increasingly turned to their regional languages as media for expansion of their views. The pride of one's own language which was often combined with antagonistic feelings towards neighbouring languages.

Language group, created a strong sense of solidarity among the class and mass of respective regions (Khan, 1970: 110). In the composite madras Presidency, the Telugu speaking area and the people were the largest when compared with the rest. But the political leadership in the presidency was held by the Tamilian leaders. Being outspoken the Telugu leaders had no will to play the role of a second fiddle. They expressed the view that they will form an Andhra Committee of the Indian National Congress. The determination of the view was lucidly expressed by Dr B. Pattabhi Seetha Ramiah, who said: 'the clear sketch of continuous territory, a common language and literature, common traditions of heroes and poets, warriors and kings and deep down a strong similarity of temper and character these languages bound communities are to be outlined each into a single race and accorded all those accessories of communal and political institutions which illustrate and feed the unity'.

The Andhra Congress leaders, against the wishes of the national leaders met at Bapatla, a town in Guntur district in May 1913, and declared the formation of the Andhra Congress Committee, under the chairmanship of Duggiral Gopala Krishnaiah. The main objective of the committee was to avoid the interference of the Tamil leadership in the Andhra problems. Apart from that, they expressed their commitment to achieve a separate provincialhood to the entire Telugu speaking people and the area, to promote, to get more freedom of action, for all-round progress of the Telugu people. The Andhra leadership pressurized the Indian National Congress through different means, as well as building public opinion through their vernacular press. Ultimately, the National Congress obliged and granted permission to establish Andhra Congress Committee on 8 April 1917. It was the first step towards the Andhra regionalism. Till our independence, the Telugu leadership shared the political power with their Tamilian counterparts, in the Madras Province.

At the Nagpur session in 1920, the Indian National Congress resolved that the Federal set up of India will be based on the principle of language. The 1928 Nehru report, keeping the 1920 resolution in view, recommended the necessity of restructuring the provinces on the linguistic basis. The report said, inter alia, that 'it comes most desirable for provinces to be re-grouped on a linguistic basis. Language as rule corresponds with special variety of culture, of traditions and literature. In a linguistic area, all these factors will help in general progress of the provinces'.

After the first general elections in independent India the Madras Province was held by C. Rajagopalachari as the chief minister. The people of Andhra in general, and the leaders in particular, started feeling suffocated and they initiated the demand of restructuring the province on the linguistic basis as recommended by the historical Nehru Committee. But the central leadership was reluctant to undertake such a move, keeping in view a variety of problems the nation was facing at that time. But, almost all the legislators from the Telugu speaking area were firmly determined to achieve their goal, the Andhra province to begin with, separation of Andhra and forming an integrated province while uniting the Telugu speaking people and areas of Andhra, and Telangana which was then a part of the Dominion of Hyderabad, as in integrated State of 'Vishalandhra'. Potti Sri Ramulu a Sarvodya leader of Gandhian order went on *niraharadeeksha* (Satyagraha by fasting) till death to attain the objective of the Andhra demand. The central leadership at Delhi did not pay much attention towards the people's demand of Andhra. The Satyagraha was continued till the death of Sri Ramulu up to the 56th day. During that period much tension was generated among the Andhras, but their agitation approach was one of the democratic ways of strife, such as demonstrations, hartal and bandhs. On the precedence of the Civil Disobedience Movement of Indian Liberation movement, the students boycotted the educational institutions and other groups also joined with the common cause of the people. The indifference of the Union Government headed by Nehru, who endorsed the proposal of restricting Indian Federation on linguistic grouping of the areas and people, and the death of Sri Ramulu, added fuel to the already existing tension among the Andhras.

The death of Sri Ramulu further aggravated the situation extremely. The people lost faith in peaceful means of agitation and resorted to violent means. There was a wave of panic and emotion among people of Andhra. The state government, at the Andhra districts, was paralysed. It is a sorry state of affairs in India that the Union Government takes an easy way, with indifference, till the democratic means of agitations in the demand of genuine public interest shape into violence. Though the Union Government refused the demand of the Andhras, stating that it could not be coerced, when scores of people were killed in the police firings at different places, and when the agitation turned into a mass scale revolt, finally it climbed down. Nehru made a statement that he was willing to take early steps to form an Andhra State out of Telugu areas but excluding Madras city. The Andhras reluctantly received the statement as it did not include their demand over the city of Madras. On 19 December 1952, Nehru announced the formation of separate Andhra State with follow-up action.

After the formation of separate state of Andhra, on the basis of linguistic regionalism, pressure started building upon the Union Government from the rest of linguistic areas. Ultimately, as a first step in the light of the Nagpur resolution of 1920 and with the spirit of constitutional recommendations of the Nehru Committee of 1928, the Government of India announced the formation of the State Reorganization Commission, with Justice Fazal Ali, as Chairman, R.M. Pannikkar and H.N. Kunzru as members, to recommend the reorganization of the states with a guidelines of linguistic approach. The dominion of Hyderabad was also, like the presidency of Madras, a multilingual state consisting of Telugu, Kanada, and Marathi speaking areas. Among them the Telugu speaking was the largest both in area and population. Being a Muslim princely state, Urdu was the official language. The people in the 20th century started raising their voice against the autocracy of feudal rule. The movement, on parallel with the freedom struggle, was started by the people. To begin with, the people of Telangana organized a literary association known as Andhra Mahasabha, to promote the linguistic and cultural interest and activities in 1920. Simultaneously, it became a cover for the underground political activities of Telangana freedom struggle against the autocracy and feudal rule. The Mahasabha expressed its desire to unite all the Telugu speaking people into a single unit, as the Telugu speaking areas of both Andhra and Telangana were contiguous geographical areas.

After 1952, both the Congress and Communist parties endorsed their previous commitment of uniting the Telugu speaking people into a single political unit 'Vishal Andhra'. The separation of Andhra State in 1953 gave fillip to that movement the states reorganization commission, proposed to form two Telugu linguistic states, that is Andhra and Telangana. The opinion of the commission encouraged certain sections of the Congress party to demand a separate Telangana State. They contended that the integrated Telugu State will hinder the economic interest of the backward Telangana people. That group included mostly the younger generation of the congressmen of the Telangana leadership. The agitation movement was headed by Dr M. Chenna Reddy, a dynamic leader among the younger generation of the Telangana leadership.

Finally, the compromise took place, and the inhabitants of Andhra and Telangana were brought under the common roof of a Telugu State. The state of Andhra Pradesh was inaugurated on 1 November 1956 and thus the Andhra or Telugu regionalism became a reality. Keeping in view the socio-economic realities of the two areas, the Government of India provided certain safeguards to the people of Telangana. The safeguards were spelt out through what is known as the 'gentlemen's agreement 1956'. The safeguard included social, employment, educational, economic and political aspects. The agreement included the provision to create a Telangana regional council to supervise over significant Telangana interest. Clause 13 is politically very significant, and it reads: 'If the chief minister is from Andhra, the deputy chief minister from Telangana and vice-versa. Two out of the following portfolios will be assigned to ministers from Telangana: (a) home, (b) finance, (c) revenue, (d) planning and development: and (e) commerce and industry'. It also indicated that the surplus revenue from Telangana would be allocated for Telangana development. The gentleman's agreement paved a smooth way for the process of integration of Telugu speaking people, the second largest linguistic group in India. Though, in 1956, the Telugu people were politically integrated, still there was a lacuna in the administrative and social areas. The government employees belonging to the two areas developed a feeling that there was a wide gap between each other.

The employees from Telangana developed a feeling that the Andhra employees were exercising hegemony over them, and the Andhra officers were discriminating against them; the gentleman's agreement was not followed in its true spirit. There was a lapse in the implementation of the 'Mulki Rules' also. The vacant post from Telangana quota, thought to be reserved for the Telangana people, with a plea that suitable candidates were not available, were being filled by Andhra's. Slowly, the Telangana regional council had become a nominal body. On the other hand, the government employees from Andhra area, who were posted in Telangana areas, also developed discontentment against the Telangana employees and they started thinking that they were privileged class of people, but the Telangana employees with less efficiency were getting more opportunities against them. Another problem was also before them – that is due to the necessity of the mulki or domicile certificate for the admission into the educational institutions in Telangana, they felt that their children were deprived of educational facilities in Telangana.

Meanwhile, overlooking the Telangana safeguards, the government of Andhra Pradesh prepared an integrated list of seniority of their employees for the purpose of promotions. The Telangana employees were totally unhappy as that was a violation of the gentleman's agreement, and hindered their prospects. Hence, they challenged the list in the Andhra Pradesh high court and brought a stay order against the implementation of the integrated promotion list.

To bring the village administration at par with Andhra area, modification orders were issued under the legislative act abolishing the hereditary right of succession of the Telangana village officers. The Telangana village officers association challenged the act in the High Court of Andhra Pradesh and the judgment was in their favour. That action of the government of Andhra Pradesh purchased displeasure at the grass-root level administrative personnel.

The incidents had created an unwarranted fear complex among the Andhra employees. Ultimately, they challenged the validity of the Mulki Rules in the High Court. The judgment went in favour of Andhra employees, the Mulki Rules were declared as a violation of fundamental rights.

The judgment of the High Court declaring the 'Mulki Rules' ultra vires caused a great anxiety and frustration among the student community and the non-gazetted employees of Telangana. The students called for a strike with a demand of separation of Telangana from the integrated state of Andhra Pradesh. The students of the area organized relay-hunger strikes. They demanded the resignations of Ministers from Telangana, as they failed to safeguard the Telangana interests. Further they started pressuring the legislators to resign from the legislative bodies. But no favourable results were achieved.

The Supreme Court of India withheld the election of Dr M. Chenna Reddy, who at the time was a cabinet minister in the Union Government, where he had appealed against the judgment of the Andhra Pradesh High Court which previously had made a similar kind of judgment. Under the People's Representative Act, he was disqualified to contest any election for a term of six years. Hence, he resigned from the central cabinet. During the time the dissident leaders of the Congress party of Telangana, and non-Communist opposition party leaders, formed the Telangana Praja Samithi, a platform and organization to achieve the goal of separate Telangana. Immediately after the formation of Telangana Praja Samiti, the agitation was spread to the nook and corner of the area. The masses, unprecedented agitation by the matured leaders and, the younger generation, who felt more affected, turned violent. It caused a great concern of law and order situation in the entire Telangana.

Though the Government of Andhra Pradesh was awaiting the Supreme Court judgment where they had appealed against the judgment of high court regarding the withholding of the Mulki Rules as unconstitutional, the Telangana non-gazetted officers association launched a strike to press their demand of safeguarding their service conditions. Separation of Telangana was also one measure, they felt, as a protection towards their service conditions. The strike continued for 46 days. During that period practically the government machinery was at standstill and there was no government order in effect in Telangana. Subsequently, the Supreme Court admitted the plea of the state government and declared the Mulki Rules as valid under the constitution. Telangana ministers persuaded the non-NGO association to call off the strike, and convinced them that the government was interested to protect their service conditions. The government also assured them, that the Andhra employees, if they were hosted in the vacancies of Telangana would be transferred to Andhra area by creating superannuary posts and the vacancies would be filled by the Telangana personnel. Subsequently, the government fulfilled the commitment. With these assurances, the Telangana NGO association called off their 46-day old strike.

The government allocated 90 million rupees as an additional grant for the economic developments of Telangana districts. An-all party meeting was called by the government to find the solution to clear off the tension and the conflict of Telangana problem, on 19 January 1969, at Hyderabad. The all-party meet examined the irritant problems such as employment, revision of the integrated intact of seniority, utilization of Telangana surplus funds for their economic development of Telangana, to remove the existing economic imbalances. They resolved that 'we of different political persuasions firmly resolve to bend our energies towards achieving quicker development and follow integration of our state. Andhra Pradesh holds a predominant position in the map of India and in order to be able to contribute our own share of our national integration of the country, it is of paramount importance that within our own state we achieve full unity. We, therefore, vehemently and unequivocally condemn the slogan that is raised in certain quarters for the creation of separate state' (*Telangana, A Challenge of Masses,* Telangana Graduate Convention Warangal, July 1969: 81–82).

But the all-party meet and its resolutions did not convince the agitators in Telangana to depart from their agitation. The people in general and the youth in particular lost faith in the promise of the politicians. Furthermore, the agitations started to take a more violent course of action. Buses were burnt; government and semi-government buildings were burnt. 'Telangana people are in a state of worry and Andhra in a state of fear. Already much damage has been caused. Any further delay would worsen the situation' was the observation made by Ram Reddy during the situation. He further summarized, 'the Telangana agitation which was launched in January 69 turned out to be long drawn out. Its nature and contest have also undergone substantial changes; started as an agitation of students, it has spread to politicians, trade unions, intellectuals, businessmen and finally to the government Non-Gazetted Officers'.

In a new democracy like India, which is striving to give a participatory mass base and representative character to its structures of governance the internal implications of building and sustaining a modern State are many (Khan, 1970). A general feeling was developed that the leaders of Telangana were not given due share in political power in the United Andhra Pradesh State administration. Thus the political elite had developed a sense of frustration and it was practically responsible for anti-Andhra behaviour (Reddy and Sharma, 1979).

The Telangana Praja Samiti persuaded Chenna Reddy to join them to strengthen the cause of 'separate Telangana', and unanimously offered him its presidentship. Being a skillful and experienced organizer, Chenna Reddy was able to bring most of the dissatisfied political groups into the fold of Telangana Praja Samiti. It should also be noted that young and dynamic leaders, who were not either encouraged or patronized by the earlier Chief Ministers, mostly coming from the backward castes of Telangana, strengthened the agitation in Telangana and played a very important role to accelerate the tempo of agitation. They functioned as a bridge connecting the student and youth force and the seasoned politicians of the areas.

The Government of Andhra Pradesh detained several leaders of Telangana Praja Samithi, including Dr Chenna Reddy. But the writs filed by the detenues in the Andhra Pradesh High Court, challenging their detention, got the release orders from the High Court. At this juncture, the Central Government intervened and proposed measures to establish normalcy in Andhra Pradesh. But the central leadership did not adhere to the demand of 'Brahmananda Reddy as Chief Minister to go'. The Chief Minister K. Brahamananda Reddy, shuffled his cabinet; P.V. Narsinga Rao, the senior-most minister from Telangana, was appointed as the Deputy Chief Minister. For the first time, due share was given to the backward castes in the Council of Ministers of Andhra Pradesh. The Central Government appointed 'Lalit Committee' to find out about the Telangana's surplus funds.

The leaders, who dropped from the council of ministers, were in a dilemma, and they had their own reasons. They did not subscribe to the idea of separate Telangana, but were unhappy with the action of the Chief Minister. In due course, they joined the agitation demanding the change of leadership and the protection of Telangana Mulki Rules with other safeguards. In 1972, a prominent leader from Telangana, P.V. Narasimha Rao, replaced Brahmananda Reddy as the Chief Minister. He was reputed as staunch integrationist from the day of Andhra Mahasabha. At that time Narasimha Rao was the only acceptable leader from Telangana, to both the areas, to head the Congress Party in the State as the Chief Minister.

After becoming the chief minister, P.V. Narasimha Rao brought two very important and progressive legislations. They dealt with the ceiling over the agricultural landholdings and urban land ceiling in the state of Andhra Pradesh. Land reforms to some extent were followed in Telangana along with the abolition of Jagirdari system in 1952. The extension of such ceiling on the landholding in entire Andhra Pradesh, caused much anguish among the bourgeoisie in Andhra. It also goes to the credit of Narasimha Rao that he implemented the Mulki Rules and the Telangana safeguards in the letter and spirit. His ministry gave berths to new faces who were so far denied such a political privilege, and most of them were the backward castes of Andhra Pradesh.

The implementation of Mulki Rules caused an anxiety among the people of Andhra region, particularly among the government employees and the student community of that area. The leaders who felt that their political identity was been narrowed, organized dissident groups.

The political dissent, the bourgeoisie economic interest, the anxiety of the student for both educational and employment facilities and the unhappiness among the Andhra employees, all culminated into political distrust and thus an agitation was launched in Andhra area. The demand was for a separate Andhra state. The 1974 Andhra separatist agitation was a cyclical rotation of the Telangana movement. Kakani Venkatarathanam, a veteran leader from Krishna district, who belonged to the influential Kamma caste, and Peddireddy Timma Reddy of Chittoor district, who became unpopular due to his sharp remarks about the Harijan community in one incident at Kanchikacherla village in Krishna district, became important leaders of the 'separate Andhra' agitation. This time, the national leadership acted swiftly and in time. President's Rule was imposed at that time, the state legislative assembly was kept in suspension and P.V. Narasimha Rao was deposed from the office of chief minister. These measures had immediate effect on the agitators. Subsequently the agitations were called off. Slowly the state returned to normalcy. After revoking the President's Rule, J. Vengala Rao, an Andhrtes residing in Telangana since decades (earlier to the independence) was elected unanimously as the leader of Andhra legislative assembly and headed the council of ministers.

In 1978, Dr M. Chenna Reddy, the veteran Telangana leader spearheaded the separate Telangana movement. He was twice elected as the Chief Minister of Andhra Pradesh. After becoming Chief Minister of integrated Andhra Pradesh he declared that separation was a past history and his stewardship would provide impartial approach for the all-round development of the people of the entire state of Andhra Pradesh. In-built tensions and conflicts of the subregional units should be minimized if not entirely removed. These are destroying the very edifice that we are building. The continuing concern and debate of these very fundamental issues should be considered by the authorities that bear a genuine manifestation of the democratic ethos of the country. After the formation of the Andhra state, the social inter-reaction between the two regions were not favourable to any harmonious relations. After Hyderabad (a Telangana city) became the capital of the new state, people from the Andhra area migrated to it in a large number as government servants, businessman and job seekers. There were stereotype perceptions about each other's cultural levels, economic capacities and political motives. 'The Telangana personality, according to protagonists of the movement, is based on refinement, cultural synthesis and what they called cosmopolitanism in their hierarchy of values, human relations seems to rank higher than worldly successes. Telangana people are generally unambitious and mercantile a major criticism of Andhrites is that they are 'nouveaux riches' and throw their money about'.

The emphasis on a different cultural identity was a distinctive and a significant feature of the Telangana movement. The justification of the movement, on which the cultural identity was based, was the assertion that Telangana was backward as compared to other regions. As pointed out earlier, Telangana was part of a princely state, having fewer educational facilities than the rest of Andhra region. It is still educationally backward.

There was a clear, visual, impression of Andhra becoming prosperous, while Telangana remained stagnant. The coastal area had always been more prosperous, but the massive strides in the field of agriculture in the areas along the Godavari and Krishna rivers widened the developmental gap between the Andhra and Telangana regions. In the costal areas of Krishna, Guntur and Godavari districts, tobacco production increased and new agro-industries were established to process tobacco, rice and sugar. At the same time, main Andhra landlords disposed of their lands at high prices in Andhra and purchased lands at lower price in Telangana (partially in the Nizamabad area) which was then coming under the new irrigation schemes. Telangana peasants were hardly touched by the green revolution, because all the agricultural and irrigation schemes started much later in their region. Most industries established in the Telangana region hardly benefited the people from Telangana area. Business started by Andhra people recruited staff from the Andhra and those started by the Government recruited staff on all-India basis, thus putting Telangana people in a marginalized state.

It was in every field of special life that the Andhra people had achieved a controlling position. The feeling developed among the Telangana people that earlier they were governed by the Nizam protected by the British Raj, and after Andhra Pradesh was formed they came to be dominated by the Andhra people protected by the Central Government. There were at least three social classes who were feeling an acute sense of relative deprivation because it was no longer possible for them to obtain benefits. The students in Telangana were dissidents because of different reasons. Literacy rate was rising and the number of graduates had increased. These educated youth were seeking employment at a time when there was a recession in the job market and the Andhra people held most of the office jobs. Peasants of Telangana, particularly of Nizamabad and Nalgonda districts, were dissidents because earlier they had sold land to richer Andhra migrants and were now resentful of these rich neighbours. Middle-class government employees, particularly non-gazetted officers, were resentful of their colleagues from Andhra and who had obtained promotions and were an obstacle in their possibility of promotions. It has to be kept in mind that these three social groups were very closely linked with each other. Many of the lower level civil servants were related to landholding peasants, and the students were the children of these two groups. All these people look at opportunities for themselves as finite.

The Telangana separatist movement was basically an economist proposition. The glaring disparities between the two regions of the state that had evolved as a result of an uneven process of development could not have been eliminated overnight. It is generally believed that other factors such as caste, religion, culture, language and primordiality shed much of their traditional appeal in a welfare-oriented process of development. In Telangana, there is no substantial claim to fight for or against primordiality and when such claims introduced as welfare prizes and development allocations, the subregion in Andhra Pradesh was no longer based on linguistic lines but on economic demands. The fact that the economic factors constituted the main cause of this movement was, in fact, confirmed by the solution that ended the agitation. The agitation ended on the basis of Prime Minister's eight-point formula: the identification of the new development schemes; the increasing association of regional bodies with decisions on development of the region; securing of adequate safeguards for service opportunities of Telangana people, etc. All of this was nothing else but a programme for the more faithful implementation of the regional assurances that were not originally fulfilled, giving a rationale to the separatist demands.

Sri Krishna Committee (Committee for Consultations on the Situation in Andhra Pradesh)

Pursuant to the Union Home Minister's meeting with the eight recognized political parties of Andhra Pradesh on 5 January 2010, the Government of India constituted a committee for consultations on the situation in Andhra Pradesh (CCSAP), with the following composition, to hold wide ranging consultations with all sections of the people including all the political parties and various groups, with a view to examine the demand for a separate State of Telangana as well as for maintaining the present status of a united Andhra Pradesh:

(1) Shri Justice B.N. Srikrishna, Chairman, Retired Judge, Supreme Court of India; (2) Professor (Dr) Ranbir Singh, Member, Vice Chancellor, National Law University, Delhi; (3) Dr Abusaleh Shariff, Member, Senior Research Fellow, International Food Policy Research Institute, Delhi; (4) Professor (Dr) Ravinder Kaur, Member, Professor, Department of Humanities and Social Sciences, Indian Institute of Technology Delhi; (5) Shri V.K. Duggal, IAS (Retd.), Member Secretary, Former Union Home Secretary.

The Chairman was accorded the status of the sitting Supreme Court Judge and the Member Secretary, the rank of a Union Minister of State. The Terms of Reference of the Committee were:

(1) To examine the situation in the State of Andhra Pradesh with reference to the demand for a separate State of Telangana as well as the demand for maintaining the present status of a united Andhra Pradesh.

(2) To review the developments in the State since its formation and their impact on the progress and development of the different regions of the State.

(3) To examine the impact of the recent developments in the State on the different sections of the people such as women, children, students, minorities, other backward classes, scheduled castes and scheduled tribes.

(4) To identify the key issues that must be addressed while considering the matters mentioned in items (1), (2) and (3) above.

(5) To consult all sections of the people, especially the political parties, on the aforesaid matters and elicit their views; to seek from the political parties and other organizations a range of solutions that would resolve the present difficult situation and promote the welfare of all sections of the people; to identify the optimal solutions for this purpose; and to recommend a plan of action and a road map.

(6) To consult other organizations of civil society such as industry, trade, trade unions, farmers' organizations, women's organizations and students' organizations on the aforesaid

matters and elicit their views with specific reference to the all-round development of the different regions of the State.

(7) To make any other suggestion or recommendation that the Committee may deem appropriate.

Andhra Pradesh (29 November 2009 – 31 December 2010): The events and happenings in the state in the last one year starting from 29 November 2009 are still quite fresh in public memory. To recall, as announced earlier, Telangana Rashtra Samithi (TRS) President, K. Chandrasekhara Rao started his fast-unto-death on 29 November 2009 demanding that the Central Government should introduce the Telangana Bill in Parliament. Prior to his undertaking the fast, TRS called upon student bodies, employees unions and various non-gazetted officials organizations to join the movement. After the Telangana issue had resurfaced around Assembly elections of 1999, the students, non-gazetted officials and other organizations at this point of time once again got involved in the Telangana movement. On the day of his fast, i.e., 29 November 2009, K. Chandrasekhara Rao was arrested and taken to Khammam. On 30 November 2009, he reportedly broke his fast but resumed it soon thereafter under pressure from vociferous and agitating pro-Telangana elements. Following these developments, there was simultaneous and widespread agitation and violence in Telangana region for a few days, particularly on 6–7 December 2009, resulting in major damage to public and private property and loss of life including a number of suicides. Around the same time, a Joint Action Committee (JAC) was formed by the students of Osmania and Kakatiya universities. The JAC started seriously agitating for the cause of a separate Telangana, demanding an assurance for the same. The agitations led to the closure of educational institutions and business establishments throughout the Telangana region. Public transport services were also suspended. During this period, reportedly over five thousand persons were taken into preventive custody with a view to bringing the law and order situation, created by the agitations, under control.

With the situation becoming grim, a meeting of the floor leaders of the political parties in the State Legislature was convened by the Chief Minister, K. Rosaiah on 7 December 2009. It is learnt that all political parties, except Communist Party of India-Marxist (CPI-M), were in favour of a proposal to adopt a resolution in the

State Assembly for creation of a separate Telangana. The CPI-M apparently referred to the stand it had taken at the time of the Pranab Mukherjee Committee. The All India Majlis-e-Ittehad-ul Muslimeen or the All India Council of the Union of Muslims (AIMIM) on the other hand observed that the proper forum to express its views would be the Legislative Assembly. Taking into account the situation in the state and the deliberations in this all party meeting, the Union Home Minister, P. Chidambaram in the late evening of 9 December 2009 at New Delhi announced the decision of the Central Government to initiate the process of forming the state of Telangana, adding that an appropriate resolution would be moved in the State Assembly. Based on this development TRS President, Chandrasekhara Rao gave up his fast and the agitation was called off.

The above announcement, however, created a backlash in coastal Andhra and Rayalaseema regions, resulting in agitations and eruption of violence in many districts. The agitations included bandh calls by political parties, road blockages, fast-unto-death programmes, relay hunger strikes, etc. A near total bandh was organized in all the districts of coastal Andhra and Rayalaseema on 11 December 2009 at the call of political parties. The agitations continued during the second and third week of December, 2009. Reportedly, nine MPs, one hundred forty-three MLAs and forty-one MLCs submitted their resignation in protest against the announcement on the formation of a separate Telangana.

Looking at the totality of the situation, including the intensity of the backlash and the strong sentiments expressed through agitations in all the regions of the state, as also the near vertical division on the issue among the major political parties in the state, the Union Home Minister made another statement on 23 December 2009 that the situation in the state had altered since 9 December 2009 when the Central Government had announced that the process of the formation of a separate state of Telangana would be initiated and an appropriate resolution would be moved in the State Assembly (meaning perhaps, thereby, that moving such a resolution in the State Assembly appeared to be difficult at this point of time). The Home Minister, therefore, in this statement emphasized the need for wide ranging consultations with all political parties and groups and promised to take steps to involve all concerned in the process. Although this statement led to ending of agitations in coastal

Andhra and Rayalaseema regions, agitations restarted in Telangana region due to the perceived change in the stand of the Government of India. At this point, reportedly sixty-three MLAs belonging to Telangana region (Congress – thirteen; Telugu Desham Party (TDP) – thirty seven; TRS – ten; Bharatiya Janta Party (BJP) – one; Praja Rajyam Party (PRP) – two) submitted their resignation.

During the period starting from 29 November 2009 till the end of April 2010 the state witnessed agitations of varying kinds, the most intense being from late November 2009 up to January 2010. Initially, these agitations were in Telangana region, then after the 9 December 2009 announcement, in coastal Andhra and Rayalaseema regions, and again back to Telangana region, post- 23 December 2009 statement. The law and order machinery of the state took appropriate action to bring the situation under control. A large number of cases both under preventive and substantive sections of law were registered and the needed arrests carried out. Since the agitations in Telangana region were for a much longer time compared to coastal Andhra and Rayalaseema regions, the number of cases registered against the agitators from Telangana was also much higher. In all, over 1,600 cases were registered involving more than 8,000 agitators. The cases were classified in two categories, i.e., simple cases such as 'Rasta Roko', 'Rail Roko', making provocative statements, instigating violence, violation of prohibitory orders, insulting national leaders by garlanding their statues with objectionable material and attempt to suicide, etc., and serious cases involving damage and burning of private properties, government properties and assault on public servants. The State Government has recently withdrawn all simple cases totaling to 565 pertaining to the first category in the interest of the career prospects of the youth and the students. The region-wise details of cases withdrawn are as: Telangana – 440; Coastal Andhra – 58 and Rayalaseema – 67.

As indicated in the announcement of 23 December 2009, the Central Government invited the presidents/senior leaders of the eight recognized political parties of the state for a meeting on 5 January 2010 to deliberate on the mechanism of the proposed consultations and to lay down a road map for the same. In the meeting chaired by the Union Home Minister on the said date at New Delhi and attended by the presidents/senior representatives of eight recognized political parties, the opinions on the issue were quite divided. It is learnt that while TRS, BJP and CPI expressed the view that no further consultations were necessary and that the process of creation of a separate state of Telangana, as announced, should be initiated, the Congress Party, CPI-M, AIMIM and the PRP conveyed that wide ranging consultations would be an appropriate option at this stage. The TDP was represented by two leaders who took divergent positions; with one favouring consultations and the other supporting a separate state. Notwithstanding the diversity in their views on the further steps to be taken, there was clear recognition of the need of the hour, which was to ensure that peace and calm should return to the state at the earliest. Understanding the serious law and order problems the state was facing, all the parties issued an appeal to the people of Andhra Pradesh (AP), to maintain peace and public order.

One of the major arguments for a separate state of Telangana has been that since the formation of the state of AP, this region has been neglected and even discriminated against, resulting in economic and social hardship. Compared with coastal Andhra, it is alleged that Telangana has low per capita income, lower access to employment, lower business opportunities and low access to education and so on. It is also alleged that most of the higher level economic opportunities are appropriated by those belonging to coastal Andhra. At the outset, some or all such allegations appear true when absolute amounts, numbers and percentages are reviewed. Yet, when a study of rate of change, growth rate and shares in the state economy is evaluated, nothing unusual emerges. Telangana excluding Hyderabad, currently has a share of 36 per cent in state population and 41 per cent in state landmass. Any development parameter that is consistent with these shares can be considered on par or at parity with the population/share of land mass. Indeed, one finds that at a reference point in the past, such as the census 1956 or 1961 or 1974 since when factual data are available, the shares for Telangana were far too low. In recent years, however, the shares of Telangana for many common development parameters are in league with the share of population/area, often being higher. There are a few crucial indicators on which Telangana is lagging behind, and they appear to have occurred due to structural causes of the economy and also due to concentration of economic activity in Hyderabad district/urban agglomeration.

Although three new states (Uttarakhand, Chhattisgarh and Jharkhand) have recently been created in the Indian Union, and are being cited as a precedent for creating more new states, Telangana may present a very different and unique case. One major difference in AP from the other states is that the apportioning of the capital city is in contention here. While Hyderabad forms a geographical component of Telangana region, it has been the capital of the state since 1956 and all three regions have contributed to its development. A major issue in the present conflict is how the three regions would protect their rights in and access to Hyderabad. Also, Andhra Pradesh consists of three distinct regions and any proposed division of the state must take into account the repercussions on all three regions. Thus, the demand for bifurcation of AP presents a much more complex case requiring a specific and appropriate solution. The case of Andhra Pradesh would probably reveal that demands for autonomy and separate statehood must be considered on a case by case basis, while keeping in mind issues of fundamental importance to state formation. Here we agree with the States Reorganization Commission (SRC), which recommends against a monistic approach to the problem of reorganization.

Regional sentiment or identity is not "given" and comes into play only when a region (which may be part of a larger unit, a state, or spread over several states) experiences feelings of neglect or discrimination in relation to other regions of the political unit of which it is a part. At the root of this feeling usually lies a sense of being marginalized by other groups or regions which seem to dominate either culturally, economically or politically. There may be a sense that the dominant region, due to greater economic or political power receives greater attention or a larger share of resources and benefits from the government. It may also have political power to enable it to divert a greater share of resources and benefits towards itself. Some of this is true in the case of Telangana, which perceives domination by the coastal Andhra region.

As Duncan Forrester (1970) famously said 'The tragedy of Telangana is that so little was done to identify or deal with the legitimate grievances of the area for so many years. The consequences, we may hope, may be a new sensitivity to similar situations developing in other states'. While Forrester may have been right when he wrote in 1970 and no doubt what he said remains important as a lesson even in the current context, the fortunes of Telangana have changed substantially since then. It is also clear that the sense of discrimination is not experienced equally by all groups. Thus, C.H. Hanumantha Rao (2010) says in the context of Telangana, 'The feeling of injustice is greater among the educated classes, i.e., students, teachers, NGOs and professionals in general. This is explained by the increasing awareness leading to greater sensitivity to discrimination among such classes in respect of employment and promotions or career prospects, especially because of the rising importance of the services sector at higher levels of development. It is not surprising, therefore, that the separatist movement has gathered momentum in the post-reform period when the opportunities for such classes have proliferated in the services sector and the role of the state in influencing development and regional equity has vastly increased. For the same reasons, it should not come as a surprise that the separatist sentiments are stronger in the relatively developed areas like North Telangana. Therefore, it can be concluded that far from development programmes – more precisely, welfare measures currently being implemented – countering separatist sentiments, the movement for separation may become stronger with the spread of development as long as the perception of injustices due to discrimination in development within the integrated state persists'. The Committee's findings on various allegations and grievances have been presented in the preceding chapters; it considers it important that the demand and sentiment for separation has to be dealt with by rectifying not only the actual discrimination but also the sense of discrimination (Rao, 2010).

Regional movements provide diverse groups and sections of society comprising the region with an opportunity to voice grievances and demands which may be particular to them. Thus, while a regional movement may present an external unity and a common goal, various groups join it to express their particular needs from their own vantage points. Here, one has to remember that although Andhra Pradesh became the first state to be formed on the basis of language, new linguistic units which were subsequently carved out (including AP), often fractured ecological cultural regions which continue to spread over several states. Thus, the closer connections of Ananthapur in Rayalaseema with Bangalore (now Bengaluru) and Tirupati with Chennai; Adilabad's, Khammam's, Vizianagaram's and Srikakulam' s shared concerns with tribal areas of Maharashtra,

Madhya Pradesh, Chhattisgarh and Orissa reveal that regions within the territorial boundaries of linguistic states do not necessarily perceive themselves only with reference to the state and its capital. Intra-state regional homogeneity can thus be quite frayed at the edges and show fault lines even within, due to development disparities or envied prosperous groups of migrants.

After going into all aspects of the situation as well as keeping in view the local, regional and national perspective, the Committee considers that the following solutions/possible options may offer the best way forward:

(i) Maintain status quo.
(ii) Bifurcation of the State into Seemandhra and Telangana; with Hyderabad as a Union Territory and the two states developing their own capitals in due course.
(iii) Bifurcation of State into Rayala-Telangana and coastal Andhra regions with Hyderabad being an integral part of Rayala – Telangana.
(iv) Bifurcation of Andhra Pradesh into Seemandhra and Telangana with enlarged Hyderabad metropolis as a separate Union Territory. This Union Territory will have geographical linkage and contiguity via Nalgonda district in the south-east to district Guntur in coastal Andhra and via Mahboobnagar district in the south to Kurnool district in Rayalaseema.
(v) Bifurcation of the State into Telangana and Seemandhra as per existing boundaries with Hyderabad as the capital of Telangana and Seemandhra to have a new capital.
(vi) Keeping the State united by simultaneously providing certain definite Constitutional/Statutory measures for socio-economic development and political empowerment of Telangana region – creation of a statutorily empowered Telangana Regional Council.

Operational Conceptual Framework

Post-Industrial Cities

Cities stand out at the apex of the service economy as the major articulating nodes. They form a distinct system of their own which lies atop a more intricate urban system and an even more comprehensive total settlement system.

The post-industrial cities integrate the regional economies with the state capital. Apart from this integrative function in a broader in a contextual perspective, the interrelations of these post-industrial cities with adjacent areas are of immense importance in enforcing reciprocity in the spatial economy. The post-industrial cities act as the organizing foci for the economies of their respective hinterlands. This interrelated system of cities and their hinterlands constitutes the basic fabric of any post-industrial set-up. Agglomeration economies tend to attract industries to these large centres. Trade and commerce are also attracted to these centres more so as they invariably lie at transportation and communication junction and by virtue of their large population size offer a vast consumer potential. Thus, the metropolises in these underdeveloped countries, project an image of hypertrophy of urban development.

The post-industrial cities including Hyderabad are the hard-core centres of economic activities, especially service economy. Owing to its intense economic activities and occupational opportunities, Hyderabad has become the centre of attraction for the people of different regions and origin. What binds people of Hyderabad despite regional diversity is commonality of economic opportunities.

Cosmopolitanism

The word derives from Greek 'cosmos' (the universe) and 'polis' (city). The etymological meaning thus would be the whole universe to be one city. Broadly speaking, cosmopolitanism, transnationalism and glocalism are concepts associated with, for example, global economy, communication, migration and environmental problems (Beck, 1992, 2000a, 2004). There is little doubt whether these examples are global issues; however, there is less agreement regarding the consequences of this trend for society on a global, national and individual level; and it is also rather unclear how these concepts relate to each other, as well as how they should be investigated empirically. In the first issue of *Current Sociology* for Victor Roudometof discusses three aspects of cosmopolitanism: first he tries to clarify some of the conceptual indistinctiveness surrounding the subject; second, he exemplifies the consequences of a changed reality in people's attitudes; and finally, he offers an operationalization of transnationalism inspired by Ulrich Beck. Roudometof (2005a) operationalizes transnationalism as attitudes related to different geographical and cultural levels, and he argues that it might be possible to empirically position people on a one-dimensional scale, ranging from local to global, according to their attitudes.

Hyderabad is one of the fastest growing cosmopolitan city with people of different cultural and ethnic communities coming together and living. Since city life generates its own lifestyle and value system, at an apparent level the regional and cultural diversities seem to sink. However, at a latent level regional identities are of tremendous significance. When the ethnicity of the regional groups is hit by globalization, regional identities are threatened and they become rigid and thus start the process of questioning cosmopolitanism.

Regionalism

Regionalism is a feeling or an ideology among a section of people residing in a particular geographical space characterized by unique language, culture, etc., that they are the sons of the soil and every opportunity that exists in their land must be accorded to them first but not to the outsiders. Regionalism definitely offers the advantage of ethnocentrism and till a point in continuum is a unifying factor. However, when regionalism becomes inclusive of violence it leads to regional conflicts. Conventional theories of development, economic as well as political, are insensitive to regional demands and aspirations. Regionalism is treated as a threat to national integration and coherence and, only occasionally, a positive role is conceded in generating political participation through regional mobilization.

Review of Literature

Elaborating on cosmopolitanism, Auguste Comte held that, after the French Revolution, prior to the global age, the entire old world had been destroyed, including its religion, and that the new, post-aristocratic order needed its own gospel and its own church. This he found in positivism and the *église positiviste*, in which the new rulers (the bourgeoisie) serve the nation through science and technology. As a new ethos for a global era, cosmopolitanism holds that, the post-national order needs its own gospel, which it discovers in cosmopolitan teachings of giving credit to strange intellectuality, knowledge of different cultural patterns of group life and inclusion of others. As an ethos of world citizenship, cosmopolitanism legitimates the inclusion of strangers by stating that strangers are not strange, deviant or dangerous but have their own human goodness, *despite* their social characteristics.

Cosmopolitanism legitimates this claim by investing humanity with an intense religiosity, in the sense that it elevates humanity to the authority status that the world religions would typically attribute to God or the sacred (Berges, 2005; Hill, 2000). Richard Falk holds that cosmopolitanism is 'an essentially religious and normative undertaking, faith in the unseen, salvation in the unseen, salvation in a world to come, guided by convictions, beliefs, values' (1994: 139–40).

The feelings and forces of cosmopolitanism pervade almost all the societies. The awareness of global forces seems to be increasing. Durkheim thus says: 'No matter how devoted men may be to their native land, they all to-day are aware that beyond the forces of national life there are others, in a higher region and not so transitory, for they are unrelated to conditions peculiar to any given political group and are not bound up with its fortunes. There is something more universal and enduring ... . National aims do not lie at the summit of this hierarchy – it is human aims that are destined to be supreme' (Durkheim, 1992: 72–73). Furthermore, in his work with Mauss, Durkheim shows a keen understanding of the necessity to switch in and out of the national frame depending on the objects under investigation and argues that '... not all social phenomena are equally apt to internationalize themselves. Political institutions, juridical institutions, the phenomena of social morphology constitute part of the specific character of each people. On the other hand, the myths, tales, money, commerce, fine arts, techniques, tools, language, words, scientific knowledge, literary forms and ideas – all of these travel and are borrowed' (Durkheim and Mauss, 1998: 153).

There have been several interpretations of "social" by various sociologists and interestingly it has been associated with cosmopolitanism. Durkheim shows us that his notion of the social connects to forms of Kantian universalism – certainly a form of cosmopolitan imagination – rather than to a narrow nationalism. Durkheim is adamant that existing nation-states will have to be the agency for the evolution of world patriotism, or cosmopolitanism; but this does not make him a methodological nationalist, any more than Beck is when he admits that the nation-state must remain an indispensable analytic unit in any realistic political analysis ('the cosmopolitan outlook retains a reference to the nation-state but situates and analyses it within a radically different horizon' (Beck, 2006: 33). Durkheim realizes that much of the development of culture and civilization must be studied from a global perspective, and his position here not only adopts a Kantian argument with an emphasis on pacifism and internationalism, but also emphasizes a degree of complementarily between the nation-state and cosmopolitan ambition.

Contemporary studies of global culture that focus on post-colonialism often connect this kind of cosmopolitanism to the political culture of human rights activism as evidence of the post-national spatialization of politics. For example, Arjun Appadurai has grouped transnational NGOs and philanthropic movements, diasporic communities, refugees, and religious movements under the rubric of actually existing 'post-national social formations', arguing that these organizational forms are 'both instances and incubators of a post-national global order' because they challenge the nation-state and provide non-violent institutional grounding for larger-scale political loyalties, allegiances and group-identities (1993: 421). It is claimed that these global social and political movements emanate from the grass-roots level and exhibit autonomy from dominant global economic and political forces ('grassroots globalization' or 'globalization from below') and that they can be the sustaining basis for transcending or overcoming the constraining discourse of nationalism/statism (Appadurai, 2000).

The connection between transnational migrant experiences of global cultural diversity and institutionalized forms of cosmopolitan solidarity, however, remains largely unelaborated. The world is undoubtedly interconnected and transnational mobility is clearly on the rise. But this does not inevitably generate meaningful cosmopolitanisms in the robust sense of pluralized world political communities. One should cast a more discriminating eye on the various emergent forms of cosmopolitanism and distinguish them in terms of how they are connected to the operations of neoliberal capital. For instance, over and above interventions on behalf of underprivileged migrant minority groups on an ad hoc basis, to what extent can activist cosmopolitanisms take root in the latter in a consistent manner to generate a genuinely pluralized mass-based global political community within the Northern constitutional nation-state as distinguished from the defensive identity politics of ethnic, religious or hybrid minority constituencies? Can these cosmopolitanisms be embedded in a global community in the South forged from transnational media networks?

Victor Roudometof tries to clarify the relations between the concepts cosmopolitanism, transnationalism and localism, and he poses the questions whether transnationalism leads to increased cosmopolitanism and if localism is a negation of transnationalism and cosmopolitanism. To answer these questions, he tries to identify the social processes responsible for undermining the boundaries of the nation-state, describes the reality of living in a social reality with structural relationships extending beyond national borders, and finally, tries to outline the changed features of individual attitudes by suggesting an operationalisation of what he calls the cosmopolitan–local continuum (Roudometof, 2005a). Roudometof argues that cosmopolitanism can be divided into 'thick' or 'rooted' cosmopolitanism, which is attachment to a specific country or locality that has developed from transnational interaction (on the level of 'social fields'), and 'thin' cosmopolitanism, which is not associated with a particular country or region, but indicates a change of values that has effects on both a local and at global level. Thin cosmopolitanism can be seen as an attitude towards life and the world that is not rooted in country specific experiences but in global and glocal experiences. Roudometof argues in favour of the second version, and he suggests an operationalization of cosmopolitanism according to the 'thin' version (ibid.).

Roudometof (2005a) criticizes Beck's lack of consistency in terminology and epistemology. According to Roudometof, Beck intertwines cosmopolitanism and transnationalism by using indicators of transnationalism under the heading of cosmopolitanization and he also treats the two concepts as interchangeable sometimes. This is connected to the epistemological problem, namely that Beck is simultaneously using cosmopolitanism as a process and as an outcome. The process of cosmopolitanization leads to a cosmopolitan society, i.e., Roudometof suggests that cosmopolitanization as a result cannot be explained by referring to cosmopolitanization as a process leading to its outcome (Rosenberg, 2000).

Instead of using concepts like 'banal cosmopolitanism' and 'glocalism', Roudometof prefers transnationalism. He claims that as nation-state boundaries are challenged through processes of globalization, glocalization and/or internal globalization, social life within these contexts is also transformed and leads to changed individual attitudes. Transnationalism, then, can be defined as the emerging new *reality* of social life under these conditions, where people can chose either to develop an open, or cosmopolitan attitude, or a closed, or local, attitude. That is, transnationalism is not affected by individual feelings or attitudes, it is the changed reality in which people live and form their lives. Furthermore, Roudometof (2005a) distinguishes between three levels of transnationalism: transnational interaction within social spaces, social fields and networks. Transnational social spaces are made up through transnational interaction, i.e., interaction between people and institutions in two or more nation-states. In this way, social relations become institutionalized and transnational practices and institutions develop, framed by Roudometof as transnational social fields, (e.g., regulating translational interactions). People in these fields are not necessarily transnational, but there are transnational communities or networks, created by immigrants and other people travelling and living 'globally', i.e., across state borders (Turner, 1992). So this is the transnational reality people in the western world find themselves living in, and Roudometof claims that they can either adopt an open or a closed attitude, according to which he categorizes people as either being *cosmopolitans* or *locals*. This appears as a bifurcation of public attitudes that can be operationalized according to a single dimension, the cosmopolitan-local continuum. However, cosmopolitan and local attitudes should not be seen as a dichotomy but as a continuum, i.e., cosmopolitans and locals occupy opposite ends of the same dimension but there is room for individual variation between the two ends. Locals should not be seen in isolation or in opposition to cosmopolitans, because they are both the result of a new glocalized reality (Beck, 2004).

Social changes cannot be limited to parts of the population; locals are just as modern as cosmopolitans, since cultural protectionism might, for example, be a consequence of a kind of cultural imperialism that only exists in the globalized world. Adopting the thin understanding of cosmopolitanism, Roudometof (2005a) argues that cosmopolitanism is not based in a specific country or place.

Roudometof defines cosmopolitans and locals as clusters of people with particular attitudes corresponding to the cosmopolitan-local continuum; i.e., individual attitudes are clustered around the two ends of the continuum like ideal types. The continuum is then operationalized into four continuous variables, according to which locals should differ from cosmopolitans (Roudometof, 2005a): degree of attachment to a locality, e.g., neighbourhood or city; degree of attachment to a state or country; Degree of attachment to and support of local culture (ethnocentrism); and finally, degree of economic, cultural and institutional protectionism.

Cosmopolitanism is too complex and multidimensional to be reduced to a single cosmopolitanism-localism continuum; a person might, for example, be both locally attached in a geographical sense and at the same time open to foreign traditions, and vice versa (Gubert, 2000).

Cosmopolitanism signals a shift from sociality to humanity, which eyes an all-inclusive society of strangers as its end result. Cosmopolitanism is discussed as a manifestation of the mentality of the global elite, as world citizenship, as a politics of human rights, as a religion of humanity and as global mores. In these distinct dimensions, cosmopolitanism appears to pave the way for the society of strangers (Berger, Berger and Kellner, 1974).

Joseph de Maistre famously claimed that human beings endowed with nothing more than their humanity are nowhere to be found and, to all practical intents, unimaginable. 'In the course of my life,' he said, 'I have seen Frenchmen, Italians, Russians, etc. I even know, thanks to Montesquieu, that one can be a Persian. But as for man, I declare that I have never met him in my life; if he exists, he is unknown to me'. Maistre's observation provides the basis for sociology. The concept of the human being without social characteristics is too vague to serve as a sociological framework, and is also tainted with a slight odour of enlightenment ideals and rootless individualism (Elias, 1991: 163). Because human beings cannot only be defined by their *humanity*, but any self-definition has to include *sociality*, identity is perceived as being dependent on social roles within a local or national group. Humanity cannot be set apart from, let alone against, the social roles through which members can express themselves. It is a sociological claim that 'humanity', as a non-empirical assumption, and sociality are balanced in a stable identity that can only emerge in stable local groups (Wrong, 1961).

The nameless human being without social characteristics, however, is, in cosmopolitan thought, the starting point, motivation and aim of cosmopolitanism. In its self-definition, cosmopolitanism is an ethos of world citizenship, a way of thinking about the relationship between human beings, and, therefore, a way of treating ourselves and others. In Ulf Hannerz's words, cosmopolitanism is the 'willingness to become involved with the Other, and the concern with achieving competence in cultures' (Hannerz, 1990).

In the midst of cultural diversity and a divided world, cosmopolitanism seeks to recognize *human goodness*, undeterred by traits that are strange, and is eager, through cultural competence, to understand and appreciate humanity in its strange guises (Delanty, 2000; Nussbaum, 1996). Cosmopolitanism argues that in order to appreciate humanity, the social bonds between locals must somehow become weaker, less binding and less partial, and more abstract, universal, indeterminate and virtual, so that the Other can be included (Habermas, 2001).

While Simmel and Schütz introduced the typology of the stranger in Sociology to investigate triadic relationships and the social positions of strangers in groups, the cosmopolitan-local distinction has been part of sociological vocabulary since the writings of Robert Merton (1968: 441–74) and Alvin Gouldner (1957, 1958) in the 1940s and 1950s (Hannerz, 1990) and more recently has been used in ethical polemics by Martha Nussbaum (1996, 2002). By distinguishing between the cosmopolitan and the local, they reveal a social conflict within the group, between contrasting interests, values, representations and commitments. Merton distinguishes between the local and cosmopolitan as two types of *influential* persons. These two types hold different social positions within the same group. The local holds a social position through participation in the local neighbourhood and the cosmopolitan holds a social position through participation in the larger structures of national society.

Like Simmel and Schütz, Merton links social position to objectivity. While Simmel's stranger is granted status through his or her knowledge about mediation, and Schütz's stranger is marginalized by locals through his or her lack of local acquaintances, Merton distinguishes between local and cosmopolitan influences as two different sources and uses of knowledge. The local's influence rests on *knowledge of acquaintance*, on *who* he or she knows, while the cosmopolitan's influence rests, like Simmel's stranger, on *knowledge about*, on *what* he or she knows. The source of knowledge of acquaintance, which is not open to the stranger because the stranger is excluded from local history, is the local's original conditioning. According to Merton's typology, the local grows up in the local neighbourhood, reads the local news, has many friends, meets as many people as possible and is actively involved in local affairs. The local uses knowledge of acquaintance to acquire a social position in the group, through personal contacts within the structure of the local setting. The source of *knowledge about* things is study.

Cosmopolitans enter some local group as strangers, equipped with special knowledge, credentials and social status obtained elsewhere, outside the local group setting. What matters to them is not the *number* of people they meet, but the *kind* of people with whom they can share their knowledge about things (Hannerz, 1990: 246). Cosmopolitans are accepted by the locals, because the locals credit their knowledge about things. They *need* that knowledge, often specialized knowledge, which they do not possess themselves, to develop their own neighbourhoods.

While Merton's typology serves to show different patterns of *influence* in local neighbourhoods, Gouldner distinguishes between locals and cosmopolitans to reveal two types of *attachments* within the workplace. While the local is committed to the workplace, colleagues and shop-floor solidarity (through which knowledge of acquaintance is socially organized), the cosmopolitan is committed to degrees, credentials, profession and career. Local workers value routines, collegiality and interpersonal contacts on the shop floor.

Because locals value their colleagues, they are inclined to be involved in the internal affairs of the organization, for the benefit of the shop floor. By contrast, cosmopolitan workers are more reserved or distanced towards others. They prefer to remain *strangers*, not to be included by locals.

But in the global era, cosmopolitans have emancipated themselves not only from their neighbourhood roots and their workplace, but also from their national grouping. Locals, on the other hand, are left behind, because their knowledge of acquaintance cannot transcend local boundaries (Vertovec and Cohen, 2003). Outside the neighbourhood and workplace, they know nothing.

In the sociological scholarship of Merton and Gouldner, the cosmopolitan type has been portrayed as a bourgeois, who, as a manager or a professional, transcends local boundaries to improve his or her position, to move upwards, to new and better places. In the global era, the cosmopolitan not only transcends local boundaries, but also *national* boundaries. In the global era, the cosmopolitan has more in common with partners in Manhattan, London, Singapore or Hong Kong than with locals or nationals who are not plugged into a network of global connections (Lasch, 1995).

Sennett suggests that, in the global era, the cosmopolitan controls the local's knowledge of acquaintance. Through reorganizing the workplace, often as interim managers, cosmopolitans have divided the locals, forcing them out of their routines and compelling them to move to alternative places, where they become strangers. Hence, the locals have lost their knowledge of acquaintance and, correspondingly, their interpersonal influence and collegial attachment. Without knowledge of acquaintance, the locals are thrown back upon themselves, on their own subjectivity, where they are confronted with their own alienation, from which they must dredge up the meaning and stability that they require to exist. When knowledge of acquaintance disappears, cosmopolitans are no longer newcomers within a locally established neighbourhood or workplace, but enter a corroded, fragmented or structureless living and working condition, which is continuously under construction and which they can influence.

Locals cannot survive without knowledge of acquaintance. The neighbourhood cannot survive without neighbours and the workplace cannot survive without shop-floor collegiality. When knowledge of acquaintance is destroyed, the local's character corrodes and a deep uncertainty arises about identity or self-image. Cosmopolitans, on the other hand, do not need neighbours and colleagues. For them, the breakdown of group boundaries opens up new possibilities for remapping the social order, in which they rule without local and national restraints. Without the limitations and social control of neighbours and colleagues, it is easier for cosmopolitans to achieve their professional or managerial objectives. As their knowledge does not rest on acquaintances, it is easy for them to relativize the stability, coherence and concreteness of the group. While the corrosion of knowledge of acquaintance enables cosmopolitans to move successfully through social disorganization and insecurity, their 'built-in identity crisis' (Berger, Berger and Kellner, 1974: 92) enables them to move onwards and accelerates mobility – not only physical, but also social, mental and ethical mobility. Though cosmopolitans are constantly surrounded by cultural differences, they do not immerse themselves in these, they do not enjoy them. The globalized cosmopolitan is flexible, not because he or she attributes *meaning* to cultural identities, but because he or she considers cultural differences as superfluous.

Cosmopolitans are objective, in the sense that, like Simmel's stranger, they are able to distance themselves from existing loyalties. Being a stranger in all places, the biography of the cosmopolitan's career does not need to adjust to any group or place: the cosmopolitan is now able to flexibly adjust his or her knowledge to the global order, without local influences and without local attachments.

Rosabeth Moss Kanter (1995: 23) observes that in the global era, cosmopolitans reveal their knowledge about management and profession through the development of new concepts, new standards of managerial and engineering competence and excellent network connections. While the knowledge of the cosmopolitan type developed by Merton and Gouldner was still limited by national borders (American knowledge), today's globalized cosmopolitans are able to take their knowledge everywhere with them, outside the national structures. As a result, the cosmopolitan's concepts, competences and connections (Kanter's three Cs) are universal, in the sense that they transcend all localities. As a result, cosmopolitans, in contrast with locals, are able to gain access to knowledge anywhere in the world (Kanter's three Cs are globally recognized) and even develop knowledge of global acquaintances through network management.

For Sennett, the World Economic Forum (WEF) is the ultimate cosmopolitan symbol of the victory over the local. The WEF has all the cosmopolitan traits of the global bourgeoisie: it is an exclusive global network that is kept at a distance from intruders, including the press, so that the global order can be remapped without local influence or attachment that might limit the opportunities of the global bourgeoisie. Sennett observes that the WEF does not seek to improve the condition of the locals, but, on the contrary, seeks to reinforce its own concepts, competences and global connections. Through exchanging information within global networks (not groups), the global bourgeoisie seeks to extend the possibilities of the cosmopolitans' knowledge within their own multinational corporations and international organizations, without being hindered by concrete relations, established authority structures, traditions or norms.

Cosmopolitanism as an ethos focuses on the 'world citizenship'. In sociological scholarship, cosmopolitanism has not only been criticized as a manifestation of the mentality of the global bourgeoisie, but it has also been interpreted as a new ethos, suitable for 21st-century global life (Featherstone, 2002; Roudometof, 2005a). Sennett and Kanter have described cosmopolitanism in its corporate form, in terms of the victory over the local or the corrosion of the cultural pattern of group life. As an ethos, and this is how cosmopolitanism is defined by its advocates, it indicates the willingness of world citizens to become involved with the Other (Hannerz, 1990).

From a world citizenship perspective, the cosmopolitan-local distinction may be valid for investigating influence (Merton, 1968), loyalty (Gouldner, 1958) or corrosion (Sennett, 1998), but such a typology offers a rather limited vision of the moral dimension of cosmopolitanism. In fact, world citizenship positions itself as the ethical antithesis of the cosmopolitan type described by classical and current sociology.

World citizenship seeks to include strangers, through identification with many places and histories in an open-ended global space that spans many local groups (Anderson, 2001). World citizenship seeks to transcend strangeness through giving credit to strangers. It turns against a global bourgeoisie which exploits cosmopolitanism, cosmopolitan concepts, competences and connections – the language of universalism – for their own narrow interests (Nussbaum, 2002). Claiming to speak from no place, no social position and no identity except as 'friend of humanity', world citizenship defines itself as a deliberate attempt to abolish exclusion (Arjomand, 2004).

To keep one's conscience clear, cosmopolitanism proposes to cultivate the goodwill of locals or nationals to become engaged with strangers, to cultivate a global sense of responsibility for the fate of strangers in distress, regardless of their group identity or social distinctions. World citizenship implies the elimination of the 'accident of birth', the undoing of the original local conditioning and transcendence of the restraints of local influence and attachment, for the inclusion of strange intellectuality *into* the locality. In Nussbaum's curriculum, the stranger is, like Simmel's third person, given credit by the world citizen for her or his specific wisdom and expertise, and derives special status because of this. The stranger is welcomed, not as a third person, but as a cosmopolitan teacher to world citizens, who has managed to undo any fixed identity as a Jew, bourgeois or black and remake the self, anew again as a world citizen. The stranger teaches the locals, on their way to becoming world citizens, to loosen their local attachments, to establish a critical distance towards their own locality and to assume an intellectual stance of openness toward strangers and strangeness. Transformed into world citizens, locals will be able to stand as naked individuals before the group, stripped of status, social position and power, and reveal their nakedness in their very sameness in strangeness (Arendt, 1968: 89) – 'as human beings bound to all other human beings by ties of recognition and concern' (Nussbaum, 2002: 295).

As an ethos of world citizenship, cosmopolitanism describes itself as an intellectual attempt to understand the common denominator – humanity – in the worldwide chaos of cultural diversity and competing groups. Cosmopolitanism points to different, strange ways of being human, through giving credit to different local philosophies, poetry, prose, music and arts, in order to 'recognize common aims, aspirations, and values and enough about these common ends to see how variously they are instantiated in the many cultures and their histories' (Nussbaum, 1996: 9).

Pratap Bhanu Mehta argues that the cosmopolitan ethos may 'open new horizons' and 'new criticisms' (Mehta, 2000). New horizons are opened when it is discovered that all manifestations of global life, such as cosmopolitan law, world citizenship, cosmopolitan education and cosmopolitan cities, emerge, as Bauman says, from 'the birth act of humanity itself (which) lies in the acceptance of the precept of loving one's neighbour' (Bauman, 2003: 78). The new horizon is located far beyond the neighbourhood or workplace: it encompasses the whole world, cutting through old limits of time.

Through adopting the stranger's view from nowhere, world citizens criticize local practices while not being included in local groups. Though world citizens certainly do not believe that such local practices are superfluous, unlike the global bourgeoisie, they do believe that such practices should be criticized when they are exclusive or hostile to strangers. By forcing their strangers to obey their rules of knowledge of acquaintance, locals, without world citizenship, deny the potential goodness of the stranger. As a potentially good human being, both locals and strangers do not need social control through the cultural pattern of group life, but by compassion.

Without world citizenship, and by defining themselves in opposition to strangers, locals tend to think of strangers as lowly, as inferiors, which is a guarantee that they will not treat the strangers well. Ulf Hannerz, however, is rather critical of how cosmopolitanism legitimates its programme for inclusion, observing that cosmopolitanism 'often has a narcissistic streak' (1990: 240). Cosmopolitanism judges all cultural patterns according to its own idea of humanity, to its own belief in human goodness. Martha Nussbaum (2003), for instance, defines Hinduism as an intellectual tradition of 'pluralism, tolerance and openness', which, thus defined, can be easily reconciled with the cosmopolitan ethos. But when it comes to caste, gender inequality, racism and the worship of violent gods (Nussbaum identifies Hanuman as 'an aggressive monkey god'), then such exclusive practices are identified as the practices of locals, which are not inherent in the intellectuality of Hindus, but in the sociality of their tribal life. In other words, Nussbaum delegitimizes Hindu group life that violently excludes strangers, but gives credit to Hindu intellectuality. Despite all the extreme cruelty and victimhood that she observes in what she calls 'genocide in Gujarat', she does not criticize the humanity of those involved in mass rape, torture and killing, but their exclusive local bonds.

Classical sociologists recognized in the cultural pattern of group life, that is, in particular customs, habits, manners, mores, values, folkways, meanings, beliefs, ideas, sentiments, taste, symbols, language and local patriotism, the elements of sociality. They realized that common experiences and shared cultural characteristics, shared memories and a sense of common destiny only had *meaning* for locals. If the cultural pattern did not have the same meaning to the stranger as to the locals, then the stranger could only form an 'ethnocentric judgment' of the situation (Sumner, 1979) – judging one cultural pattern with the norms of another.

Ulrich Beck holds that the clash of beliefs between locals and strangers has ended in total disbelief, in nihilism, in a total rejection of the cultural pattern of group life. Now that global processes cut through the borders of the nation, cosmopolitanism insists that nationality no longer binds citizens. Because citizens are no longer attached to the national pattern of group life, political bonds can no longer be established through nation building. To bind citizens in a global era, nation-states must legislate 'cosmopolitan law' that aims at the inclusion of strangers in the political group (Beck, 2002b).

When Merton and Gouldner constructed their cosmopolitan types in the 1940s, what they had in mind was a type of influential and disloyal person who, with mobile knowledge about things, is able to operate within the larger structures of the nation-state, transcending the limits of local neighbourhoods and workplaces. Merton and Gouldner could not imagine a group larger than the nation-state. In their eyes, the most abstract form of social cohesion was the nationality that ties cosmopolitans and locals together in a common political membership or citizenry. When global processes cut through the borders of the nation, the inclusion of strange ideas, objects and images are experienced, imagined, consumed and fantasized, so that strangerhood and friendship, over and above the nation, becomes a social reality for many (Skrbis, Kendall and Woodward, 2001: 121).

Cosmopolitanism denies nation-states the right to exclude strangers and to act on behalf of its own national interests that are considered too narrow. As cosmopolitanism grants political priority to the inclusion of strangers above national and political unity, it rules out the possibility of national enemies. As a result, cosmopolitan law forbids nation-states waging war against perceived political enemies. Cosmopolitan law grants the nation-state the use of its powers against the enemies of humanity. But since all human beings belong to humanity, the enemy of humanity must be degraded to the category of bestiality or insanity. Those who commit 'crimes against humanity' are, therefore, not really human or have not really developed their human potential for goodness.

Cosmopolitanism's critic, Carl Schmitt (1996), believes that cosmopolitanism aims at abolishing the 'political' in nation-states. According to Schmitt, nation-states need the presence of enemies in order to establish political bonds and constitute a political unity. According to Schmitt, in the political world there are only those who have established a political bond (citizens). Those who are excluded from the political bond are defined as *enemies*. As the stranger is not included in the citizenry, he or she is turned into an enemy. Schmitt criticizes cosmopolitanism for abolishing the enemy in the name of common humanity – hence weakening the political bonds between citizens (Cohen, 2004). By subjecting nation-states to an 'overarching cosmopolitan legal framework' (Held, 2003: 521), the meaning of citizenship is reduced from the building of political bonds to the administration of human needs.

Cosmopolitanism argues that the political role of nation-states has changed with the birth of the global era, in the sense that the purpose of citizens is no longer to establish political bonds and bring about their own good life, but to loosen their bonds to rescue those that have been conquered – the victims. Political groups must adapt to the global reality of diaspora, genocides and refugees. In the global era, nation-states must, in the name of humanity, open a new horizon for 'saving strangers' (Wheeler, 2003). In the global era, the cosmopolitan ethos states that the new role of nation-states is borderless inclusion and humanitarian control. In sum, cosmopolitanism's political argument is that in the global era, the legitimacy of nation-states exclusively rests on rendering service to humanity and its goodwill to continue doing so, without regard for political unity, balance of power or political interests (Ignatieff, 2000).

Cosmopolitanism does not seek to destroy political unity, but rather to extend political unity from the nation to a global scale, so that all strangers are included in that unity. Cosmopolitanism seeks a borderless political unity, in which all strangers, no matter their nationality, are, as an end in itself, politically included as citizens – as world citizens. This global political unity or world polity is the *cosmopolis* (Heater, 1999; Toulmin, 1990) or *cosmocracy* (Keane, 2003).

The cosmopolis is based on the 'model of the world society' (Meyer et al., 1997), of the 'world as a whole' and 'awareness of the "global"' (Szerszynski and Urry, 2002). The world polity is not patterned on a 'cosmopolitan model of democracy' as developed by Daniele Archibugi and David Held (Archibugi, 2004; Archibugi and Held, 1995; Held, 2003). Their 'cosmopolitan model of democracy' is based on international cooperation between sovereign powers and institutionalized in social forms like international treaties and supranational institutions. Political groups like the European Union are not borderless, but establish their own 'fortresses for their own members. Cosmopolitanism seeks to sack the fortress' (Benhabib, 2002).

The world polity is not established through international treaties, but through global recognition of 'sameness in strangeness' – through detecting common humanity in particular strangers (Arendt, 1968: 81–82). Stephen Toulmin (1990) argues that, in a divided international society of sovereign powers, the world polity functions to reconcile locals and strangers in a common political and ethical purpose. While nation-states and international systems of governance may include strangers through the legislation of *cosmopolitan laws*, the cosmopolis includes strangers through the legislation of *cosmic laws*. According to Toulmin, the very project of modernity is the scientific discovery of cosmic laws, through geometry and physics. The lingua franca of the cosmopolis is not Latin or English, but the language of science. Jacques Derrida (1997) defines the cosmopolis as a safe haven for strangers, receiving them as neighbours and extending local and national resources to them. Strangers are included in the cosmopolis through hospitality.

In other words, the influx of refugees and immigrants, as such, does not constitute the cosmopolis: the cosmopolis is a powerful identification with the stranger, organizing local life around the theme of the stranger. Ash Amin (2004) suggests that the borderless inclusion of strangers indicates the ongoing interaction between locals and strangers. For Amin, the cosmopolis becomes rooted in the locals' self-understanding, when they are able to transgress all group boundaries, in order to be continuously on the path with strangers, as dislocated nomads and strangers to themselves, as always *becoming* new persons.

Friedrich Meinecke (1970) recognizes in the cosmopolis an ethical ideal of justice as unlimited inclusion with dangerous *political consequences*. According to Meinecke, in its political form, cosmopolitanism ultimately points at *borderless imperialism*. Instead of unlimited inclusion of strangers in the world polity, the establishment of the cosmopolis is the conquest of the world by strangers who break down the political bonds of citizens.

Meinecke believes that the worldwide legislation of cosmic laws, valid for universal humanity, does not so much include strangers as they destroy those laws that place limits on unlimited and uncontrolled ambitions. Cosmic laws, once discovered, fail to provide compelling arguments against cosmopolitan pretensions becoming political. Without limits, the cosmopolis would not be a political world community, but an empire of strangers, a strange legion, or an imperial administration of the stranger's needs.

The critics of cosmopolitanism believe that adherence to cosmic laws or membership in the world polity does not so much lead to the inclusion of strangers as to the corrosion of local life. And a life, including a global life, can only be lived in some locality, even if that locality is globalized. With the globalization of national societies, cosmopolitanism has now become 'something of an urgent reality' (Arendt, 1968: 82) and 'an actual social condition of many today' (Mazlish, 2005b: 106). Even though humanity, as a reference for the we-identity, is still a blank area on the emotional maps of the many, local groups are increasingly confronted with a *widening of identification with strangers and the strange*.

As an ethos for the global era, cosmopolitanism delegitimizes essentialist identities that are always group related, relativizes the locals' struggle for survival in particular social contexts and subdues local attachments to a higher purpose, that of unlimited attachment to humanity. The cosmopolitan challenge is to develop the intellectual ability to establish a distance from their cultural pattern of group life and detach themselves from their old selves, their old cultural patterns, in order to understand themselves as human beings in themselves – without knowledge of acquaintance. In the borderless society of strangers, the distinction between locals and strangers, locals and cosmopolitans, friends and enemies, civilization and barbarism, and the West and the rest is abolished: cosmopolitanism invites each human being to become friends of humanity.

Cosmopolitanism stresses that in the era of global interconnections, human beings are expected to live, survive or flourish without local, immediate, concrete and exclusive bonds. Cosmopolitanism is a deliberate attempt to make space for strangers, to have world citizens rule in the cosmopolis. Ignorance and fear of strangers is a lack of the will to be part of the world. Such an attempt, however, fails to do justice to classical and current sociology.

When locals become strangers to themselves and to others, and no longer know who they are or who they are to become, no relationship between strangers can be established that would allow the effort of self-definition, as the selves would be unknown. It goes without saying that this condition of loss of integrative meaning, which is the essential ordeal of cosmopolitanism, is psychologically hard to bear. For this reason, a longing for the reintegration of local groups and the resistance against strangerhood, through nostalgia, protest, terror and hope, is one of the most powerful realities of globalizing societies (Mazlish, 2005b; Roudometof, 2005a).

The burgeoning literature on cosmopolitanism suggests that advocates of cosmopolitanism are attempting to transcend the meaning of social diversity in order to carve out a universal sense of humanity based on the quest for world citizenry (Nussbaum, 2002). This quest concerns not only the widening outlooks of globe-trotting individuals but also the implications of a deeply interconnected world for the attainment of universal justice and harmony. Intricate connections arising from diasporic flows, transnational networks and global markets can be considered the factors underlying the impetus for envisioning cosmopolitanism in terms of a new world order. Yet this vision which assumes the transcendence of national boundaries (Beck, 2006) has been described as misleading and inadequate (Calhoun, 2003: 532, 550) or still open-ended (Roudometof, 2005a: 121). In a recent survey of cosmopolitanism in Europe, Pichler (2008) concluded that its social reality was ambiguous. On a theoretical level, Kendall et al. (2008: 414) argued that cosmopolitanism was 'a fragile and incomplete political settlement'. For them, the major challenge to cosmopolitanism lies in the ways social solidarity and the sense of belonging are generated. As they put it, 'There can be no cosmopolitanism without effective solidarity mechanisms' (ibid.: 411). On this note, they emphasized the necessity of including the concepts of belonging and solidarity in future research in the sociology of cosmopolitanism.

Cosmopolitanism is essentially a city phenomenon which has multiple activities. This stands equally true for the post-industrial cities. According to Richardson 'City size is positively linked with the number of activities located there and since economies of scale and market area threshold differentials rule out the presence of each industry in each city, we obtain cities of different size. The largest city will be that which captures the highest proportion of national (and international) market industries while, at the same time, encompassing most other industries, with smaller market areas'. Richardson further maintains that the 'national hierarchy of leading cities is an instrument for achieving national growth. First, the urban hierarchy is an efficient vehicle for transmitting new technology, managerial expertise and general economic functions from the centre of the economy to the periphery. This permits social and economic change to "leapfrog" over distance and avoid the slower gradual diffusion over space from the central city. This transmission function is aided by the fact that many modern forms of business organization (in commerce, finance and industry) are themselves hierarchical with head offices and centres of decision making in the metropolitan centres and their decision trees spread out spatially down the urban hierarchy' (Richardson, 1972).

According to Kiuchi and Ishimizu a 'big concentration in a specific place brings about an accelerated urbanization and metropolitanization'. This is a consequence of what they refer to as 'the principle of accumulation effect' (Kiuchi and Ishimizu, 1963).

'The growth of post-industrial cities is the realization of the considerable (and in the case of the biggest cities) economic potential which is imparted by economic development to specific "points" of the territorial structure' (Gohman et al., 1976: 29). However, an excessive concentration of functions in some select centres in a region might lead to a situation that could aptly be described as apoplexy in one place and anaemia at the others. It hampers the development of a system of settlements and there is a paucity of small and medium sized towns. This reflects a disconcentration in the hierarchy of centres. However, in spite of efforts at decentralization of economic activities, 'the Government has not been able to break away from the advantages of industrial constellation or from the assumption that the future lies with big and medium sized cities. Countervailing forces against inevitable attraction of those established places remain weak' (Mehta, 1961: 417.)

Hyderabad has been regarded as the 'pre-given focus of the emergent urban-system of Andhra Pradesh. In addition to its administrative importance as the capital of the state, Hyderabad is also the largest urban agglomeration with a distinct and diversified economic structure' (Alam and Khan, 1972: 5–6). However, it has to be conceded that Hyderabad is not reflective of the level of development of the region. The high level of economic attainment is due to the locational advantage which the city possesses, in relation to the convergence of the transportation routes. Nevertheless, its dominance in Telangana is undisputed.

Thompson has provided for 'irreversible urban growth' after a certain threshold size. This irreversible urban growth contributes to cosmopolitanism.

- Industrial diversification is attendant on a large size and growth of the urban area; with diversification comes a near-synchrony between the growth rate of the city economy and the regional or national economy.
- Power politics which accompanies a large population size can also be instrumental in diverting the flow of financial assistance to large cities.
- Large amounts of fixed capital are invested in the social and private overheads in large cities, e.g., in streets, drainage systems, schools, electricity, housing, etc., thus locational inertia plays a major role.

- Large cities also contain a large number of potential customers and as such offer vantage points for new consumer-goods industries to take root.
- Large cities also have a constant supply of industrial leader-ship. 'Sheer size may stabilize the supply of the key human resources, necessary to economic growth and development' (Thompson, 1965).

According to B.K. Roy Burman a part from the ethnic, cultural and political questions, the people of Assam and North-East India as a whole have long standing grievances against the policy followed by successive governments in the matters of extension of various amenities, creating infrastructure of growth, generating productive activities and fixing prices of raw materials extracted from the region and processed elsewhere. Continuation of the legacy of colonial rule; geopolitical constraint, adaptation of a development model, where growth and justice are virtually treated as mutually unrelated processes; ramification of linkage with neo-colonial powers in the form of internal colonialism and one or two arguments of the same order have been advanced (Majeed, 1984).

As an analyst of the social sense B.K. Roy Burman observe that the national sentiments in Assam or in other parts of North-East India have become explosive in the context of a serious lacuna in the cultural policy with particular reference to the linguistic states, inadequately explored dimensions of citizenship, institutional inadequacy for resource mobilization and utilization keeping in view the structural specifications of the region and non-recognition of the role of Brahmaputra Valley as the nucleus in regionalization process in North-East India. The states in India have been constituted primarily on linguistic principle but as indicated earlier, in the wake of economic development or as a part of national and international political process the demographic composition of some of the states impair change. On the other hand there is no provision in the constitution that demographic shifts will not erode the special prerogatives of specific cultural and linguistic identities historically associated with specific areas (ibid.).

In an article 'Obstacles for Nationalism in North-Eastern India: An Overview', B. Rahamathulla (ibid.) says that the perpetual instability in the North-Eastern India for more than two decades has threatened the peace and security, notwithstanding the centre's efforts to promote national integration and unity with the means and devices which are in conformity with the economic needs and social aspirations of the tribal people. Various reasons have been ascribed for obstructing the process of national integration in the entire tribal area of 1, 74,505 sq kms. The autonomy demand launched by Zaphu Angami Phizo of Nagaland with a few extremists as late as in 1956 inspired other disgruntled underground tribal leaders to demand sovereignty from 'the Indian Yoke' on the ground that their ethnic cultural background derived from the Austro-Mongoloid origins and their territory was subjugated by the Government of India in 1947. The tribals claimed that neither the Hindu norms nor any Indian traditional pattern matches with a conglomeration of myriad ethnic tribes in the region. This has been the feeling among the tribes of Northern-Eastern India, which led to launch an armed struggle against the Indian security forces. Apart from the insurgency, the growth of maldevelopment in the economy and administration, external assistance to the underground hostiles and over ground political bickering further obstructed the process of nationalism in the region.

Assam has also been facing several spells of regionalism. Taking into consideration the time span and its level and degree, migration into Assam has few parallels in the world. The question of 'Assamiya' identity has got mixed up with the migration problem, which has a long history and has been a central theme in the Assam politics, at least since the 1930s. The earlier hope that migration would be 'an instrument of cultural diffusion and social integration' has miserably failed. With the advent of modernization, all the avenues of profit-earning were monopolized by the migrant communities.

The Assamese have failed to effectively compete against the migrants in matters of employment, trade and commerce. Most of the time, the migrants are also culturally distinct and can be easily blamed for failures. Demands for nativist-protectionism have manifested out of an aggressive cultural nationalism and antagonistic regionalism. These policies and techniques are natural for a people to 'suffer from status deprivation, feel culturally threatened and lack the skills and outlook to compete in the economic market place' (Weiner, 1978). The question of the Assamese nationality has helped the formation of an ideology for the anti-migrant moment. This ideology articulates the aspirations and apprehensions of a subnationality, and provides a powerful assertion of Assamese cultural identity. With the help of this ideology, and by using Assamese historical and cultural symbols, the Assamese society is trying to emerge out of its past. It may be a false consciousness. There may be false aspirations, but it grasps their subconsciousness and provides them with opportunities to symbolically overcome their doubts, their fears, their inabilities and their failures.

L.S. Bourne, in his generalized model of urban system has maintained that the cities and urban regions of a modern industrial economy constitute a set of interrelated subsystems nesting in a complex hierarchy of increasing scale upwards from individual urban areas to a national settlement system (1975: 11). He has conceived of a three-tier hierarchy of urban system, i.e., national system, regional system and daily urban system.

According to Stohr (1974), every city has a local/regional component and a national/State-wide one. These components of the urban space-economy manifest themselves in the form of intra-regional and the inter-regional activities. The intra-regional activities are mostly of a central nature, where the central place functions as a cluster in the city and the adjacent areas look towards it for the fulfilment of their requirements. The city in turn depends on the hinterlands for a variety of goods. The functional complementarities between city and hinterland thus depends on a good transportation and information system and finds reflection in terms such as commutation, commodity movement, spillover of industries, etc. In extra-regional terms, the city forms a unit in the national system of cities. The activities of extra-regional level are flows of commodities, information, capital, technological and social innovations, migration and decision-making power, Stohr contends that if these flows 'took place between all points of origin and destination directly, too expensive a transport network would be required. They, therefore, tend to bundle along routes of highest interaction, usually between major cities' (ibid.: 21).

In a study of metropolitan Hyderabad and its region Alam, S.M. and others have used the following indices to delimit the hinterland of Hyderabad city: (1) circulation of daily newspapers, (2) university enrolment, (3) regional accessibility and traffic shed, (4) supply zone of vegetables, (5) milk supply region and (6) fruit supply region. Also, the area of direct participation or the metropolitan district has been delimited which represents the core of this region. The measures adopted in this case may broadly be classified as the 'principal' and 'reflective' elements. The principal elements are: (a) suburban transport; (b)commuting areas of workers to factories; (c) retailing; (d) water supply; (e) electricity; (f) telephones; and (g) postal service.

People are living with a difference in the contemporary city and its attention to notions of citizenship within a global context is important. In recent years, urban theorists and policy makers, alike, have become increasingly convinced that urban society is in a state of crisis. What Castells (1997) refers to as 'the social glue' that binds society together is believed to be dissolving. Castells points to privatization, residualization and globalization to explain this disruption in society; policy has tended to focus on *differences* that are problematized for promoting division. At the local level, the community cohesion agenda has generated a set of criteria against which to judge the communal values of different groups.

Contemporary cosmopolitanism may be regarded as a new humanism whose premise lies in the fact that the emergence of the universal idea of humanity in the modern age has always been accompanied by intellectual and political movements dedicated either to the justification of exceptions or more radically to the destruction of the idea of humanity itself (Arendt, 1986). As the right of hospitality indicates, cosmopolitanism is an argument for the recognition of the essential humanity we all share – not so much despite our differences but by virtue of our differences. It is through the act of looking through the eye of the Other, through a flourishing of Otherness, that we are able to see the nature of humanity (Nussbaum, 1996).

In his article, 'Communal Dimension of Regionalism in Indian Federation: – A study of Trends in Akali Politics', Pradeep Kumar says: ... I have tried to argue here is that while Akali regionalism is still primarily 'communal', it has become pragmatic, modernized and negotiable and the term 'communal' is now understood as for one's own community rather than any communal chauvinism. As Rasheeduddin Khan has rightly pointed out, thus, one direction of the competing politics of bargaining at the local State and central level is the transformation of communities, or parts thereof into pressure groups. While the Akali regionalism is still communal and is aimed primarily at deriving more benefits for the Sikh community alone, it has transformed itself from a mere communal group to a more modernized, pragmatic, bargaining, and negotiable regional movement which at times has worked in collaboration with some non-religious or even religious parties (like CPM). The regionalism of the Akali is now more issue-oriented and less regional-oriented. Such a communal domination of regionalism in any socio-economically diverse society like India may not be looked with any contempt. It is not only desirable but also essential for the working of a federal system where the government is otherwise centralized and unitary in many ways. The bargaining culture which is slowly developing in the federal polity of India, is certainly to gain a lot from the modernized form of any communal regionalism which can rightly be regarded as an essential ingredient of federal system (Majeed, 1984).

Akhtar Majeed (1984) in the article 'Sons of the Soil Agitations' is of the opinion that agitation over linguistic issues is not something new in India, and it has exercised a good influence over national policy since independence. But there was something new about the 1965 agitation of Madras. The earlier language agitation concerned the setting up of linguistic states the Madras agitation involved the issue of the official language to be used by the government. What was in doubt was not the protection of Tamil language, but the future of Tamilians in a nation with Hindi as its sole official language. The Dravidian language of the South, particularly Tamil, is highly developed with a good classical literature. The present century witnessed a minor renaissance of Tamil culture, manifesting itself to purify the Tamil language of all Sanskritic influence. This cultural revival, leading to new self-confidence, led to an awareness of Tamilian identity with a deepening suspicion of all things North-Indian. The feeling developed that the region had been dominated by the North which was neglecting and exploiting the former. Even traditional Hinduism was regarded as an imposition from the north, and anti-Brahmanism found ardent exponents. The Brahmins commanded, up to the early 20th century, dominant political and economic position in the south because of the superior social position. The dominance was displaced with the rise of Tamil nationalism through the justice party, the Dravida Kazhagam (DK) and the Dravida Munnetra Kazhagam (DMK). Many Tamil nationalist even went to the extent of 'opposing independence to India' (Hardgrave, 1965: 402). Economic and industrial exploitation of the South by the North was feared and decried, and Hindi was considered to be the tool of the subjection of the south, becoming the symbol of Southern apprehensions. All this generated an attitude of Tamil chauvinism.

The process of cultural renaissance and reawakening in Maharashtra roused regional pride and consciousness, a process of rediscovering of heroes of the past, laying down the foundations of regional chauvinism. But when the linguistic states were formed, Maharashtra's claims for a separate state of Bombay led to the 'Samyuktha Maharashtra movement', in which the type of propaganda carried on in an emotionally charged atmosphere, using myths, legends and stereotypes, had far reaching consequences. It revived the memories of Maratha nationalism, created a mass paranoia as Maharashtrians began to suffer from a delusion of grandeur and an acute sense of persecution complex. They felt that they were being persecuted by the central government with the help of people speaking other languages. In this historical cultural context, developed a chauvinist outlook leading to the feeling of 'Mumbai Ham Cha Hai'. But the pattern of socialization was irreconcilably inconsistent with these Maharastrians ambitions. They found that the palatial mansions, business and commercial concerns were mostly owned by non-Maharastrians who were an overwhelming majority in Bombay. They became aware that Bombay was hardly theirs. As a Shiv Sena spokesman said there were 'bitter feelings of frustrations talking hold of the rank and file of young Maharashtrians they, who are the sons of the soil and as such must get full opportunities to develop their look of life, do not get them even in small measure. They find their interests woefully neglected' (*Marmik* Shiv Sena weekly) quoted by Ram Joshi (1970: 908). The worsening socio-psychological situation in Mumbai had become conducive for the growth of organizations like Shiv Sena. Classic problems of urban congestion, slums, shortage of housing, job scarcity, and continuous pressure on civic amenities resulted from large scale and continuous migration to Mumbai from all parts of India. A distorted view of exclusiveness became more pronounced among those who came from rural Maharashtra to the Mumbai city, where the reality was entirely different. The phenomenon of the rise of Shiv Sena in its xenophobia against non-Maharashtrians becomes intelligible if viewed in this social context.

G. Haragopal (1987) opines that Andhra occupies the first position in being carved as a province on the linguistic basis in the post-Independence era, while Punjab came into existence in the last major phase of reorganization of provinces. In the case of the third State, the already existent Assam, it had to simply go through an incredible degree of fragmentation, so that what is left can be homogeneously Assamese. 'The 'incredible degree of fragmentation' of Assam is perhaps a feature which it shares with Punjab. Punjab has similarly undergone a stupendous population change, related initially to the partition of the Indian subcontinent and subsequent successive reorganizations of the State until it assumed its present form of a Sikh-majority State in 1966. Thus, under focus are three States whose economies can be categorized on a relative scale into three stages: Punjab has a more or less developed economy in terms of its agricultural wealth. The economy of Assam can be termed on a relative basis as 'stagnant' or 'underdeveloped'. In between these two economies lies the Andhra economy which is in what may perhaps be called the 'transitional' or rapidly developing phase.

There is vast literature on cosmopolitanism and regionalism (including all the regional movements). However, in Indian context, the studies on cosmopolitanism are very limited. Further studies relating to cosmopolitanism and regionalism with specific reference to India is also very limited. There is an immense need to understand how cosmopolitanism and regionalism reflect in post-industrial societies especially when the global forces are rising and regional identities are becoming prominent simultaneously.

Statement of the Problem

The globalization of economies, migration, culture and communications, combined with a worldwide reassertion of diverse cultural affiliations, are producing intense pressures on the coexistence of different national, ethnic, religious, racial, and linguistic groups who share the same cities. This has its implications on the development process of urban areas. In cities throughout the world, social tensions and open conflict over region, culture and identity are overwhelming all other aspects of normal urban life. The post-industrial cities suffer different degrees of social disintegration and physical destruction, sometimes so severe that the future possibilities for peace, security and sustained urban development cannot be foreseen. The present study aims to understand how cosmopolitanism is related with regionalism. Further, it also tries to understand that how negatives of extreme regionalism lead to regional conflicts. It is significant to understand whether cosmopolitanism helps in reducing or exaggerating regional conflicts. Moreover, the notions of cosmopolitanism and regionalism are associated with the process of urban development. The study aims to understand the nature of their association and its implications in general and Hyderabad in specific.

Importance of Study

The proposed study has long-lasting implications. From policy perspective, the research reflects upon the issues of extreme regionalism and its ill effects on urban development so that efforts can be made to contain it. The urban centres are centres of economic activities and extreme regionalism has the threat of leading to regional conflicts which hampers the development prospects of urban centres. Secondly, from theoretical point of view, this study proposes to present a continuum of cosmopolitanism and regionalism.

Objectives

- To understand the process of cosmopolitanism and the various parameters of cosmopolitanism and the evolution of Hyderabad as cosmopolitan city
- To identify the relation between cosmopolitanism and urban development
- To study the various facets and indicators of regionalism and its impact on urban development
- To understand the relationship between variables like income, education, employment, caste, age and cosmopolitanism and regionalism

Hypothesis

The process of cosmopolitanism is complex in nature and there is a highly significant relation between cosmopolitanism and urban development. Moreover, extreme regionalism leads to regional conflicts which have a negative impact on urban development. Cosmopolitanism and regionalism are influenced by variables like age, education, nature of employment, income, religion, caste and migration status. Cosmopolitanism helps in balancing regionalism and thus reducing regional conflicts. The specific statements of null hypothesis are:

- There is no significant relationship between income and favourability towards cosmopolitanism
- There is no significant difference between educational qualifications and feelings towards regionalism
- There is no significant difference between age and feelings towards cosmopolitanism
- There is no significant difference between language and feelings towards regionalism (regional identity)
- There is no significant difference between caste and feelings towards cosmopolitanism
- There is no significant difference between nature of employment (govt/private) and feelings towards regionalism

Conclusion

The present chapter introduces the concepts of post-industrial cities, cosmopolitanism and regionalism. The review of literature shows that with reference to the Indian context there are substantial studies on regionalism but not on cosmopolitanism. The other topics covered in the introductory chapter are statement of the problem, importance of the study, objectives and hypothesis. Keeping in view the nature and complexity of the study it was felt appropriate to state null hypothesis. The area of study is Hyderabad. The succeeding chapter deals with historical development of the city and its evolution as a cosmopolitan city with shades of strong regional identities which have become more prominent in the past few years.

2 Hyderabad and Its *Tehzeeb*

Cities evolve with people of multiple cultures coming together. Cities are not only economic and administrative centres, they are cultural centres too. They present a unique and magnificent picture of cultural accommodation and assimilation. The heterogeneity of a city carries with it, its historicity, and amalgamation of several cultures of natives, settlers and migrants. Though all modern cities show similar cosmopolitan culture, the foundations of native culture are so strong that its aroma is more predominant. All the culture influences collectively merge in to the city mannerisms – *Tehzeeb* of the city.

In its historic evolution and development, Hyderabad city has experienced many changes since its foundation as the capital of the medieval kingdom of Golconda in the 16th century to its present status as the metropolis of a modern state. Each historic phase of development has significantly influenced its physical, social, economic and cultural growth. Hyderabad under the influence of Deccan, Irani and native culture synthesized and evolved its very own *Hyderabadi Tehzeeb*. It truly represented the assimilation (yet uniqueness) of diverse cultures which inhabited Hyderabad. More than four hundred years later HITEC (Hyderabad Information Technology Engineering Consultancy) city, Hyderabad today presents a different picture. Whether it is its structural and spatial expansion, infrastructural development or its socio-cultural ethos, contemporary Hyderabad has evolved phenomenally and, for many natives, beyond recognition. There is a need to understand the cultural journey of Hyderabad.

The city of Hyderabad was founded by Muhammad Quli Qutub Shah, the fifth ruler of the kingdom of Golconda, in AD 1591 on the south bank of the river Musi which is a major tributary of the river Krishna. Hyderabad–Bhagyanagar the city of luck symbolizes spectrum of obsessions – love, pearls, cuisine, *pan*, Irani *chai*, beautiful monsoons and many more. The icing, however, is the *nawabi* style and splendorous *Ganga-Jamuna Tehzeeb.* Hyderabad culture is knitted through its history and thus to understand the various facets of *Hyderabadi Tehzeeb* it is worthwhile to walk down the memory lane of Qutub Shahis and Asaf Jahis, the dynasties which laid down the foundation of modern Hyderabad.

History of Hyderabad

A multitude of influences have shaped the character of the city. Its palaces and buildings, houses and tenements, gardens and streets have a history and an architectural individuality of their own, which makes Hyderabad a city of enchantment. The history of Hyderabad can be broadly categorized under Qutub Shahi and Asaf Jahi period. In 1948, after the police action, Hyderabad was amalgamated into the Indian territory and eventually became capital of Andhra Pradesh in 1956. The *Hyderabadi tehzeeb* is essentially the result of its rich cultural history and heritage which shaped the destiny of the city.

Qutub Shahi Dynasty

Hyderabad founded in the year 1591 by Mohammed Quli Qutub Shah, the fifth sultan of Qutub Shahi dynasty, offers a fascinating panorama of the past, with richly mixed cultural and historical tradition spanning over 400 years. It is one of the fastest growing cities of India and has emerged as a strong industrial, commercial, technology centre, and presents glimpses of past splendours and the legacy of its old history. The history of Hyderabad begins with the establishment of the Qutub Shahi dynasty. Quli Qutub Shah seized the reins of power from the Bahamani kingdom in 1512 and established the fortress city of Golconda. Inadequacy of water and frequent epidemics of plague and cholera persuaded Mohammed Quli Qutub Shah to venture outward to establish the new city with the Charminar at its centre and with four great roads fanning out in four cardinal directions. Hyderabad's fame, strategic location and

Golconda's legendary wealth attracted Aurangzeb who captured Golconda after a long siege in 1687.

The Qutub Shahis ruled the Deccan for almost 171 years. All the seven rulers were patrons of learning and were great builders. They contributed to the growth and development of Indo-Persian and Indo-Islamic literature and culture in Hyderabad. During the Qutub Shahi reign, Golconda became one of the leading markets in the world of diamonds, pearls, steel for arms, and also printed fabric. This brought people of different cultures together. The glory of the Golconda kingdom ended in 1687, after a valiant struggle. Aurangzeb, the last great Mughal ruler, captured Golconda after a siege that lasted eight months.

The city of Hyderabad was established mainly to mitigate congestion in the fortress town. With the stability of the kingdom during Ibrahim Qutub Shah's reign and due to its growing prosperity, the population of Golconda increased phenomenally. Consequently, the water supply became inadequate and the housing problem acute. The situation was further aggravated by the influx of refugees in large numbers after the fall of the kingdom of Ahmednagar in AD 1600. This is corroborated by Bhaunani who remarked, 'In the days of the fifth Qutub Shahi King, Muhammad Quli, Golconda became overcrowded and unhealthy, and supply was scanty. This led to the selection of a new site for the city. The, choice fell in 1591, upon the site of the present city of Hyderabad (Bhaunani, 1917).

It may be pointed out that the situation had considerably worsened even during the time of Ibrahim Qutub Shah who had also attempted to found a new city. This is brought out by Mr Sherwani who observes, 'Ibrahim Qutub Shah, the fourth king of the dynasty (1550–1580), tried to found a city to be named after him at the foot of two hillocks, a couple of miles to the north of Golconda which have Taramathi's pavilion and Premavathi's mosque. But the site chosen was uneven and stony and the king thought it was not possible to found a city in such a terrain. He therefore began by constructing a bridge over the Musi in 1578, "Purana Pul" or old bridge, which it still serving the needs of the people' (Sherwani, 1967).

The fort of Golconda which is now in ruins is of earlier origin than the city of Hyderabad. It was, in its heyday, one of the most magnificent defensive structure. The Golconda fort was originally built by the Kakatiya Rajas of Warangal in the thirteenth century AD and ceded it together with its dependencies to Muhammad Shah Bahmani of Bidar in AD 1364. Qutb-ul-Mulk Muhammad Quli, the first king of Golconda who had migrated from Iran to Bidar, was appointed as 'Tarafdar' (Governor) of Telangana by Muhammad Shah Bahmani. After the disintegration of the Bahmani kingdom, he declared himself an independent sultan in AD 1496. He came from a Persian Tribe family, originally belonging to the Black Sheep Tribe from Lake Van, Iran. The original fort was made of mud and brick by Kishen Rao, probably a local chieftain. Afterwards, Ibrahim Qutub Shah, father of Quli Qutub Shah, ordered it be built with stone and lime on the advice of his Peshwa, Mustafa Khan. The entire fort was constructed over a period of 62 years from AD 1518.

Asaf Jahi Dynasty

After Aurangzeb's siege the importance of Hyderabad declined and the city fell into partial ruins. As the Moghul Empire decayed and began to disintegrate, the viceroy, Asaf Jah I proclaimed himself the Nizam and established independent rule of the Deccan. Hyderabad once again became a major capital city, ruled by successive Nizams of the Asaf Jahi dynasty until the state was merged into the Indian Union in 1948.

The seven Nizam's of the Asif Jahi dynasty ruled the Deccan for nearly 224 years, right up to 1948. The origins of the Asif Jahi dynasty can be traced to Chin Qalich Khan who was the grandfather of the first Nizam and the commander of the Mughal army during Aurangzeb's reign. Chin Qalich Khan led the attack of the Mughal army into the Deccan under his Emperor's ambitious plans of expanding the Mughal empire. During Aurangzeb's last siege of Golconda in 1687, Chin Qalich Khan was wounded. He died in Attapur village near Himayath Sagar. Chin Qalich Khan's son, Nawab Ghaziuddin Khan, married the daughter of Sadullah Khan, Prime Minister of Aurangzeb. A son was born, and the Emperor named him Mir Qumaruddin. At the age of six, Mir Qumaruddin accompanied his father to the Mughal court. Aurangzeb awarded him a Mansab, and said to his father, 'The star of destiny shines on the forehead of your son'. Mir Qumaruddin displayed considerable skill as a warrior and at the age of nineteen, the Emperor bestowed on him the title 'Chin Fateh Khan'. At 26, he was appointed Commander in Chief and Viceroy, first of Bijapur, then Malwa and later of the Deccan.

Subsequently, the Mughal Empire declined. There was much confusion after the death of Aurangzeb, and Mir Qumaruddin established his position as Viceroy. Farukh Siar who was the Mughal Emperor for a brief tenure conferred on Mir Qumaruddin the title *Fateh Jung*. He thus became the first Nizam. A subsequent Emperor, Muhammad Shah bestowed on him the title *Asif Jahi*. The dynasty of the Nizams of Hyderabad thus came to be known as the Asif Jahi Dynasty. Hyderabad was ruled by the following Asaf Jahis popularly known as the seven 'Nizams':

I	Nizam-ul-Mulk	1724–1748
II	Nizam Ali Khan	1762–1803
III	Sikander Jah	1803–1829
IV	Nasir-ud-Dowla	1829–1857
V	Afzal-ud-Dowla	1857–1869
VI	Mahboob Ali Pahsa	1869–1911
VII	Mir Osman Ali Khan	1911–1948

During the Asaf Jahi period, Persian, Urdu, Telugu and Marathi developed simultaneously. The highest official positions were given to deserving persons irrespective of their religion. Persian was the official language up to 1893 and then Urdu up to 1948. When the British and the French spread their hold over the country, the Nizam soon won their friendship without bequeathing his power. The title 'Faithful Ally of the British Government' was bestowed on Nizam VII. The British stationed a Resident at Hyderabad, but the state continued to be ruled by the Nizam.

Hyderabad's twin city Secunderabad shares a similar history, even if it is quite different culturally, in contemporary times. In 1798, a subsidiary alliance for military and political cooperation was signed between the Nizam and the British East India Company. Thereafter an area north of what is now the Hussain Sagar was established as a cantonment. The area was named Secunderabad after the then Nizam, Sikander Jah. The essential difference between Hyderabad and Secunderabad is that the former was a feudal Muslim city, while the latter was a cosmopolitan colonial town. Hyderabad was where the Nizam lived; Secunderabad housed the British Resident who wielded the real power in the state. The Nizam's prime ministers were selected or approved by the Resident before the ruler formally appointed them. Every prime minister first called on the Resident who returned the call.

The Nizams were popular for their riches and wealth. Speaking about the seventh Nizam, Narendra Luther reflects 'The seventh – and the last ruling – Nizam, Mir Osman Ali Khan, was reputed to be the world's richest man of his time. He had no idea of his wealth, not surprising for a man whose personal estate yielded 2.5 million rupees and whose privy purse was five million rupees a year. Besides, in 1919, he published and became the sole selling agent for the six collections of his poems for one guinea each. (Yes, the price was fixed in guineas! It was equivalent to twenty-one rupees). He was also presented a *nazar* whenever someone was given the privilege of an audience. Every senior official of the state presented him a *nazar* twice a year – on Eid and on his birthday. The honour of a present of even one mango from his private estate, or a part of his khasa-dinner, sent ceremonially to a noble or a randomly chosen subject had to be acknowledged gratefully with a *nazar* the next day. The minimum amount for a nazar was one gold and twenty silver coins – twenty-four rupees' (Luther, 2008)!

The Nizam's rule saw the growth of Hyderabad economically and culturally. Electricity, railways, roads and airways developed. Huge reservoirs and irrigation projects such as the Tungabhadra, and Nizamsagar were completed. The early work on Nagarjunasagar was undertaken. The Osmania University and several schools and colleges were founded throughout the state. Nearly all the public buildings currently known as the Osmania General Hospital, High Court, Central State Library, Assembly Hall, Jubilee Hall and other buildings in the Public Garden were built during Osman Ali Khan's reign. Soon after India gained independence in 1947, all princely states were invited to join the Republic. Nizam VII was reluctant to do so; but in 1948, after the Police Action (Operation Polo), his state was merged into the

Indian Union. Mir Osman Ali Khan, the last Nizam, died on Friday 24 February 1967. It was the end of the princely era.

> The Police Action has been very assertively described by Mohan Guruswamy in his work On the morning of 13 September 1948 five infantry battalions and an armoured regiment of the battle hardened Indian Army under the command of Maj Gen J N Chaudhry entered the princely state of Hyderabad, over a year after Independence and after the patience of the new Indian Union was tested beyond endurance. The Nizam of Hyderabad like the Maharaja of Jammu & Kashmir too entertained notions of an independent state and had so far managed to avoid accession. In the meantime the Nizam sought to widen the issue by moving the United Nations, took the advice and assistance of Pakistan, and began stockpiling arms. The Times in London reported on 9 August 1948 that the Hyderabad army was strengthened to 40,000 and supplies of arms were being received, presumably from Pakistan. The Prime Minister of Hyderabad Mir Laik Ali boasted that if "the Indian government takes any action against Hyderabad, 100,000 men are ready to fight. We also have a hundred bombers in Saudi Arabia ready to bomb Bombay!" Within the Nizam's realm, Razakars led by Kasim Razvi, had stepped up their campaign. Within five days the "police action", actually a military operation, was all but over and the Hyderabad army commanded by Maj. Gen. El-Edroos formally surrendered. The Indian Army's "police action" was as violent as it was swift. It killed 1373 Razakars and captured 1911. In addition Hyderabad State Army lost 807 killed and 1647 captured. The Indian Army's losses were never officially revealed but a figure of less than 10 killed is commonly accepted. It was a sudden and crushing blow to a movement that had vowed to hoist the Asafia flag on the Red Fort (Guruswamy, 2008).

At the time of India's independence, Hyderabad was the largest Indian princely state in terms of population and GNP. Area-wise it was as big as England and Scotland put together. The State had its own currency, mint, railways, and postal system. There was no income tax. Its territory of 82,698 sq miles was more than that of England and Scotland put together. The 1941 census had estimated its population to be 16.34 million, over 85 per cent of who were Hindus and with Muslims accounting for about 12 per cent. It was also a multilingual state consisting of peoples speaking Telugu (48.2%), Marathi (26.4%), Kannada (12.3%) and Urdu (10.3%). Its diversity and broad heritage could be seen in the historical monuments at Ajanta, Ellora and Daulatabad in Marathawada; Bijapur, Bidar, Gulbarga, Anegondi and Kampili in Karnataka; and Warangal and Nagarjunakonda in Telangana. Hyderabad, not only had its own Army, but also had its own railways, airline, postal service, radio broadcasting network and currency. The Nizam and his court ruled over it with the British Resident keeping a close and watchful eye over everything.

Post-1947 Hyderabad

The years 1947 to 1956 were very crucial in the history of Andhra Pradesh. When India got independence on 15 August 1947, the three main regions of Andhra Pradesh – Coastal Andhra, Rayalaseema and Telangana were not part of Andhra Pradesh State. Coastal Andhra and Rayalaseema belonged to Madras Presidency as a province of British India. Telangana was part of Hyderabad state, which was an independent native Indian state. Though, there were 568 native Indian states, Hyderabad State was the most important native state and was administered directly by the Governor General of India.

Telugu speaking people demanded for their long cherished Visalandhra formation, but people of Hyderabad State were unanimous in their demand for splitting the state into three parts. The States Reorganization Commission headed by Syed Fazal Ali heard the views of different people and organizations. Based on the Commission's conclusions, the Congress Party High Command preferred Visalandhra and enlarged the state by including nine Telugu speaking districts of Hyderabad State to eleven districts of Andhra state to form Andhra Pradesh with 20 districts. In the process, the Hyderabad State was split among Maharashtra, Karnataka and Andhra State. Aurangabad division merged with Maharashtra and Gulbarga division merged with Karnataka. The rest of the two divisions of the state – Gulshanabad or Medak and Nizamabad merged with Andhra State.

Thus, the state of 'Andhra Pradesh' emerged merging all the districts of Coastal Andhra, Rayalaseema and Telangana on 1

November 1956, with Neelam Sanjiva Reddy as the Chief Minister and C.M. Trivedi as the Governor.

Culture of Hyderabad – *Hyderabadi Tehzeeb*

The culture of Hyderabad – *the Hyderabadi Tehzeeb* is the result of evolution and assimilation of several cultures some of which were transitory and some cultures which made Hyderabad their home and thus assimilated with other cultures. The arrival of different cultures though dates back to period much before Qutub Shahis, the present *Hyderabadi tehzeeb* foundations were laid during this time. Different communities from north and south India migrated to Hyderabad during different periods of the Qutub Shahi and Asaf Jahi rule and subsequently Hyderabad became the meeting ground of practically all the elements of the population of the country. Many families from the north came in the early 10th century with the benign Asaf Jah-I to the Deccan and some in the 19th century. These communities played a significant role in the political, social and cultural life of Hyderabad.

Dharmendra Prasad articulates the impact of Iranis on the culture of Hyderabad. Iranis were a part of the cultural make-up of Hyderabad ever since the founding of the city in AD 1591. This was natural because the ruling dynasty of the Qutub Shahis came from Iran and the most important positions in the administration of the Kingdom were held by the nobility from Iran. This factor had a tremendous impact on the art, architecture, literature and culture of Hyderabad for nearly two hundred years after its foundation and the influence is clearly visible in all these areas. There was hardly any facet of life in Hyderabad which did not bear the mark of Iranian influence. There may have been a decline in the Iranian influence, but it never wholly disappeared and individuals and families of Iranian origin continued to wield a great deal of influence until very recently and continued to shape the way of life at least among the higher classes in Hyderabad (Prasad, 1986).

Sheela Raj while communicating the cultural heterogeneity of Hyderabad says that Hyderabad's heterogeneous society included both Muslims and Hindus, and men of diverse ethnic, racial, religious and social backgrounds. Hyderabad was full of diverse groups belonging to different castes and classes. They were influenced more or less by one another's culture (Raj, 1987). It is this influence which has shaped the *Hyderabadi tehzeeb*.

Bilkees Latif says that through the centuries the ethnic Telugus of the region have intermingled and amalgamated with people who have come and been made welcome to this region of the Deccan. The fusion has brought about a special composite Hyderabadi culture that has evolved between its Telugu population and the Mughals from the north of India with whom Hindus of the Kayasth community came in the 16th century, and occupied important posts in the state. There was a further influx of Turkish and Persian scholars, artists, craftsmen and traders who came between the 16th and 19th centuries, invited by the rulers to embellish the forts, tombs and other structures. This interaction and mingling amongst those of different regions and lands also led to the emergence of a beautiful language, Urdu, with its colourful locally spoken Hyderabadi Urdu or 'Dakhni Boli' which often includes an element of humour at one's own expense (Latif, 2008).

Though Asaf Jah I introduced Mughal culture into Deccan, it no longer remained predominant, as it had undergone changes with the needs of the changing society, and particularly with the association of the Marathas and the residing natives. The society which developed during the late nineteenth century in Hyderabad had distinct features. It was, in fact, a unique one due to the integration of Hindus and Muslims. The study of the customs and traditions followed by the people of the Hyderabad will show the peculiarities, which are not found anywhere else in India.

The composite culture is reflected in varied dressing patterns, food habits, customs and traditions. In medieval Hyderabad, *Hyderabadi tehzeeb* was greatly reflected in simplicity. People were very simple and mostly stuck to their religions but they paid due respect to each other's religion as well. Sheela Raj writes that this simplicity of the culture was also reflected in the people's attires. Generally speaking, the ordinary forms of the dress in the rural areas of Hyderabad was *dhoti* or waist cloth, a short jacket or coat of cotton, a red or white turban in the Marathwada region, and always white in Telangana. They carried *Kambal* or blanket. This was worn by both Hindus and Muslims. Hindu women used to wear saris and *cholis* (blouses) but Muslim women often wore a *lehanga* or petticoat, with a *choli* and *dupatta*. The *dastars* or the head-dress of the people of Hyderabad was of different types. Different types of family or traditional dastars used by the people was the identification of their profession, caste and family. Wearing of another's *dastar* was considered to be uncultured. Those whose fathers were dead, wore white dastars and others used colours according to their whims. Of the entire dress, *dastar* was supposed to be symbol of respect. If it fell from the head or the hanger, it was considered as a bad omen. At such times it was customary to weigh the *dastar* against the wheat, and the quantity of wheat was distributed among the poor. The weight of *dastar* was probably considered as a counteraction. Unless it was weighed, it was never again put on the head. Today *dastar* is no longer the head-dress of the people (Raj, 1987).

Among Telugu community *langa odhni* (half sari) was a very prominent attire of young women and girls. The plaited hair decorated with jasmine flowers projected a beautiful picture of *Hyderabadi tehzeeb*. But the onset of globalization has brought in new attires which are relatively modern.

The traditional Muslim family in Hyderabad had a separate Zenana. *Zenana* or the interior part of a house particularly meant for the women was a separate place in the house of a common man. Privacy was secured by means of thick wadded curtains which are called *parda*, generally made of coarse cloth according to individual taste. *Parda* was strictly observed among the Muslims, and few Hindu families. Besides parda, the openings between the pillars had blinds made of bamboo strips, woven together with coloured cords. These were called *chilman*. Many of them were painted green.

The *Hyderabadi tehzeeb* has its own charm and attraction. Narendra Luther says 'the charm of the old-world ambience was still lingering when I arrived in the city a decade after the integration of the old state of Hyderabad with India in 1948. The origin of this flavour can be traced back to over four centuries. In 1591, the fifth Qutub Shahi Sultan of Golconda, Mohammad Quli built a city as "a replica of heaven". He named it *Bhagyanagar*, after his beloved Bhagmati. In 1983, the German architect Jan Pieper quoted chapter and verse to argue that the city was indeed an architectural metaphor for the Quranic heaven' (Luther, 2008).

Great temples for pilgrimage, famous diamond mines, and international trade attracted people from many regions. There was contact with distant lands through coastal trade that included the export of precious stones, and printed textiles, especially of the famous chintz that was so popular with the ladies of Rome and further into Europe. Bilkees Latif writes that the beautiful Dakhni style of miniature painting, the famous Kalamkari handpainted textiles depicting the Persian tree of life as well as scenes from our Ramayana is equally a legacy of Hyderabad's cultural fusion (Latif, 2008).

The romanticism of Hyderabad is so much inherent in *Hyderabadi tehzeeb*. There is something romantic in the air of Hyderabad which has been highlighted by Bilkees Latif and Narendra Luther. Narendra Luther while comparing Hyderabad and Taj Mahal says Hyderabad is to cities what Taj Mahal is to buildings – a monument to love. Both were named to commemorate the respective beloveds – Taj for Mumtaz, Bhagyanagar for Bhagmati. Whereas Taj symbolized a pining for a departed beloved, Bhagyanagar was a celebration of a union of lovers. Taj was to enshrine a resting place for a departed queen, Bhagyanagar to provide living space for her subjects. Mohd. Quli was the first *saheb-e-diwan* Urdu poet of India. He bequeathed a secular legacy to the city. His poetry also celebrated the monsoon season when the city is at its best. Its onset is officially decreed on 7 June though it often violates that injunction with impunity (Luther, 2008).

Latif writes, Hyderabad with its lakes, white-domed buildings, the rugged rocks of the Deccan and its beautiful multi-coloured sunsets spread romanticism in the air of Hyderabad. The Golconda Fort is where the Qutub Shahi Sultan sat on the terrace, listening to the voice of the singer Taramati, wafting from her Baradari across the hills. Premavati, the other favourite, is said to have danced on a set of wires stretched right across these hills till she reached the terrace of the fort. Today the Baradari is once again a cultural centre where singers perform (Latif, 2008).

The *Hyderabadi tehzeeb* is *Ganga-Jamuna tehzeeb* which shows glaring example of synthesizing Hindu–Muslim culture and obviously which had its roots in the history of Hyderabad.

In 1869, Mehboob Ali Khan became the sixth Nizam when he was not yet three. He was the first Nizam to be educated on modern lines under British supervision. He spoke English and wore western dress. He grew into a fine ruler and never wore the same dress twice. Unsurprisingly, he had the world's largest wardrobe – some 70-metre long hall with double-storey almirahs. To stop the worst floods in Hyderabad in 1908, as advised by some Hindu *pandits*, Mehboob Ali Khan placated the goddess Bhavani by performing her *arti*. His subjects venerated him.

The seventh Nizam, Mir Osman Ali Khan became ruler at the age of twenty-five after his father's demise in 1911. The era of modern development in the state began thereafter. The young ruler, well educated by select scholars, was fond of writing poetry. Stylishly dressed, he was at ease with social graces and even enjoyed formal ballroom dancing. He announced that he would be a caring and just ruler. He issued the *Nizam's Asafia* creed stating,

> Whatever be the religion of my house and my own personal beliefs, I am, as a ruler, the follower of another religion as well, which must be characterized as "love towards all" because under me live people of different communities, and the protection of their houses of worship has for long been part of the constitution of my state. I do not desire therefore, to injure with narrow-mindedness the susceptibilities of any community or faith, or to distort the practice of my religion in such a manner as to earn the title of a bigot. In my capacity as a ruler, I consider myself an atheist, but in the sense of being without ties as a ruler for or against any religion or community. In that faith, I and my forefathers have taken just pride and will continue to do so.

He started of by building houses for the poor to prevent slums, and constructed artificial lakes and dams for adequate water supply. There were 32,000 temples and 6,000 mosques in the state, 11,355 Hindu and 5,024 Muslim religious institutions, as well as churches, and the famous Sikh gurdwaras at Nanded, most of which were given annual grants by the Nizam's government. Hindu officials managed 90 per cent of these temples as well as mosques. There was much criticism of the seventh Nizam for his personal frugality. One of the richest men of his time, he chose to spend his wealth on his state and on various causes rather than on himself. He appointed good administrators and experts such as Vishveshwaraya, and prime ministers such as Maharajah Kishen Pershad, Sir Akbar Hydari, as well as advisers like Imad-ul-Mulk and Faridoon Jung, the latter a Parsi gentleman whose descendants and their families still symbolize the best traditions of Hyderabad, and the closeness and caring that form the soul of Hyderabad (Luther, 2008).

Hyderabad city is a centre of different cultures and religions. It is evident from its history, that from the founding of the city, Hindu nobles and jagirdars had an active part in celebration of Muharram festivals. They used to instal *alams* and *tazias* in their places as soon as they observed the new moonlight for their Muslim brethren. Maharaja Kishan Pershad, Raja Rao Ramba, Maharaja Raj Bahadur, Raja Ray Rayan, Bansi Raja and other Hindu jagirdars contributed much to the celebration of this festival. Special majlises (assemblies/conventions) where held in the house of Hindu nobles. On the ninth day of Muharram, Maharaja Sir Kishen Pershad used to arrange a special dinner at his place and invite high dignitaries of the state, the British Resident and other European officials. On the tenth day of Muharram at about 11 a.m., sweets, *sharbat* and fine food were distributed among the poor. The most striking aspect of the Muharram festival in Hyderabad was of Hindus coming to the city from rural areas during this month. They had a staunch belief in it, as much as the Muslims (Vedantam, 1971).

Highlighting the diversity of the ruling elite Narendra Luther writes that Aurangzeb's hated *jaziya* – poll tax – was never imposed in the South. On the other hand, a broad streak of secularism runs through its history. In 1805, a Kayasth noble, Raja Bhavani Pershad, built the first Kayasth temple at Rambagh near Attapur. The third Nizam, Sikander Jah, performed the installation ceremony of the idols of Rama, Sita and Lakshmana. He also granted a *jagir* of 12,000 rupees for its maintenance. The population of the state of Hyderabad was predominantly Hindu. Its founding dynasty, Qutub Shahi, subscribed to the Shia sect of Islam. The Asaf Jahis were Sunni. Of the ten highest noble families under them, one was Sunni, five Shia and four Hindu. Out of the Hindu families, two were Deccani, and two from North India – one Kayasth and the other Punjabi Khatri, tracing their ancestry to Todar Mal, Akbar's celebrated revenue minister. This diversity of the ruling elite imparted a distinctive flavour to the Hyderabadi culture (Luther, 2008).

Apart from multiple indigenous and Asian cultures which imparted distinct flavour to *Hyderabadi tehzeeb*, European culture set the direction for the modern-day Hyderabad.

Both British as well as French have equal importance in setting up many institutions that became the root of solid Western education system in Hyderabad, back since 17th century itself. This also helped in expanding the city with Western culture in the northern side of the Musi river. The Nizam, during various times, had both French and British as part of his army, but maintained in separate locations outside his main city. Only the money required for maintaining the army was provided by the Nizam.

Both the armies have built the area – from the scratch – all by themselves. Since the foreign armies were not forced to build their cantonment areas resembling native cities – they built them as a city of their own respective country. Thus, the cantonment areas had all facilities that a cantonment city of a French or British nation used to have. These facilities included prominent institutions, industries, schools, etc., that made their culture to prevail even after decades of their leaving the city. The French were the earliest of the two, to have resided in the city along with their army. The most noted officers of the French were Monsieur Raymond, also called Musa Ram by the natives. He was the then French General, in the service of Nawab Mir Nizam Ali Khan, the second Nizam of Hyderabad. It was he who set up a place, around which many major institutions of the city prevail even today. The place was Gunfoundry, a factory that manufactures cannon and cannonballs – a modern institution set up in 17th century of the Hyderabad city.

Raymond soon established a great credibility and stature for himself among Nizam and his subjects. His distinction, temper, talent and character marked with a rare spirit of sainthood made him so much beloved of the Nizam and his subjects that the British envied it. His cannon factory used to manufacture world class guns and cannons, as per historians. All this effort had paid off well, as the area became the anchor for many modern institutes, and thus the people here got access to western culture, living, thinking, etc., which helped the city very much during globalization.

The Gunfoundry was set up around in 1786. However, in 1798, Raymond's death resulted in disarmament of the French by the British who overtook the area. The oldest church of the city, St. George's church, was built by the British in 1844 in the same area. This structure later became a boy's school and the church expanded into a beautiful monument in same area.

Then, the St. Joseph's Cathedral was constructed in 1872 in the same locality beside All Saint's. Then, Rosary Convent was set up in 1904 beside this church. There is also another girls' school adjacent to the St. Joseph's Cathedral, Hyderabad, also run by the Franciscan Missionary Sisters of Mary named St. Joseph's High School. Though the French army left Hyderabad, the French missionaries set up All Saint's School, existing even today as one of the premier institutes of Hyderabad. It then also became the reason for establishment of 2 more premier institutes – Little Flower High School (1953) and St. Paul's High School (1954).

All these institutes resulted in inculcating scientific thought in the mindsets of people of Hyderabad. The republican nature of the French has probably resulted in weak feudalism and casteism in Hyderabad compared to other parts of Telangana area. When Nizam wanted to start a bank, he chose the same locality rather than some other part of the city. Today, the same bank has become the headquarters of the State Bank of Hyderabad, the largest associate bank of the SBI.

Though Gunfoundry is not in the similar prominence today, it was definitely the reason for establishing an area and culture that made Hyderabad match with the ideals of the modern civilization in Global village culture (http://hyderabad-india-online.com).

In recent years not only major government institutions, but business houses too have been established. Hyderabad is now Cyberabad owing to multiple firms catering to IT and IT-enabled services. The influx of people from all over India and the world continues. Hyderabadis still retain their composite culture and cosmopolitan outlook with warmth of hospitality. There is a consciousness of being part of a confluence of varied streams and shared values. This confluence, warmth and hospitality is reflected in the present-day *Hyderabadi tehzeeb* which received global appreciation for its hospitality during the Biodiversity Convention (CoP XI) in October 2012 which was hosted by Hyderabad.

Architecture is quite literally, the face of civilization; it largely depends on cultural, technological and economic imprints. *Hyderabadi tehzeeb* imbibes the architectural splendour. The glorious period of architecture in Hyderabad began during the reign of Qutub Shahi dynasty. Vedasri Kada in her article 'Of Minarets, Towers, Spires and High Rises' is of the opinion that the Deccan Islamic architecture saw a multitude of Islamic explorations with Western styles and Mughal ideals. The blend gives rise to a new style in form, some labelled the Indo-Sarcenic, while others, the Indo-Persian. It was during this time that the famous Golconda Fort was built. The Qutub Shahi tombs are fine examples of this period. The monument that the city is now very famous for, the Charminar was built during this dynasty, as was the famous Hussain Sagar lake. All the monuments were built using limestone and granite mortar. They also exhibit fine workmanship and detailing, an import, definitely from Persia (Kada, 2012).

Makkah Masjid is one of the architectural splendours of Hyderabad. Mughal emperor Aurangzeb completed the Makkah Masjid in 1694, the foundation for which was laid by Sultan Mohd. Qutub Shah in 1614. The mosque is said to have bricks from Mecca. During Asaf Jahis (Nizam) it was a glorious period of architecture, and under whose reign Hyderabad's Twin City, Secunderabad was founded. The Osmania University, the Chowmahallah Palace, the King Kothi Palace, the Falaknuma Palace are few examples of grand architecture during the Nizam age. During the same era, Secunderabad was built as a station for the French and later British troops. The Army barracks, clubs and homes in Secunderabad exhibit tremendous inspiration in architecture style from the English. The highly adaptive city took the newness of dotcom boom in its stride when a part of the city was rechristened Cyberabad and Hitec City. In 21st century Hyderabad, the jewel in the crown is the Rajiv Gandhi International Airport. Further, several structures in Gachibowli including IT companies and convention centres like HITEX are magnificent examples of modern-day infrastructure.

Hyderabadi Food – The *Dastarkhan Tehzeeb*

Food is an eminent part of any culture. Hyderabad is known for its world popular *Haleem and Biryani.* Hyderabadis love to eat. Bilkees Latif writes that most conversations seem to end with a discussion on food! In restaurants all over town or even if one is walking down a street at dusk, one gets the aroma of saffron and cardamom from a hot *kachi biryani* of fine rice and succulent meat, of which it is said that once eaten it will draw you back to the city for more! Hyderabad food has its own character depicting its composite culture. The food has the flavours of saffron, cardamom and nutmeg from Persia, the rich fried spices in ghee from northern

India, enhanced by its basic, piquant, local Andhra ingredients of sour tamarind fruit, curry leaves and hot red chillies in meat, seafood, fowl or crisply fried vegetables and spicy, chilli-hot dishes. Chilli-hot food is followed with a helping of plain yoghurt and boiled rice to cool down the fiery fumes, and the rich *masalas* in the *baghare baingan* and *mirchi ka salan* become easy to digest because of the addition of tamarind, so popular in Telangana (Latif, 2008).

All meals were served on the floor where *dastarkhan (white cloth spread over carpet for traditional meal)* were spread, but knives, forks, spoons, glasses or napkins, considered essential to the enjoyment of a meal by the Europeans, were never used. *Dastarkhan* of both Hindus and Muslims had great importance, with a variety of food in the day-to-day life of the people of Hyderabad. It was part of the social life of the people, who were known for their hospitality. This was a mark of the magnificent Deccani culture. Whether poor or rich, all were equal in showing hospitality. Cooking in Hyderabad was an art in itself in former times and to some extent, even today. The neat and clean *dastarkhan* decorated with skilled techniques were marks of the host's good taste.

Traditionally, the people of Hyderabad ate rice and sour things in plenty without caste and class distinction. A proportionate quantity is put in specific food, which improves its taste and is said to be good for health. Shahid Sidiqui, in this article "Hyderabad ki Biryani", wrote 'If sherwani is our national dress, then biryani is our national dish' (Here the word national is used in a limited sense). Parties either in connection with the marriage or circumcision even today are supposed to be incomplete without Biryani. Different types of vegetables were cooked (and are cooked) either separately or with mutton. *Baghare baigan* and *Mirchi ka salan* is a peculiar dish of Hyderabad. It could be kept for a number of days. Similarly, *kut* prepared with tomatoes and *kulti* was the oldest and most popular Hyderabadi dishes (Raj, 1986).

All these dishes are even today current in the region. European dishes like bread, biscuit, cake, pastry, pudding, ice cream, fruit salad, were introduced during the late nineteenth century. The Nizam had a department known as *amra,* which arranged state dinners, lunches and at-homes by experts of the department. For example, Berganaza from Goa was a specialist in European food. With the advent of Europeans in Hyderabad, different types of drinks were introduced. With "cyber culture" developing in Hyderabad, contemporary Hyderabadi food includes all types of food including intercontinental food (Italian, Mexican, Mediterranean etc).

Hyderabadi's Irani chai is so much part of its *tehzeeb*. The Irani cafes best delight is *Irani chai, Osmania biscuits and Irani samosa*. Among other beverages south Indian coffee, *bandi chai* addiction is common among Hyderabadis. The modern Hyderabad is witnessing *bandi food culture* and curry point culture. Morning breakfast (Idly, Wada, Dosa etc) and evening snacks on *bandi* is becoming quite common.

The city is not only known for its hospitality but also friendliness, sociability and affability. Jyotirmayi Sharma narrates his experience highlighting this cultural trait. He recounts 'I came to Hyderabad at a juncture in life when it becomes increasingly impossible to make new friends. One, at this point, likes to retain the few good ones that are there, consolidate these bonds, and enter middle age in anticipation that middle age would at least last longer than youth and old age will not dawn as rapidly as the teenage years went by. Hyderabad proved me wrong. I have made more friends than I ever did in my entire life. These friends are from all parts of the country as there are those who trace their beginnings to this city. Those from elsewhere do not hanker after returning to a 'promised land' (not even the Bengalis), nor do they indulge in misplaced nostalgia. They live in Hyderabad, belong here and think of the city as the centre of the universe. There is a great element of truth in the often heard phrase, 'Gandipet ka paani piya hai (He/she has drunk the waters of Gandipet Lake). He who drinks these waters stays in Hyderabad forever' (Sharma, 2008).

The description of *Hyderabadi tehzeeb* is incomplete without mentioning the typical Hyderabadi argot. It is so much part of Hyderabad's culture. Karthik Pasupulate in his article *Hum aiseich hai* mentions about interesting words and phrases of Hyderabadi lingo – *Jump Jilani* (runners who ran to save their lives), *de thadi pochamma gudi* (not backing down, what may come), *hand ichadu* (pure Telugu slang for when someone ditches you), *bada hath de diya yaron; kya baingan ke baata karre ji, khamush baitho*.

Elaborating on usage of word *purson* in Hyderabad, Narendra Luther says 'Old people used to tell me that the worst floods in the city occurred *purson* – the "day before yesterday". They meant 1908. In the Hyderabadi lexicon, the term covers all remembered past' (Luther, 2008).

The famous Laad bazaar is so much sought for pearls and bangles especially the lac bangles which is a vital identity of Hyderabad.

Cultural Diversity of Hyderabad

Cultural diversity is the very soul of *Hyderabadi tehzeeb*. The various religious and social institutions in Hyderabad have been vital in promoting the cultural diversity of Hyderabad. The religious, social and educational institutions of Hyderabad have through the ages, acted as powerful magnets to attract people from diverse parts of India and of varied cultural backgrounds. They have also played a key role in integrating these diverse elements of Hyderabadi culture and *tehzeeb*. These institutions reflect the cultural heritage of India.

The dargahs or shrines of Muslim Sufi saints, on the one hand, throw light on the importance Islam has attained in the area they are located, and on the other hand, they testify to the cultural unity of India for, among the devotees of these Muslim Sufi saints, there are both Muslims and non-Muslims. In addition, these shrines have acted as magnets for attracting people and settlements. The temples of Hyderabad, like the dargahs, have played a significant role in promoting social harmony, religious tolerance and as the nuclei of settlement for certain communities which settled down in Hyderabad.

The Christians constitute a significant minority in the twin cities even though their total number forms only a small percentage of the population. Among the Christians, the Roman Catholic are large in number than the protestants including all denominations. The Christian population of the twin cities has significantly clustered around the churches which are concentrated in certain localities. It is in these localities that besides churches there are Convent and Grammar Schools run and maintained by Christian organizations and churches. The origin of the gurudwaras of the Sikhs in the twin cities of Hyderabad and Secunderabad is closely associated with the arrival of the Sikhs in the erstwhile state of Hyderabad during the period of Nizam-III, Nawab Sikandar Jah Bahadur (AD 1803–29).

Hyderabad – "The City of Nawabs" is a perfect combination of traditional and modern outlook. The city is a melting point of various religions and cultures imparting cultural diversity. Its well-preserved cultural heritage creates nostalgia among old residents for its fine arts and architectural ambience. Pt. Jawaharlal Nehru described the city as "Microcosm of Indian culture". It is a city of joy; a charming city where secularism has been existing for centuries. The Muslim culture is fused with the South Indian tradition and it has manifested a symbol of secularism in India.

Hyderabad is a unique cosmopolitan city with secular diversity where the followers of all religions following Christianity, Hinduism, Islam, Jainism, and Zoroastrianism reside happily. Hyderabadis have developed their own distinctive culture, which is a fusion of the centuries old Islamic culture and the Hindu traditions of the Telugu people. Urdu and Telugu are the most commonly spoken languages of Hyderabad. A large section of the Telugu speaking population lives here who have migrated from different parts of Andhra Pradesh. Hyderabad's rich cultural heritage of Telugu and Urdu literature, music and dance is perpetuated in universities and different performing art centres located at various parts of the city. The Osmania University, located in the heart of the city, was the first Urdu medium university in India.

Festivity pours happiness to the lives of millions of Hyderabadis. The city celebrates a number of fairs and festivals which signify unity and prosperity among people. Apart from religious festivals it also organizes several modern dance and music festivals to raise the cultural creativity among people. Diwali, Eid, Christmas, Ganesh and Durga Puja, annual Urs at Moulali and Yousufain are celebrated by all the city dwellers with equal fervour and enthusiasm. Dance and music are popular events during these occasions and special food items are prepared to make the celebrations more captivating. Afrin Humayun says that Hyderabad is believer's haven There's miraculous little dargah, mandir, chapel or gurudwara around every other street corner made famous by local, legend and lore, and the power of sheer faith. These sacred places are abodes of our resident gods who take care of our small and big things. Be it the Khairtabad

Ganesha or Our Lady of Health, Khairtabad; the Visa Balaji of Chilkur or the Yousufain, Moulali dargah, some of these places have become synonymous with the church or temple or mosque located there. "Ganapati Bappa Moriya" scream young teenage boys from the trucks as they escort mighty, friendly looking Ganesha seated at the centre. Passers-by only too familiar with the chorus of festive season, stare to look at the Ganesha that's zooming past. The tallest and largest Ganesha makes his presence felt in Khairtabad. Simultaneously, the feast of Our Lady of Health in Khairtabad is visited by lakhs of devotes including Hindus. One of the oldest mosques – Mecca Masjid where people of all religions and faith come here for various reasons either to admire architecture that took 50 years to complete or to look at the strand of hair of Prophet Muhammad that is kept in one of the rooms or to simply feed the numerous pigeons that settle on the stone flooring of the front courtyard. The Bonalu and Bathakamma celebrations and Mahankali *Jatra* are attended by hundreds of people. People in processions follow the brightly painted Potharaju who dances wildly to the beat of the drums, the oracle who makes predictions for the coming year (Humayun, 2012).

Social Changes and the Missing Element

In its historic development, Hyderabad city has experienced many changes since its foundation as the capital of the medieval kingdom of Golconda in the 16th century to its present status as the metropolis and megacity of a modern state. Each historic phase of development has markedly influenced its physical and cultural growth while the Golconda period was known for the promotion of Shiite Iranian culture, it encouraged equally the development of the native Telugu culture in the city which is indicated by the fact that the rulers themselves were conversant with the Telugu language and some of them even composed poetry in this language.

In more than four centuries of its existence Hyderabad has seen innumerable socio-cultural changes. In the past two decades its expansion has been phenomenal, so much so, that it reflects multiple identities even if it subsumes in identity of Hyderabad. Christina Francis says that the "Twins" (twin cities of Hyderabad and Secunderabad) have grown so much that they have developed four very distinct identities over the years. Distinct enough to seem like four mini cities – Old city, New city, Tech city and

Secunderabad – masquerading as one colourful Hyderabad. Hyderabad acquires a new identity and Hyderabadi flaunts a new personality, every 25 odd kilometres. While the old city is the true Hyderabad, with centuries-old traditions and Nawabi way of living still intact in its colourful and chaotic streets, the new city (from Begumpet to Banjara Hills and Jubilee Hills) is the face of urban Hyderabad, with its swish lifestyle, global outlook, page 3 culture and impressive affluence. With the IT industry and corporate culture becoming a parallel life-line, a Tech city (Madhapur, Kondapur, Gachibowli) has formed for new age Hyderabadi who has chosen to stay in the city for the opportunities it provides. It has an identity of its own, what with its futuristic infrastructure and residents who are from all over the country. Secunderabad, meanwhile, celebrates its own unique identity which has been shaped by a 200-year old colonial history and distinct features like convent schooling culture, Christian and Parsi settlements, army lifestyles and more (Francis, 2012).

Alongside the undoubted contributions of the Nizams, and ministers like the Salar Jungs, or the English in the setting up of the twin city of Secunderabad, modern-day Hyderabad, as the capital of Andhra Pradesh, has been transformed by substantial infusions of capital, both material and intellectual, in the post-independence era. Site of important public sector units such as the Bharat Heavy Electricals Limited (BHEL), major defence establishments like the Defence Research and Development Organisation (DRDO), Council for Scientific and Industrial Research (CSIR) labs like the Centre for Cellular and Molecular Biology, academic centres like the Central and Osmania Universities, as also research institutes like the Administrative Staff College of India, National Institute of Rural Development (NIRD), International Crops Research Institute for the Semi-Arid Tropics (ICRISAT), and more recently the Indian School of Business, the National Institute of Information Technology or National Academy of Legal Studies and Research (NALSAR), just to name a few, Hyderabad today is a vibrant megapolis, attracting vast numbers of young professionals for both employment and skill enhancement. Hyderabad also houses National Police Training Academy and several other institutions of national and international importance. These institutions have contributed immensely in bringing about positive social change and development.

A critical factor which will bring social change is Hyderabad Metro Rail popularly called Metro. In its efforts to improve the intra-city transportation, Metro has been suggested as the panacea. The need for Metro has been expressed to meet the needs of megacity of Hyderabad that covers 625 sq km of municipal corporation area and 6,852 sq km of metropolitan area. It is fast emerging as the hub of Information Technology/Information Technology Enabled Services (IT/ITES), Biotech, Pharma and Tourism sector. Its strategic geographical location, multilingual and cosmopolitan culture, tremendous growth potential and investment-friendly economic policy are all making it an attractive destination for corporates, entrepreneurs, academicians and homemakers alike. The present population of Hyderabad is 8 million and is projected to touch 13.64 million by 2021. Currently, over 2.8 million personalized vehicles ply on Hyderabad roads, with an addition of 0.20 million vehicles every year. Around 8 million motorized trips are made every day, of which, only about 3.36 million or 42 per cent are made by the Public Transportation System (PTS), i.e., buses and local trains. That means the rest of the trips are made by personal vehicles leading to traffic bottlenecks, high pollution levels and a steep increase in fuel consumption. Thus, Metro is expected to overcome these shortcomings. However there should be all possible efforts to secure and safeguard the heritage buildings which are so much part of its culture and *tehzeeb*.

Anyone who is born and brought up in Hyderabad and has seen its evolution in the past 2–3 decades shall definitely vouch that there is some element of our culture, our *Hyderabadi tehzeeb,* which is missing, though it is difficult to identify the exact missing element. The social and secular tolerance which defined *Hyderabadi tehzeeb* seems to be diluted even though many residents still retain the secular spirit.

Narendra Luther very precisely and emotionally brings about the change in Hyderabad and the *missing element.* He says that Hyderabad was conceived in the image of heaven. All its gardens and low buildings have been gobbled up by new apartment buildings. Multi-storey malls have sprung up even in the exclusive residential areas. Its arteries are choked, its breath polluted, its heritage all but vanished. The 2.5 billion-year-old, fascinating rocks are being recklessly destroyed. Paradoxically, while people's income is going up, their quality of life is coming down. Nostalgia is for that lost heaven of broad concrete roads, of a low skyline, and of gardens. It is a longing for a world of laid-back life, of courtesies, of *mushairas*, *qawwalis* and *chowki* dinners. It is a yearning for the sepia tones of yesteryear. I too suffer from nostalgia. I came to this city five decades ago. I still live in Hyderabad, but where is Hyderabad, *O bird of time?* (Luther, 2008).

The traditional attire of *langa odhni* is almost extinct. The real estate has taken such a form that concrete jungles are getting denser keeping at stake the ecological and environmental balance of the city.

Secularism is the very fabric of *Hyderabadi tehzeeb*. Though we have been living and projecting the secular spirit, it is sad to see that religious festivals have become means to reflect strength and power. The warmth of the people and relaxed attitude is missing. Vanaja Banagiri says that gone are the days of *nawabi* attitudes and laid-back lifestyles. Everything is on a fast track. From economic development to attitudinal change, Hyderabad has undergone a tremendous metamorphosis. Steering the growth are the city's young. With their restlessness to be a part of the hip and happening, and energy levels to match, they have redefined all things hitherto known as Hyderabadi (Banagiri, 2007).

The apartment culture has become a necessity keeping in view the space crunch. It has been debated that apartment culture is discouraging the people of diversified religion and castes staying together. Till recently, Hyderabadis couldn't relate to apartment culture. After much resistance, they have succumbed to the housing demand and escalating land rates, and one finds high rises mushrooming in and around the city. Fortunately, some areas like Jubilee Hills are protected from the onslaught of modern-day wonders and still retain the charm of homes with gardens.

The societies undergo change. In fact change is the permanent feature of society. The forces of modernization have become predominant owing to globalization. There is not only exchange of goods and services but also cultural diffusion taking place at a very fast pace. In the past one decade the topography of Hyderabad has witnessed sea change with IT companies and malls becoming an imminent part of the culture. The mall culture has popularized its own distinct lifestyle. Jyotirmayi Sharma while writing about the change in Hyderabad says 'The city has grown since I came here. The IT and biotech boom has brought in people from all over the country. They don't drink water from the Gandipet Lake and, mercifully, will go away in a few years. They live in gated communities, sit in soulless offices, hardly ever mingle with the local community, retire on weekends to the antiseptic but noisy confines of pubs, and return to their pigeonholed existence on Monday morning. They ignore the city and the city ignores them' (Sharma, 2008).

The expansion of the city has lead to increased travel time. The social interactions between people have assumed new dimensions with weekend parties and pub culture making its strong presence feel. There seems to be an unending race in which rikshaws are out of sight.

It has been asserted by many passionate Hyderabadis at various platforms, in several write ups, monographs and ethnographies that *Hyderabadi tehzeeb* evokes images of charm and romance, a grandeur and splendour woven with legend which over the years has continued to inspire contemporary folklore. Popular renditions of the city, much like those of its counterpart city in the north, Lucknow, reminisce about the syncretistic Hindu-Muslim culture, a Ganga-Jamuni *tehzeeb*, and an elite drawn across denominational divides that left behind not just iconic wonders like the Charminar, the Chowmahalla and the equally marvellous palaces and *baradaris* but a fusion cuisine marked for its distinction and the attractive speech, Deccani Urdu.

All these descriptions are true but somewhere undermining the present reality. Beyond the glories of the Nizami era, buildings, pearls and the enjoyable *cuisine* the contemporary Hyderabad has expanded and thus are its challenges and predicaments which bring forth the clashes between castes, class, religion and regions. The usual *najaakat*, mannerisms and courtesies which were part of day-to-day social interactions between common people seem to be missing. The best example is the way *autowallahs* (auto drivers) rough up the commuters. The relaxed pace of the city has transformed drastically. The attires have changed. Traditional attires have been replaced by western and modern ones. The concrete jungles and pollution have taken away the brightness from the stars and has dimmed the pole star.

Not only is contemporary Hyderabad, an eight million plus agglomeration, more and different from the erstwhile capital of the Asaf Jah dynasty, we need to revisit its history to grasp both the energy and tensions marking the populace and its popular culture. Equally, without understanding the relations between the city and its hinterland, more extractive than synergistic, we may miss out on its future.

The city in its frenzied pace is choking its resources especially land and water. The city which was known as 'City of Lakes' is witnessing destruction of local water bodies and phenomenal change in land use pattern.

It has been asserted at several seminars and discussions 'Like all large cities, Hyderabad too displays many faces, with people inhabiting many worlds simultaneously. There are the glories of the past – the buildings, the crafts, the food and the tehzeeb. There is the vibrancy of the present, new modes of wealth creation and consumption, increasingly involving a cosmopolitan workforce' (http://www.india-seminar.com).

In fact cities change; but change should not snatch the identity and the *tehzeeb* which defines the identity. For a visitor, Hyderabad may present a very satisfactory picture but for those residents who see Hyderabad changing at such high pace, the change is not always welcome. In fact in the winds of these changes the basic nuances of *Hyderabadi tehzeeb* is missing.

Nevertheless despite the missing element, the Hyderabadis love and adore the city but do sigh for the missing element. Just to conclude and quote the content in a seminar write up (City of Hope – a symposium on Hyderabad and its syncretic culture, May 2008) '... What shape this will take remains uncertain, but the city still retains its soul and generates fierce pride among its resident *mulkis* and migrants. Even if somewhat frayed, in part more myth and memory than fact, there is no gainsay the languorous grace and welcoming spirit, just what makes Hyderabad so special.'

Demographic Details of Hyderabad

As per 2011 Census of India, population of Hyderabad in 2011 is 6,809,970; of which male and female are 3,500,802 and 3,309,168 respectively. Although Hyderabad city has population of 6,809,970;

its urban/metropolitan population is 7,749,334 of which 3,985,240 are males and 3,764,094 are females.

There was change of 4.71 per cent in the population compared to population as per 2001. In the previous Census of India 2001, Hyderabad district recorded increase of 21.74 per cent to its population compared to 1991. The initial provisional data released by Census India 2011, shows that density of Hyderabad district for 2011 is 18,480 people per sq km. In 2001, Hyderabad district density was at 17,649 people per sq km. Hyderabad district administers 217 sq km of area. Average literacy rate of Hyderabad in 2011 was 80.96 compared to 78.80 of 2001. If things are looked at genderwise, male and female literacy was 83.35 and 78.42 respectively. For 2001 census, same figures stood at 83.74 and 73.50 in Hyderabad district. Total literate in Hyderabad district were 2,906,923 of which male and female were 1,540,195 and 1,366,728 respectively. With regards to sex ratio in Hyderabad, it stood at 945 per 1000 male compared to 2001 census figure of 933. The average national sex ratio in India is 940 as per latest reports of Census 2011 Directorate. In 2011 census, child sex ratio is 938 girls per 1000 boys compared to figure of 943 girls per 1000 boys of 2001 census data (http://www.census2011.co.in/census/district/122-hyderabad.html).

As per data released by Govt. of India for Census 2011, Hyderabad is an Urban Agglomeration coming under the category of Million Plus UA/City. Hyderabad city is governed by Municipal Corporation and is situated in Hyderabad Urban Region. The total population of Hyderabad UA/Metropolitan region is 7,749,334. The male population is 3,985,240 while female population is 3,764,094. The literacy rate of Hyderabad Agglomeration is 82.92 per cent which is lower than National Urban average of 85 per cent. Literacy rate for male and female for Hyderabad stood at 86.14 per cent and 79.51 per cent respectively. Total literates in Hyderabad UA were 5,736,575 of which males were 3,064,389 and remaining 2,672,186 were females.

The Greater Hyderabad Municipal Corporation (GHMC) comprises the erstwhile Hyderabad Municipal Corporation, plus 10 municipalities and 8 panchayats in Ranga Reddy district and 2 municipalities in Medak district.

The municipalities in Ranga Reddy district are: L.B. Nagar, Gaddi Annaram, Uppal Kalan, Malkajgiri, Kapra, Alwal, Qutubullapur, Kukatpally, Serilingampalle and Rajendranagar. The panchayats in Ranga Reddy district are: Shamshabad, Satamarai, Jallapalli, Mamdipalli, Mankhal, Almasguda, Sardanagar and Ravirala.

The municipalities in Medak district are: Ramachandrapuram and Patancheru. The areas under Hyderabad Metropolitan Development Authority includes 16 mandals in Hyderabad district (entire Hyderabad district), 24 mandals in Ranga Reddy district – Shamshabad, Rajendranagar, Sherilingampally, Balanagar, Quthubullapur, Malkajigiri, Alwal, Lothkunta, Keesara, Ghatkesar, Uppal, Saroornagar, Medchal, Shameerpet, Hayathnagar, Shankerpally, Chevella, Shahbad, Moinabad, Maheshwaram, Ibrahimpatnam, Manchal (Part), Yacharam (Part), Kandukur, 10 mandals in Medak district – Patancheru, Ramachandrapuram, Sangareddy, Jinnaram, Hathnoora (Part), Narsapur, Shivampet, Tupran, Wargal, Mulug; 5 mandals in Nalgonda district – Bhongir, Bibinagar, Pochampally, Bommalaramaram, Choutuppal; 2 mandals in Mehboobnagar district – Kothur, Farooqnagar (Part) (http://www.apind.gov.in/library/district/hyderabad).

Hyderabad district, in its present shape, was formed in August 1978, when all its rural areas were included in Ranga Reddy district. The area of Municipal Corporation of Hyderabad (excluding a small part), Secunderabad Cantonment, Lalaguda and Osmania University are included in Hyderabad district. All the 65 revenue villages with its erstwhile taluks of Charminar, Golconda, Musheerabad and Secunderabad have been regrouped into 16 mandals. Hyderabad being the state capital is highly developed in all aspects. It is situated at an altitude of 536 metres and offers pleasant weather conditions. The total geographical area of the district is 199.60 sq km (present area is 217 sq km). River Musi, a tributary of river Krishna, runs through the city, dividing it into old and new city. Drinking water needs of the city are met by the water from Osman Sagar, Mir Alam Tank and from Manjeera River in Medak district. Proposals to supply drinking water from Nagarjuna Sagar to meet city's demand are also under active consideration of the government (http://www.hyd.co.in/ government/).

The city of Hyderabad today is a megacity and is currently the capital of Andhra Pradesh. The city is run by the Greater Hyderabad Municipal Corporation (GHMC), headed by the City Mayor who has a few administrative powers. GHMC's geographical area covers most of the city's urban development agency, the Hyderabad Metropolitan Development Agency (HMDA). It was formed on 16 April 2007 when 12 municipalities and 8 villages were merged. Today, it is in charge of the infrastructure as well as the civic needs of the city, with all of Hyderabad's 150 municipal wards overseen by a corporator. The administration corporators, on the other hand, are elected by popular vote, and almost all of Hyderabad's political parties field their own candidates. Hyderabad's municipal limits cover three districts, and the administration of each district is headed by a District Collector whose tasks include updating property records and revenue collection for the central government, as well as overseeing the elections held in the city. The three districts that are covered by Hyderabad's municipal limit are Hyderabad, Rangareddy, and Medak. The HMDA, on the other hand, is headed by the Chief Minister along with a Commissioner. Its main purpose is to undertake developmental projects in a jurisdiction of above 6,250 sq metres.

Previously, the Mayor of Hyderabad had been selected by the legislative body of the GHMC but the state government modified the Hyderabad Municipal Corporation Act of 1955 to stipulate that the mayoral elections be held simultaneously with the corporate elections. The chain of authority goes such that the Mayor and the corporate legislative body can be dismissed by the state government, and have been in the past.

There are also some parts of Hyderabad that is under the jurisdiction of the Secunderabad Cantonment Board (SBC) mainly because of a large presence of military units. However, most of the Board's jurisdiction falls to Hyderabad's twin city, Secunderabad. The Board provides basic infrastructure such as roads, bridges, parks, water, and other municipal needs to the people of both cities residing under the its jurisdiction.

As for policing, Hyderabad's state police is divided into two: the Hyderabad Police and the Cyberabad police. Both come under the state Home Ministry and are headed by police commissioners who are officers from the Indian Police Service. The city itself is divided into five police zones, with each zone headed by a Deputy Commissioner of Police. The Traffic Police, on the other hand, is semi-autonomous, under both Hyderabad and Cyberabad commissionerates.

It is a known fact that Hyderabad stands apart in terms of developmental profile. Hyderabad, along with its peripheral areas, has largely been service-centric in spite of housing several large manufacturing units both in public and private sectors and the real estate and infrastructure development enterprises, and has been growing along this pattern. Its pre-eminence in IT exports and as the biggest software centre in Andhra Pradesh is well established. The city is also contributing to the growing share of national exports from the software talent it has pooled from across the country. The availability of basic infrastructure like space/land, transport systems, power supply, etc., provided an added advantage. It is also contended that migration of people to Hyderabad is not a new phenomena. It started in 1920s, at the invitation from the Nizam of Hyderabad to the farming community from coastal Andhra for cultivation of the lands of Nizam-Hyderabad. By 1930s, there were about 20 lakh migrants cultivating about 10 lakh acres of land in the then Hyderabad state. They were called 'settlers'. Migration to Hyderabad was not confined to persons from coastal Andhra alone. Although in comparatively smaller numbers, migration had also taken place from Karnataka, Maharashtra, Bihar, West Bengal, Orissa (now Odisha), Uttar Pradesh and Gujarat, etc. The city's cosmopolitan character had enabled consolidation of 'talent' from all parts of the country. The 'Urdu' heritage formed the backbone for the spread of Hindi which facilitated communication linkages with the northern states and which in turn attracted workforce from the north in the low income strata. Other infrastructure facilities, like availability of primary coal and power resources, lent support to encouraging investment. The city, thus, acquired a sort of national character with the spread of IT and IT-related software and service enterprises.

Hyderabad's historical distinctiveness has always been well known. As a city, it is, as Nehru said of India, 'an ancient palimpsest on which layer upon layer of thought and reverie had been inscribed, and yet no succeeding layer had completely hidden or erased what had been written previously'. The social base of Hyderabad's politics is also distinct. While different communities have historically inherited strengths and weaknesses, they have all been able to find their political niche within the city, creating a diverse political landscape of largely constructive contestation.

As a city, Hyderabad's economy operates across three levels: regional, national and international. At one level, it is strongly linked to the region, and its role as a driver of regional growth depends on its unique location, advantage of having concentration of high quality infrastructure from the period of the Nizams, extending into the present and its current position in the global economy of IT and ITES. Its role as a driver of regional growth depends on its position in the global economy of IT and ITES. Within Andhra Pradesh, the IT and ITES industry is almost solely in Hyderabad, which accounted for 99 per cent of the total exports from the state in the year 2005–06, and has consistently accounted for 98 per cent of the total exports from the state in the years 2006–07, 2007–08, and 2008–09. Hyderabad has now grown as the fifth largest centre after Bengaluru, Mumbai, the National Capital Region, and Chennai, and much ahead of locations such as Pune and Kolkata. Modern services form 39 per cent of the economic activity in Hyderabad, with transport accounting for another 19 per cent. The real estate industry, which benefits from this, is also unusually diverse, with strong participation of national players, in addition to regional firms. To complement these strengths in services, it has a manufacturing base in the surrounding Rangareddy district. It has been able to draw in talent from across the state and country, not just at the high end but across the range of economic activities. Hyderabad has been able to attract investors from across the country and indeed across the globe. In fact, a sixth of Telangana's GDP comes from Hyderabad. The pattern of Hyderabad's migration and investment reflects a growing increase in its cosmopolitan identity and social diversity. Hyderabad has also benefited from a number of public sector interventions at both the state and central level, in terms of institutions, investment and infrastructure. It is to be noted that a large number of Central institutions are Public Sector Companies/Units,

National Institutes, Civil and Military Research and Development Organisations, and Defence Forces Institutions.

Although historically and geographically a part of the Telangana region, the cultural and demographic composition of Hyderabad, with a very substantial Muslim population and migrants from all over the state and indeed the country, makes it, quite distinct from the other three regions. Hence, the political choices that the city makes and its intervention in the agitation are rather specific to its character. The demand for Telangana does not arouse the same intensity of emotions among most residents of the city; yet it cannot escape the tremors of separatist agitations; Osmania University remains the hub of the student agitation for Telangana and the fate of Hyderabad itself is of central concern to the bifurcation issue.

"Composite Culture" of Telangana and Hyderabad

An argument being made for autonomy for Telangana is that the "composite culture" of Hyderabad enveloped the whole of Telangana and cannot be sustained in united Andhra Pradesh. The composite culture emerged from the diversity of linguistic, ethnic, caste and religious groups settled in the region and was epitomized in the city of Hyderabad. Although a large majority of the population of the city has been Muslim from the Nizam period onwards, there are long standing migrant populations of Tamils, Marwaris, Punjabis and others from many other regions and communities of India, including Muslims of foreign descent. Migrants from other regions of Andhra Pradesh (AP) have also been coming to the city and the Telangana region for a fairly long period. Although the Telugu language predominates among the Hindu population of the city and Muslims are largely confined to the old city, with their own subculture, other languages and cultural forms of other communities also find acceptance in the city. In the post-1970 period, however, there was a large influx of migrants from the prosperous regions of coastal Andhra (neighbourhoods such as Ameerpet, Kukatpalle, Sanat Nagar and Patancheri are known to be coastal Andhra settlements); these migrants came for education, to join government service and start businesses. Over a period of time, a large number of such migrants have settled down having bought homes and properties and having educated their children in Hyderabad. Prosperous farmer-capitalists from the delta districts of coastal Andhra invested heavily in real estate, films, education and also made Hyderabad their home.

According to Telangana people, Andhra culture has been brought in by these migrants and by the fact that a large number of people in administration are from the Andhra area. As discussed earlier, the Telugu influence in the city became more predominant from the 1980s when N.T. Rama Rao (NTR) shifted the Telugu film industry from Chennai to Hyderabad, offering real estate and infrastructure subsidies. The shift brought many artists, technicians and investors to the city. NTR played a large role in creating a Telugu identity in the state and the city. Unfortunately, migrants from coastal Andhra, irrespective of their duration of residence in Hyderabad or in other Telangana districts continue to be termed as 'settlers' and the ire of Telangana natives is reserved for them. They are considered to be 'money-minded' even though recognized as entrepreneurial and industrious by nature. According to Telangana natives, Andhra settlers have brought in their own (idli-sambhar) culture which now swamps the original cosmopolitanism of Telangana and Hyderabadi culture. In the event of separation of the state, Andhra-Seema migrants fear that their homes, properties and businesses may be targeted.

In this context, it is important to recognize that migrants to Hyderabad are from all three regions of the state and from all classes and sections of society. They are not merely the capitalist elite. Such migrants – short and long term – see Hyderabad as a destination for education and employment. Second and third generation migrants do not see themselves as non-locals and many new arrivals become locals after four years of schooling in Hyderabad and Rangareddy, driven by parent's desire to afford them a good education in schools and colleges located in the two districts. The cosmopolitan culture of the city, which has now become a mega-city, is only set to deepen by recent in-migration from other states of India than from other regions of AP. As a city, Hyderabad will continue to be dynamic even as its character continues to evolve.

Methodology and Respondents' Profile

A methodology is a guideline system for solving a problem, with specific components such as phases, tasks, methods, techniques and tools. Research methodology is a way to systematically solve the research problem. It may be understood as a science of studying how research is done scientifically. In it, we study the various steps that are generally adopted by a researcher in studying his research problem along with the logic behind them. It is necessary for the researcher to know not only the research methods/techniques but also the methodology. Research methodology not only includes the research methods but also considers the logic behind the methods used in the context of the research study and explains why a particular method or technique is being used. Why a research study has been undertaken, how the research problem has been defined, in what way and why the hypothesis has been formulated, what data have been collected and what particular method has been adopted, why particular technique of analysing data has been used and a host of similar other questions are usually answered when we talk of research methodology concerning a research problem or study.

Methodology

The various aspects of the methodology used in this study are presented in succeeding sub-paragraphs.

Universe of the Study

The present study is primarily based on understanding cosmopolitanism, regionalism and urban development in Hyderabad. The universe includes the people of Hyderabad, a city with a deep-rooted past and with technological development. It is one of the fastest growing cosmopolitan post-industrial cities of India. With people from various regions and cultures, Hyderabad reflects unique diversity and cosmopolitanism, especially post-IT revolution.

The Sampling Frame

The sample has been collected from the people of Hyderabad who have experienced the evolution of Hyderabad as a cosmopolitan city. The sample will be collected from the natives as well as migrants in Hyderabad.

Sampling Method

The primary data from Hyderabad is collected using random sampling.

Sample Size

The district of Hyderabad consists of 16 mandals. These are Charminar, Bahadurpura, Bandlaguda, Saidabad, Amberpet, Nampally, Golconda, Asifnagar, Himayath Nagar, Secunderabad, Tirumalgiri, Maredpally, Ameerpet, Musheerabad, Khairatabad and Shaikpet. Keeping in view the requirements of efficiency, representativeness, reliability and flexibility, a sample of 225 respondents have been drawn from each mandal leading to the final sample size of 3,600 (three thousand six hundred).

Units of Observation

The various variables which have been observed and analysed apart from socio-economic profile of the respondents are food habits, dressing patterns, means of recreation and entertainment; hobbies, dynamics of purchasing groceries and shopping; changes in values and traditions; openness to new experiences; attitude towards the people of other regions and those of migrants; area of residence; language; culture and economic interests.

Data Collection

The sources of data collection are both primary and secondary sources. The tool used in the study is observation and interview schedule. Apart from the researchers own observations, the study has been supported by the observations of the experts who have been witness to evolution of Hyderabad into a cosmopolitan city and the process of its development. Literature has been collected to understand the evolution of Hyderabad as a cosmopolitan city with more than 400 years of glorious existence. The interview schedule method has been used to collect the primary data from the respondents based in Hyderabad. Since this method facilitates face-to-face interpersonal interaction in which an in-depth understanding of the problem is possible, it is an appropriate method to understand cosmopolitanism and the sensitive bases of regionalism. The interview schedule has four sections. They are:

Socio-Economic Profile of the Respondents, Cosmopolitanism in Hyderabad, Cosmopolitanism and Urban Development, Regionalism and Urban Development.

Data Analysis

The present study aims to derive certain important relationship and association between important variables and to judge the significance of their association. Keeping in view the nature of study, null hypothesis has been formulated. To check the relevance of null hypothesis, Chi-Square test has been used. The scales used in measurement analysis are Nominal scale, Ordinal scale and Likert scale. Nominal scale is one of the crudest yet simplest scales of measurement. In this scale the different scores on a measurement simply indicate different categories. It does not express any values or relationship between variables. Ordinal scale involves the ranking of items along the continuum of the characteristic being scaled. In this scale the items are classified according to whether they have more or less of a characteristic. The categories in ordinal scale have a logical or ordered relationship. This type of measurement permits the measurement of degrees of difference but not specific amount of difference. This is very common in satisfaction and attitudinal research. Likert scale is extremely popular for measuring attitudes since it is simple to administer. The respondents indicate their own attitudes by checking how strongly they agree or disagree with carefully worded statements that range from very positive to very negative attitudes towards the attitudinal object. The respondents choose from five alternatives like strongly agree, agree, neither agree or disagree, disagree, strongly disagree.

Socio-Economic Profile of Respondents

The social research is an inquisitive and systematic process with several stages and steps. One of the vital steps is that of data collection. The reliable and valid data is instrumental in validating the research results. Thus, the role of respondents becomes critical in success of the research process. The socio-economic background of the respondents is important to understand the responses given by them.

The present chapter presents the socio-economic profile of the respondents. The profile includes gender, age, caste, religion, educational and occupational background, etc. The detailed socio-economic profile of the respondents is presented in the following sections.

Gender Composition

The data given in the table below shows that number of male respondents are more as compared to female respondents. There are 1,998 males and 1,602 females, which is 55.55 per cent and 44.55 per cent of the total number of the respondents respectively.

Table 2.1 *Gender Composition*

Gender	*No. of Respondents*	*Percentage*
Male	1,998	55.55
Female	1,602	44.55
Total	3,600	100

Age Composition

The data in Table 2.2 illustrates that the age group of 41–50 years has more number of respondents, i.e., 50.63 per cent followed by the age group of 31–40 years with 39.91 per cent of respondents. There are (5.80%) and (1.58%) of the respondents in the age group of 21–30 years and 51–60 years respectively.

Table 2.2 *Age Composition of the Respondents*

Age Composition (in years)	*No. of Respondents*	*Percentage*
Below 20 Years	49	1.36
21–30 years	209	5.80
31–40 years	1,437	39.91
41–50 years	1,823	50.63
51–60 years	57	1.58
61–70 years	18	0.50
71–80 years	7	0.194
Total	3,600	100

Religious Composition

Religion has existed throughout the history of human society. It is a part of culture and an important aspect of human social life. It shapes human behaviour in a moral fashion. Religion is a system of belief in the existence of supernatural beings. Religion provides a world-view and framework to develop one's cognitive system and social ethos.

Table 2.3 *Religious Composition*

Religion	*No. of Respondents*	*Percentage*
Hindu	1,802	50.05
Muslim	1,034	28.72
Christian	447	12.41
Sikh	306	8.5
Any Other	11	0.30
Total	3,600	100

The figures in Table 2.3 indicate that the respondents of Hindu religion are more, i.e., 50.05 per cent followed by Muslim respondents constituting 28.72 per cent of the total number of respondents. The respondents of Christian and Sikh religion are 12.41 per cent and 8.5 per cent respectively. Interestingly, it must be noted that the percentages are more or less similar for Hyderabad as a whole.

Caste Distribution

The caste system in India can be described as an elaborately stratified social hierarchy distinguishing India's social structure from any other nation. Its history is multifaceted and complex. Caste is a term, which is used to specify a group of people having a specific social rank and dates back to 1,200 BCE. The Indian term for caste is jati, and generally designates a group that can vary in size from a handful to many thousands. There are thousands of jatis each with its own rules and customs. The various jatis are traditionally arranged in hierarchical order and fit into one of the four basic varnas the (Sanskrit word for "colours"). Caste is a very significant aspect of individual and group identity.

Table 2.4 *Caste Composition of the Respondents*

Caste	*No. of Respondents*	*Percentage*
SC	932	25.88
ST	509	14.13
BC	966	26.83
OC	1,126	31.27
Any Other	67	1.86
Total	3,600	100

Table 2.4 shows that respondents from OC are relatively more constituting 31.27 per cent followed by BC – 26.83 per cent. The respondents from SC and ST community are 25.88 per cent and 14.13 per cent respectively.

Language Composition

Language is an important socio-cultural factor and has strong relationship with the identity of a region. Hyderabad is multilingual. Though there are more number of Telugu speaking people, owing to Hyderabad being a metropolitan city with its cosmopolitan culture there are substantial number of Urdu, Hindi, Marathi, Bengali, Tamil and Kannada speaking population. Table 2.5 clearly asserts that Telugu speaking respondents are in majority constituting 38.83 per cent. The respondents speaking Urdu, Hindi and any other language are 28.72 per cent, 16.58 per cent and 15.86 per cent respectively. Hyderabad has substantial Urdu speaking population owing to Telangana being under Qutub Shahi and Asaf Jahi rule for few centuries. The native populations even if they are Marwaris or Telugu speaking can read Urdu fluently. Some argue that this is one of the defining characteristic of Hyderabad that reflects a distinctive melting-pot model.

Table 2.5 *Language Composition of the Respondents*

Language	*No. of Respondents*	*Percentage*
Telugu	1,398	38.83
Urdu	1,034	28.72
Hindi	597	16.58
Any Other	571	15.86
Total	3,600	100

Income Distribution

Income is an important socio-economic factor which determines an individual's status. It is usually argued that income is instrumental in determining one's opinion about cosmopolitanism since it is perceived to be associated with the material culture. Though the philosophy of universalism operates at latent level, good income facilitates the purchasing of goods and services and thus imparts a particular lifestyle.

Table 2.6 indicates the division of income levels of the respondents into five categories ranging from below Rs 10,000 to more than Rs 40,000 per month. The respondents in the income group of Rs 21,001 to Rs 30,000 are more, i.e., 48.22 per cent followed by 30.02 per cent of the respondents who are in the income group of Rs 31,001 to Rs 40,000 per month. There are 13.47 per cent respondents whose income range is Rs 10,001 to Rs 20,000 and 6.13 per cent respondents whose income is more than Rs 40,000 per month.

Table 2.6 *Income (Per Month) of the Respondents*

Income (Per month)	*No. of Respondents*	*Percentage*
Less than Rs 10,000	77	2.13
Rs. 10,001 to Rs 20, 000	485	13.47
Rs. 21,001 to Rs 30,000	1736	48.22
Rs. 31,001 to Rs 40,000	1081	30.02
More than Rs 40,000	221	6.13
Total	3600	100

Educational Level of the Respondents

Education is an important factor for development. It is instrumental in shaping the attitude towards cosmopolitanism and regionalism. Hyderabad has witnessed substantial outflow of students to foreign countries and Universities and has also brought in considerable number of students to Hyderabad. This has facilitated considerable exchange of cultural elements and thus consolidating cosmopolitanism. However, the presence of regional sentiments cannot be undermined.

It can be inferred from Table 2.7 that majority of the respondents (54.69%) possess a post-graduation degree, followed by those with professional education who constitute 20.4 per cent of the sample. Urban living in more than a way demands literacy and hence illiteracy accounts for a meagre 0.2 per cent of the number of respondents. The rest of the categories, viz. Literate, Primary and Secondary School, Intermediate, Degree, M.Phil, Ph.D, Others range between 0. 22 per cent and 10 per cent.

Table 2.7 *Educational Level of the Respondents*

Educational Qualifications	*No. of Respondents*	*Percentage*
Illiterate	8	0.22
Literate	213	5.91
Primary School	37	1.02
Secondary school	125	3.47
Intermediate	105	2.91
Degree	319	8.86
PG	1,969	54.69
Professional Education	736	20.44
M.Phil	12	0.33
Ph.D	58	1.61
Any other	18	0.5
Total	3,600	100

Occupational Background of the Respondents

Occupations are sociologically important because of the role they play in the distribution of wealth, power and prestiges among people and in the general process through which societies produce goods and services. In each occupational group, a distinct value system can be discerned. The 'occupational profile' (how people are distributed across occupations) shows a majority of respondents belong to Teaching, the number stands at 1,287 (35.75%) accounting to over one-third of the sample size. This is followed by Private Employees (25.94%, roughly a quarter of sample size) and Govt. Employees (at 684, which comes to 19% of sample size). All the remaining occupations – Administrative Services, Medical (Main), Legal Profession, Business, Retired citizens, Politics, Student community – account for less than 10 per cent of sample size (Table 2.8).

Table 2.8 *Occupational Background of the Respondents*

Occupation Background	*No. of Respondents*	*Percentage*
Administrative services	153	4.25
Medical (Main)	339	9.41
Teaching	1,287	35.75
Legal Profession	31	0.86
Business	68	1.88
Retired	29	0.80
Govt. Employees	684	19
Private Employees	934	25.94
Politics	44	1.22
Student	31	0.86
Total	3,600	100

Marital Status of the Respondents

Marriage is a cultural phenomenon which gives a more or less permanent union between partners, conferring legitimacy on their offspring(s). Depending on the society, marriage may require religious or/and civil sanction. Table 2.9 shows that 86.94 per cent of respondents are married, while the unmarried accounted for 12.69 per cent. The remaining categories – Widowed, Divorced and Separated – barely account for less than 1 per cent of the total sample size.

Table 2.9 *Marital Status of the Respondents*

Marital Status	*No. of Respondents*	*Percentage*
Married	3130	86.94
Unmarried	457	12.69
Widowed	2	0.05
Divorced	3	0.08
Separated	8	0.22
Total	3,600	100

Place of Origin of the Respondents

The 'Place of Origin' is one of the chief characteristics that builds a person's identity and is responsible for an individual's world-view, especially on the notions of cosmopolitanism and regionalism. This variable also reflects the migratory trends as a whole.

Table 2.10 indicates that while respondents from Semi-Urban and Urban areas account for 31 per cent and 10 per cent of sample size respectively, majority of them hail from rural areas. The numbers stand at 2102, about 58.38 per cent of the sample size. This consequentially vindicates the fact that much of the migration into the cities in India are of rural to urban nature.

Table 2.10 *Place of Origin of the Respondents*

Place of Origin	*No. of Respondents*	*Percentage*
Rural	2,102	58.38
Semi-Urban	367	31.41
Urban	1131	10.19
Total	3,600	100

Table 2.10a offers a micro-analysis of this aspect as far as Hyderabad is concerned. More than half of the respondents (52.41%), who trace their origin to rural areas; have been residing in the Hyderabad for more than 20 years, which reflects perpetual influx of rural migrants into Indian cities.

Table 2.10a *If Rural, Years of Stay in Hyderabad*

Stay in Hyderabad	*No. of Respondents*	*Percentage*
Less than 5 years	372	10.33
6 to 10 years	457	12.69
11 to 15 years	649	18.02
16 to 20 years	235	6.52
More than 20 years	1,887	52.41
Total	3,600	100

Reasons for Migration

Migration, the physical movement of people from one region to another, is a major component of population growth and has been the main source of urbanization in India. It profoundly affects the social composition of population, and hence plays a major role in ethnic and class relations. Theories of migration have largely been economic and have neglected the social and cultural aspects (such as migration due to marriage) of the process. However, migration is analysed as a consequence of push (negative) and pull (positive) factors. There could be both factors operating at the same time and hence, *multiple reasons to migrate.

From Table 2.11, it can be inferred the major cause for migration is economic (51.02%). One in every two respondents migrated for economic reasons. This is followed by social (45.22%) and cultural (39.08%) reasons. It is interesting to note that Psychological reasons (personal preference or migration arising out of individual perceptions) accounts for nearly 36.52 per cent, a significant number. The political and other reasons are not very substantial, i.e., at 7.88 per cent and 3.02 per cent respectively.

Table 2.11 *Reasons for Migration*

Reason for Migrate to Hyd	*No. of Respondents*	*Percentage*
Social	1,628	45.22
Economic	1,837	51.02
Political	284	7.88
Psychological	1,315	36.52
Cultural	1,407	39.08
Any Other	109	3.02
Total	6,580*	100

* Respondents have given more than one response.

Migration from Urban Area to Hyderabad

Migration has been categorized into different types – rural to urban, rural to rural, urban to urban and urban to rural. In the past one decade, Hyderabad has immensely expanded primarily due to migration of hundreds of people into it. This migration is significantly owing to pull factors of migration, whereby people have been attracted due to employment opportunities in Hyderabad especially in the service sector.

Table 2.12 *Migration from Urban Area to Hyderabad*

Migrated from Urban area to Hyd	*No. of Respondents*	*Percentage*
Yes	1,903	52.86
No	1,588	44.11
Cannot Say	109	3.02
Total	3,600	100

Table 2.12 above clearly indicates that more than half of the respondents have migrated into Hyderabad from other urban areas – 1,903 members, who account for 52.86 per cent of the total respondents while 44.11 per cent of the respondents are from other areas but urban.

Conclusion

Hyderabad is a unique city (district) which has reflections of cosmopolitanism and regionalism. It is culturally diverse with people from not only all over the country but also all over world, especially owing to large presence of multinational companies and development of service sector. In the past few years, Hyderabad is witnessing intense agitations with regard to Telangana movement and demand for a separate state of Telangana. Thus, Hyderabad provides a perfect palate for social researchers who wants to understand the issues of cosmopolitanism and regionalism in a post-industrial city like Hyderabad.

The present chapter apart from dealing with various facets of Hyderabadi Tehzeeb also deals with methodology and socio-economic profile of the respondents. The universe of the study is Hyderabad and sample has been drawn from 16 mandals of Hyderabad district. The sample size is 3,600. Interview schedule has been used as a tool for data collection. The parameters on which data was collected was age, gender, religion, caste, language, income, qualifications, occupation, marital status, place of origin, migration from any other area. The succeeding chapter is on cosmopolitanism in Hyderabad.

3 Cosmopolitanism in Hyderabad

Cosmopolitanism has got several interpretations. It can mean a city or place or person that embraces its multicultural demographics; world citizen, one who shuns traditional geopolitical divisions derived from national citizenship; Cosmopolitanism is the idea that all of humanity belongs to a single moral community; Cosmopolitan Society or Cosmopolitan City is where people of many ethnicities, religions and cultures meet and live in close proximity.

Hyderabad was known originally as Bhagyanagar, a city Sultan Muhammad Quli of the Qutub Shahi dynasty had founded and named after his beloved Bhagmati or Bhagyamati in 1591. Once she entered the royal household and embraced Islam, she was rechristened Hydermahal and as a result the city got its second name, Hyderabad. Hyderabad is one of metropolitan and cosmopolitan city of India. It is also described as a *panchanami sangam* a place where five linguistic and cultural patterns met here – Telugu, Marathi, Kannada, Tamil and Urdu have mingled and enriched a city famous for its Nawabi traditions of graciousness. Introducing a sixth culture stream to the sangam has been that of combination of French and British. However, the contemporary Hyderabad is a meeting point of several cultural strings.

Hyderabad and Secunderabad, the twin cities fused into one, is a city where north meets south, Islam meets Hinduism and consent meets cosmopolitanism. All the cultures that reigned, left indelible marks and resulted in a unique cultural amalgam, a social blend to which modernism has added its might. Major industries, educational institutions and important research and training centres, expanding service sector and several multinational companies are located in this city that is pride of Deccan and which enjoys a central location in India. A mild climate and world values of courtesy and politeness are the attractions of the cosmopolitan city of Hyderabad.

Cosmopolitanism in Hyderabad can be witnessed in its culture including dressing patterns and food habits. Hyderabadis love to eat out and this is apparent from the number of restaurants and eating-joints that dot the landscape all across the city. They cater to a wide range of tastes offering everything from spicy Andhra cuisine to exotic Thai and one can serve the delicious Hyderabadi Biryani and a fragrant cup of Irani chai from any corner stall.

Cosmopolitan Thought

Cosmopolitan thought has its roots in ancient philosophy but it emerges as a modern political and philosophical project in Enlightenment thought. One of the main sources of inspiration today is to be found in the political writings of Immanuel Kant where he presents a profound defence of cosmopolitan values and proposes a cosmopolitan order to advance the moral nature of humanity. In his 'Perpetual Peace' essay, Kant proposes a cosmopolitan order underpinned by both an international legal authority and a universal civil society to guarantee peaceful relations between sovereign states. This cosmopolitan legal order arises when sovereign states voluntarily give up their lawless freedom and submit themselves to a comforting federation. Just as the people within the territory of a nation-state abandon their lawless condition and enter into a social contract to end internal strife, so should nation-states willingly limit their freedom and submit to a legal authority beyond themselves.

There are four important aspects with reference to cosmopolitanism. First, the deep roots of cosmopolitanism in the sociological tradition are evidence of the difficult task sociology took on to maintain the universalistic legacy of Enlightenment thought while at the same time testing it against the reality of a world torn apart by national divisions and wars. As the twentieth century rolled on, this conflict between the concept of cosmopolitanism and its actual existence grew all the more fierce with the onset of totalitarianism and the transformation of violence into unprecedented terror and annihilation. Second, cosmopolitanism is a politics – not complacency with our age but an international movement to transform our world. It battles with its own uneasiness, difficulties of understanding and equivocal judgments. Political cosmopolitanism is not a series of formulae for establishing or reforming institutions of global democracy, though institution building is certainly one aspect. It is not only a moral commitment to world peace, human rights and global governance, though our judgments are certainly guided by such norms. It is a political challenge to the entities and borders we take for granted in our 'globalizing' age.

Cosmopolitanism is not an abstract theory but an approach that tests itself in relation to the pressing political issues of our day whether they are humanitarian military interventions for the stopping of genocides and other such atrocities committed by state rulers, the prosecution of crimes against humanity within the framework of international criminal law, the future of Europe as a transnational federation that can inspire confidence and enthusiasm, or the treatment of immigrants and non-nationals within our own post-national societies. Cosmopolitanism is a public and practical matter. Finally, cosmopolitanism is a cultural as well as intellectual movement. It crosses the disciplines of the social sciences but it also infuses the aesthetic vision of intellectuals and artists who, no longer willing to hide behind the purity of the nation, have the imagination and capacity to make the *cosmopolis* into an existing reality.

Cosmopolitanism in Hyderabad

Hyderabad has reflected various shades of cosmopolitanism. Though historically Hyderabad was a meeting point of several cultures from Iran and Central Asia imparting a very cosmopolitan outlook, the modern-day Hyderabad is a classic example of modern cosmopolitanism. The post-1990 economic and technological developments owing to globalization brought several multinational companies to Hyderabad. The globalization process also facilitated the movement of people across nations and continents. This was instrumental in cultural exchange and exposure to diversified goods and services. This influenced the lifestyle and value system of the people in Hyderabad. The dressing patterns, eating habits, cuisine and consumption patterns underwent a lot of change heralding in a new phase of cosmopolitanism which is relatively more western compared to the earlier phase which was more of eastern cosmopolitanism. The following sections deal with various aspects of cosmopolitanism in Hyderabad beginning with the respondents' conception of a cosmopolitan city.

Conception of a Cosmopolitan City

The presumption of people's knowledge (also understanding) on what they are being surveyed is often taken for granted. In order to avoid this pitfall, the respondents' conception of a cosmopolitan city had to be known. They were given four options and were allowed to mark more than one choice.

Respondents' perception and understanding of the term is reflected in Table 3.1. But, most of the respondents, close to 97.58 per cent, of the sample felt that it is a city which had people from different regions in India. At the risk of generalization (as the sample size is relatively small), an argument can be raised – majority of them could not think beyond the nation-state in their conception, probably because India in itself is a cultural mosaic. However, 89.19 per cent of the respondents' felt that it's a city with many cultures. And the perception that it is 'A city with people from different countries' accounted for 11.61 per cent of the sample size.

Table 3.1 *Conception of a Cosmopolitan City*

Conception of a Cosmopolitan City	*No. of Respondents*	*Percentage*
A city with many cultures	3,211	89.19
A city with people from different countries	418	11.61
A city which has people from different regions in India	3,513	97.58
Any Other	36	1.00
Total	7,178*	100

* Respondents have given more than one response

Preferred to be Identified by Region

The idea of a nation precedes that of a region or otherwise, at least as far the respondents' are concerned. This is substantiated by the data in Table 3.2 – a majority of them, 39.66 per cent of the sample have identified them as Hyderabadi and Indian followed by a 30.30 per cent of the respondents who identified themselves as from Telangana and as an Indian. It can be argued that the latter, in part, reflects the following – One, the geographical location of Hyderabad within Telangana, that attracts a majority of population in the region (the neo-classical economic theory of migrant behaviour observed that migrants generally move short distances); Two, the prevalence of the Telangana sentiment that is currently leading the agitation for a separate state. However, it is interesting to note that 2.61 per cent of the sample has identified them as only from Telangana. From other categories, 16.16 per cent of the sample have identified them as from Andhra Pradesh and as an Indian; followed by 10.55 per cent of the sample who have exclusively identified themselves as Hyderabadi. The other categories such as – from Andhra Pradesh, as a citizen of the world – hardly account for less than 1 per cent of the total sample.

Table 3.2 *Preferred to be Identified by Region*

Identified by Region	*No. of Respondents*	*Percentage*
Only Hyderabadi	380	10.55
As Hyderabadi and Indian	1,428	39.66
Only Telangana	94	2.61
From Telangana and as an Indian	1,091	30.30
From Andhra Pradesh	12	0.33
From Andhra Pradesh and as an Indian	582	16.16
As a citizen of the world	11	0.30
Any Other	02	0.05
Total	3,600	100

Socio-economic and Cultural Changes

Hyderabad has witnessed several socio-economic and cultural changes in the past three decades, especially in the post-IT phase with establishment of Hyderabad Information Technology Engineering Consultancy City (HITEC City) and several multinational companies coming to India. The process of globalization resulted in exchange of goods and services and enhanced the movement of people across countries and continents. The lifestyle of people in Hyderabad and culture has undergone significant transformation. The respondents' opinion was asked on socio-cultural changes in Hyderabad.

The socio-economic changes are reflected in changes in family patterns (both structurally and functionally), caste-class nexus, changing occupational structure and forms of employment, the purchasing power and preferences, usage of consumer goods, etc. Culturally Hyderabad has witnessed increasing night life, highly diversified food preferences, westernized dressing patterns, changes in means of recreation, etc. While administering the schedule some respondents were of the opinion that Hyderabadi (some also said Deccani) tehzeeb has changed drastically.

The Table 3.3 below indicates that most of the respondents (83.72%) felt that Hyderabad has witnessed socio-economic and cultural changes in the last one decade.

Table 3.3 *Socio-economic and Cultural Changes in the Last One Decade*

Socio-economic and Cultural Changes	*No. of Respondents*	*Percentage*
Yes	3,014	83.72
No	382	10.61
Cannot Say	204	5.66
Total	3,600	100

Culturally Diversified and Heterogeneous in the Last One Decade

Cultural diversity is the cultural variety and cultural differences which exist in the world, a society, or an institution. The inclusion of diverse people in a group or organization imparts cultural heterogeneity. The respondents strongly affirmed that Hyderabad has witnessed socio-economic and cultural changes (as seen in the Table above). It was vital to understand whether the changes have lead to greater cultural diversification and heterogeneity. Table 3.4 shows that 70.97 per cent of the respondents are of the opinion that Hyderabad has become more culturally diversified and heterogeneous in the last one decade. However, over a quarter of the respondents (25.72%) thinks otherwise.

Table 3.4 *Culturally Diversified and Heterogeneous in the Last One Decade*

Culturally Diversified and Heterogeneous	*No. of Respondents*	*Percentage*
Yes	2,555	70.97
No	926	25.72
Cannot Say	119	3.30
Total	3,600	100

Hyderabad: Emergence as a Cosmopolitan City

The respondents' opinion was sought whether Hyderabad has emerged as one of the fastest growing cosmopolitan cities. Table 3.5 shows that most of the respondents have expressed their agreement. Most of the respondents (53.36%) strongly agree and 34.41 per cent agree with the notion that Hyderabad has emerged as one of the fastest growing cosmopolitan cities in India. This is indeed the case in reality. The IT-driven economic boom attracted educated professionals from all parts of India (and the world) to Hyderabad. The city gave Bangalore (which earned the sobriquet, the silicon valley of India) a ride in attracting investment. Migration went on during this IT boom in the 2000s as it provided numerous employment opportunities. For the need of space, the city expanded geographically into the adjoining districts of Rangareddy and Medak, so much so, that the IIT located in Medak is called IIT, Hyderabad. As far as the economy is concerned, the GDP of Hyderabad (and consequentially Andhra Pradesh) has grown exponentially in this period.

Table 3.5 *Emergence of Hyderabad as One of the Fastest Growing Cosmopolitan City*

Hyderabad – Fastest Growing Cosmopolitan	*No. of Respondents*	*Percentage*
Strongly Agree	1,921	53.36
Agree	1,239	34.41
Disagree	285	7.91
Strongly Disagree	27	0.75
Cannot Say	128	3.55
Total	3,600	100

Changes in Social Living according to you

Social life comprises of several parameters and indicators. These parameters undergo change owing to cultural and technological changes. The respondents' views were sought on variables and cultural traits such as Dressing Patterns, Eating Habits, Lifestyles, folkways and mores as expressed through Norms and Values, Traditions and Customs; the other variables being – Education, Occupation, Means of Recreation and Sociability. These are briefly analysed from Tables 3.6 to 3.14. Interestingly all variables reflect polarized responses (one response is affirmed by over two-thirds of the respondents) and hence, it can be conclusively established that people feel the changes in social living and the city has been in a state of flux.

Dressing Patterns

Most of the respondents (94.55%) felt that dressing patterns have undergone changes while remaining either think otherwise or were unsure. The traditional attire of typical 'langa-odhni' (half saree) has been replaced by western outfits. This is greatly attributed to cultural cosmopolitanism.

Table 3.6 *Dressing Patterns*

Dressing Patterns	*No. of Respondents*	*Percentage*
Yes	3,404	94.55
No	148	4.11
Cannot Say	48	1.33
Total	3,600	100

Eating Habits

There are 80.27 per cent of the respondents who are of the opinion that the eating habits have been altered. This claim was rejected by roughly 18 per cent of them, while barely 1.5 per cent of the respondents were unsure of either. As has been discussed in the above tables, globalization has been instrumental in bringing diversified cuisines to Hyderabad. For instance Mexican food, Thai foods were not much popular in Hyderabad a few decades ago, but the same is not the case now. Snacks and food like pizzas, burgers are so much part of snacking. However, the inclusion of diversified food has not excluded the demand for authentic Hyderabadi food and snacks.

Table 3.7 *Eating Habits*

Eating Habits	*No. of Respondents*	*Percentage*
Yes	2,890	80.27
No	656	18.22
Cannot Say	54	1.5
Total	3,600	100

Lifestyles

Lifestyle, broadly defined as way of life, reflects the attitudes and values of a person or a group.

Table 3.8 *Changes in Lifestyles*

Lifestyles	*No. of Respondents*	*Percentage*
Yes	3,004	83.44
No	453	12.58
Cannot Say	143	3.97
Total	3,600	100

Most of the respondents (83.44%) felt that there has been a noticeable change in lifestyles, while about 13 per cent think otherwise. Around 3.97 per cent of the respondents were unsure of either. The lifestyle changes are visible in the way the free time at their disposal is spent. Night life has become an important part of Hyderabad culture. The increased usage of social networking sites has brought many changes in social communication. The concept of weekends has brought many changes in our eating habits (going out on lunch/dinner has become quite common), means of recreation and our ways of living are various facets of lifestyles undergoing transformation.

Norms and Values

What society considers right or wrong is abstract and general. These can be called values. They are social judgments. Values are group conceptions of relative desirability of things. They are the general standards and are the measure of goodness or desirability. Values provide general guidelines for the behaviour of the people and thus provide goals or ends for the members to aim for. Norms are an expression of values. These are specific guidelines or rules. Norm is not a statistical average of actual behaviour but rather a cultural/shared definition of desirable behaviour. Norms are group shared expectations and are the guidelines by which we control and evaluate our action and that of others. Therefore, both are interlinked; a change in one, automatically necessitates a change in the other.

Most of the respondents (75.11%) are of the notion that norms and values have changed. Around 21.16 per cent of the respondents think otherwise and a marginal proportion of 3.72 per cent are unsure about either.

Table 3.9 *Changes in Norms and Values*

Norms and Values	*No. of Respondents*	*Percentage*
Yes	2,704	75.11
No	762	21.16
Cannot Say	134	3.72
Total	3,600	100

Traditions and Customs

Customs are defined as established patterns of behaviour and belief. They are sanctioned by the society, informally regulated and collectively enforced. It contributes to the stability of the social order thus making it socially important. Customs are socially inherited. Traditions are long established customs, i.e., those passed on across generations. A little over two-thirds of the respondents (68.86%) believe that there has been a change in traditions and customs; while 27.08 per cent opine that the traditions and customs have not undergone changes. One of the respondent said Irani chai hasn't changed and so haven't Charminar and Hyderabadi Nawabi style.

Table 3.10 *Changes in Traditions and Customs*

Traditions and Customs	*No. of Respondents*	*Percentage*
Yes	2,479	68.86
No	975	27.08
Cannot Say	146	4.05
Total	3,600	100

Occupation

In industrial societies, occupation refers to a particular type of work, and not all work can be termed as occupation. It can be considered so only when it results in money earnings. The Table 3.11 below indicates that most of the respondents' (72%) feel that there has been a change in the type of occupation as far as Hyderabad is concerned. This can be factually corroborated by the service sector boom, during 2000s, which diversified and specialized the occupational/opportunity structure in the city region. However, 22.55 per cent of the respondents disagree on the aspect of change.

Table 3.11 *Change in Type of Occupation*

Occupation	*No. of Respondents*	*Percentage*
Yes	2,592	72
No	812	22.55
Cannot Say	196	5.44
Total	3,600	100

Sociability

Sociability is matrix of conducive or pleasant interaction. It shows whether the individuals of a society are fine with or averse to interaction among themselves. Over three-fourths of the respondents (76.27%) have noticed changes in sociability, while about 20.47 per cent think otherwise.

Table 3.12 *Changes in Sociability*

Sociability	*No. of Respondents*	*Percentage*
Yes	2,746	76.27
No	737	20.47
Cannot Say	117	3.25
Total	3,600	100

Means of Recreation

Recreation is an activity of leisure, leisure being discretionary time. The "need to do something for recreation" is an essential element of human biology, psychology and culture. Recreational activities are often done for enjoyment, amusement, or pleasure and are considered to be "fun". The term recreation implies participation to be healthy refreshing for the mind and body.

Table 3.13 *Changes in Means of Recreation*

Means of Recreation	*No. of Respondents*	*Percentage*
Yes	2,658	73.83
No	876	24.33
Cannot Say	66	1.83
Total	3,600	100

Hyderabad has witnessed significant change in the means of recreation. The mushrooming of recreation clubs and groups make this evident. In 1990s, watching movie in the theatre was considered the best means of recreation but there is now a transformation in this notion. The respondents' opinions were sought whether the means of recreation has changed or not. Most of the respondents (73.83%) have noticed changes in the means of recreation. However, 24.33 per cent of the respondents feel there is no change in the means of recreation.

Education

In every society, socialization ensures that new members know how to participate. In simple societies, such training can be given informally (say through family); but in more complex ones such as industrial (urban) societies, with diversity of functions the amount of knowledge is so vast and diverse that formal (schools, colleges, etc.) and systematic training is necessary. Sociologically, such training as against the less formal modes of socialization can be termed education. It is in this aspect that most of the respondents (79.22 %) have felt changes in education as against 16.66 per cent who have not. The changes are reflected in the courses being opted, for instance, the preference for professional courses has become paramount. The concept of attaining education and studying abroad has also become prominent. With reference to relation between regionalism and education, it can be said that education brings awareness among people of their rights and if these are deprived, regional feelings increase.

Table 3.14 *Changes in Education System*

Education	*No. of Respondents*	*Percentage*
Yes	2,852	79.22
No	600	16.66
Cannot Say	148	4.11
Total	3,600	100

Attribution of Changes to Hyderabad becoming Cosmopolitan city

Most of the respondents (70.38%) attribute these changes, (viz., the variables dressing patterns, eating habits; lifestyles, folkways and mores as expressed through norms and values, traditions, and customs; the other variables being – education, occupation, sociability and means of recreation to Hyderabad becoming a cosmopolitan city. This suggests that people have taken cognizance of changes affecting them and the underlying causes. However, a little over quarter of the sample (26.11%) do not attribute these changes to Hyderabad becoming a cosmopolitan city (Table 4.5).

Table 3.15 *Hyderabad becoming Cosmopolitan City*

Hyderabad becoming Cosmopolitan city	*No. of Respondents*	*Percentage*
Yes	2,534	70.38
No	940	26.11
Cannot Say	126	3.5
Total	3,600	100

Peaceful Coexistence of Different Cultures

Urban development requires an ambience which is provided by peaceful coexistence of different cultures. The peaceful coexistence of different cultures is one of the parameters for development of cosmopolitanism. Table 3.16 below shows that the majority of 1,631 respondents, accounting for 45.30 per cent of the respondents have felt that different cultures do not peacefully coexist in Hyderabad. This view can be possibly attributed to the conditions prevailing in Hyderabad for past 3–4 years. The respondents expressed their unhappiness over frequent bandhs and agitations and communal riots which affected some parts of Hyderabad to a great extent.

This perception is negated by 1,347 respondents that accounts for 37.41 per cent of the sample size, i.e., they are of the opinion that different cultures have peaceful existence in Hyderabad. However, a noticeable 17.27 per cent of the samples were unsure about either.

Table 3.16 *Peaceful Coexistence of Different Cultures*

Peaceful Coexistence of Different Cultures	*No. of Respondents*	*Percentage*
Yes	1,347	37.41
No	1,631	45.30
Cannot Say	622	17.27
Total	3,600	100

Changes in Purchasing Consumer Goods

By virtually any measure – household expenditures, number of consumers, extraction of raw materials – consumption of goods and services has raised steadily in industrial nations for decades and it is growing rapidly in many developing countries. The consumption of goods whether they are fast moving consumer goods or electronic goods has increased. The preference of advanced consumer goods is increasing. Table 3.17 below shows that most of the respondents (69.22%) believe that their preference of purchasing consumer goods underwent changes. About 24 per cent of the sample does not think so; while 7.22 per cent were unable to discern this aspect. This can be attributed to greater choices of means and places of purchase.

Table 3.17 *Changes in Purchasing Consumer Goods*

Purchasing Consumer Goods Undergone Changes	*No. of Respondents*	*Percentage*
Yes	2,492	69.22
No	848	23.55
Cannot Say	260	7.22
Total	3,600	100

Prefer Purchasing from Shopping Malls

Despite rising consumerism and rapid changes in shopping patterns, a majority of respondents – 2,076 of them, accounting to 57.66 per cent of the sample do not prefer purchasing from shopping malls. The respondents have shown interest in buying from retail outlets, whereby there is a personal touch and the consumers are attended personally (Table 3.18).

Table 3.18 *Prefer Purchasing from Shopping Malls*

Prefer Purchasing from Shopping Malls	*No. of Respondents*	*Percentage*
Yes	1,157	32.13
No	2,076	57.66
Cannot Say	367	10.19
Total	3,600	100

It can be argued that this in part reflects the affordability dimension of the population. About 32 per cent of the sample, however, prefers purchasing from shopping malls; the reasons are: window shopping is very much possible and comfortable which provides an idea about the products. Further the branded products are preferred to be purchased in shopping malls instead of retail outlets. Shopping malls are also places of recreation. There are 10 per cent of the respondents who were not sure about either.

Cosmopolitan Outlook

Cosmopolitan outlook reflects a wide experience of different people, places and cultures. With multiple cultures making Hyderabad its home (both temporary and permanent) the world-view of people seems to have undergone change.

Table 3.19 *Cosmopolitan Outlook*

Hyderabad have Developed Cosmopolitan Outlook	*No. of Respondents*	*Percentage*
Yes	2,994	83.16
No	582	16.16
Cannot Say	24	0.66
Total	3,600	100

Table 3.19 above indicates that most of the respondents (83.16%) are of the opinion that Hyderabad has developed a cosmopolitan outlook.

Conclusion

The present chapter deals with cosmopolitanism in Hyderabad. Cosmopolitanism in this chapter is not viewed merely in terms of philosophical outlook of universalism, instead it has also been viewed in terms of cultural and economic cosmopolitanism. The respondents' opinions were thus sought on conception of a cosmopolitan city, preference of respondents to be identified, socio-cultural changes and the diversification and heterogeneity of these changes, changes in areas of social living in terms of cultural traits such as dressing patterns, and eating habits; lifestyles, folkways and mores as expressed through norms and values, traditions, customs; the other variables being – education, occupation, means of recreation and sociability. The cosmopolitanism in Hyderabad was also understood by seeking responses on peaceful coexistence of different cultures, preference of purchasing consumer goods and development of cosmopolitan outlook. It can be thus concluded that the present-day Hyderabad has definitely evolved into a cosmopolitan city with its own traditional flavours. The foundations of present-day cosmopolitanism were laid few centuries back when migrants from various parts of central Asia and Africa made Hyderabad their home. The succeeding chapter is on cosmopolitanism and urban development with specific reference to Hyderabad.

4 Cosmopolitanism and Urban Development

Urbanization in India has had a long history and an almost uninterrupted record of urbanization for over four-and-a-half millennia. It is really surprising to find that the first city to appear in India has also been the first planned city of the world, built on a grandiose scale and the planning principles were conscientiously followed for nearly a millennium. The seeds of urbanization germinated first in the Indus plains around 2500 BC, but the sequence of events leading to this great happening is not very clear. The time gap between the first appearance of tool-making man about 600,000 years ago, (Piggot, 1961) as dated by the solar radiation method, and the formation of the earliest agricultural settlements sometimes at the end of the fifth millennium BC or, in the first quarter of the fourth millennium BC (Meadow, 1973) is far too wide for assuming any essential cultural link between them; rather, one could not have any bearing on the other.

Urban Development in India

From 600 BC onwards, urbanization in India made remarkable headway not only in the number of flourishing cities but also in their wider spatial distribution. Hitherto urban activities were mostly confined to the Ganga-Jamuna Doab, although Aryan influence had, by then, already extended to a far greater domain – from the banks of the upper Jamuna to beyond the Himalayas in the north, from the basin of Chambal in the south to Magadha in the west. By

600 BC, the political situation underwent a tremendous change and the focus of civilization shifted eastward where four great kingdoms emerged, totally eclipsing the old kingdoms developed earlier by the Aryans in the Upper Ganga-Jamuna plains. Further, the period witnessed the birth of two new religions – Buddhism, preached by Buddha (566–486 BC) and Jainism, preached by Mahavir (540–468 BC), both greatly undermining the religious supremacy of the Aryans. This had a profound effect on the political situation of India which ultimately came to define the progress of urbanization in the country. From this period onwards our knowledge and understanding about the urban development becomes more accurate and systematic. It is based on the Buddhist and Jain literature written at this time, illuminated further by the more authentic accounts of Megasthenes who came to India in about 300 BC and the chroniclers of Alexander. Here is at least one source yielding information on the progress of urbanization and this is represented by the 'Janapada States' of ancient India existing before the days of the Mauryas.

This system was prevalent in the earlier period of Aryan rule in India. The word 'Jana' refers to different tribes of the Aryans, such as the Kurus, the Kosalas, etc., who were mobile communities in the beginning but later on settled permanently in different areas and the defined territories gradually gave rise to individual Janapadas – the word 'pada' referring to the territory occupied by the tribe. Each Janapada came to be identified by the original name of the tribe, as for example, the Kuru, the Panchala, the Kosala, etc. In course of time, however, the tribal significance was lost and the name defined only the territorial units. There is no mention of Janapadas in the *Rigveda* and in the *Atharvaveda,* the earliest of the Vedic literature; they refer only to the 'Janas', which means that Janapadas had not taken form till then.

The study of the Janapadas brings something very much relevant to the urban development in the country. Few historians find 'unmistakable parallels' between the Janapada States of India and the Greek city-states, both in their origin and evolution. The Greek Acropolis or the fortified city grew out of an evolutional process, with four succeeding stages of development and this has a strange similarity with the rise of Janapada or capital-based political territory in India. In Greece, the Genos or the patriarchal clan making the primary societal unit formed the first stage of this developmental process, followed by the Phratries or the formation of families and these, viewing the necessity of defence and security, gave rise to the Phulai or the military groupings in the society, which ultimately brought the Polis or the fortified capital into existence with its jurisdiction clearly laid down by defined boundaries. All these stages are faithfully mirrored by four stages of the Jana (the clan), the Kula (the family), the Janapadin (the tribe), and the Janapada taking part in the growth of the 'Pura' or the walled city which provided the basis for the rise of Janapada states in India.

The writings of Hiuen Tsang are great sources of information on urbanization; however after him the information in the country again dries up. For a few centuries it is not possible to know what happened in the life of different urban centres and how they survived. In fact, nothing is known for certain till the arrival of Alberuni in India in the beginning of the eleventh century AD. When the curtain draws again, making the Indian stage once more visible to the inquisitor. Born in Khiva, in the present Uzbek Republic of the USSR, Alberuni or Abu-Al-Rahim Muhammad Ibn-Ahmad Alberuni came to India in AD 1017 and stayed for about thirteen years in different parts of the country, utilizing his time 'in the study of India'. Taking keen interest in Indian life and customs in its great many details and going into the depth of the Hindu religion and its philosophy, Alberuni wrote about twenty books in India, covering various fields, including the geography of the country (Bhattacharya, 2006).

The identity thus established in the case of so many cities leads to the most important fact about urbanization in the country, that is, its unbroken continuity. In four cases, the cities have survived for more than two thousand years and five other cities are nearly as old as the former.

The inadequacy of information stands as the principal obstacle in constructing any workable picture of the state of urbanization and urban conditions in the country. While it cannot be said for certain that urbanization did make any visible progress during the span of about three centuries from the time of Hiuen Tsang's visit to this country to that of Alberuni's time, it is equally difficult to establish that there had been any appreciable retardation in its development. Besides, in the absence of any specific reference to urban activities, no definite idea can be formed about the origin or the functional character of the towns and cities.

From the time of Alberuni, for about another three centuries, we have no positive information about the progress of urbanization in the country and it is only in the fourteenth century that Ibn Battuta, another Muslim traveller, gives substantial testimony to the existence of a flourishing urban life in India. Ibn Battuta crossed river Indus in September 1333 on a travelling mission to India.

According to Ibn Battuta's accounts, in the first half of the fourteenth century there were a number of cities and large towns, some of them quite admirable in their size, wealth and magnificence. The flourishing state of urbanization is further proved by the fact that India held an important place in the world trade, maintaining direct relations with Arab countries in the west and China in the east. International trade as a very important index of urban development is another convincing proof of the stability attained by many of the seaports acting the same role for a long past.

But the picture is largely incomplete when the whole country is considered. A careful analysis of the list of urban centres will show that Ibn Battuta's narratives are mostly devoted to the places situated on the western coast; apart from a few centres like Multan, Sirsa, Delhi, Kanauj, Koel, Khajuraho, Ujjain, Madurai and Sudkawan, all the towns and cities mentioned by him belong to the western coast. This does not mean that urban development was entirely absent in the remaining part of India.

In order to get a better idea about the state of urban development in the country we have to refer to much later sources, available some three hundred years after the visit of Ibn Batuta. The most valuable works in this connection are those of Abul Fazl, a courtier of Emperor Akbar (AD 1542–1605), giving more accurate information about the towns and cities of his time. He produced two voluminous works: 'Ain-i-Akbari' and 'Akbar Nama' of which especially the former may be considered as a mine of geographical information.

In the second volume of Ain-i-Akbari, Abul Fazl mentions that empire of Akbar – covering the whole of West and Central India-was divided into fifteen Subahs or provinces, subdivided further into 105 Sarkars or districts and there were altogether 2,837 townships in 1594. He does not give the names of all these towns, many of which were undoubtedly small centres, but refers only to the larger ones (Bhattacharya, 2006).

In spite of overestimation, Abul Fazl brings forward the truth with all forcefulness that urbanization was no longer an isolated phenomenon, but had become diffused throughout the country. From Abul Fazal's writing we gather that there were at least 18 large cities in India at that time. They were: Agra, Sikri, Delhi, Ahmedabad, Lahore, Cambay, Elichpur, Burhanpur, Asir, Ujjain, Mandu, Ayodhya, Lucknow, Chittagong, Varanasi, Jaunpur, Raepur and Mednipur.

The rise of European settlements in India beginning in AD 1500, with the establishment of the first Portuguese factory at Calicut, ended ultimately in the subjugation of the country by the English within the succeeding three centuries. Such a political change in closely linked up with the course of urbanization during that period. The European settlements added a new dimension to Indian urbanization.

The Europeans brought with them a different sense of urban life which found expression in the buildings and the other constructions as well as in the layout of the settlements they established or reconstructed. The Portuguese influence remained confined to the western coast and the State of Goa is a living example of this where most of the churches, both old and new, have preserved the architectural beauty till today. The French Pondicherry was built on a different plan, with straight and wide roads, with buildings in rectangular blocks interspersed with public gardens. The Dutch Nagapatnam was neatly laid out with squares and characteristic canals. But compared to all these foreign influences, especially that of English is much more significant in introducing new elements in the style of architecture and overall get-up of the towns.

The progress of English settlements in India makes an interesting study. At the beginning of the eighteenth century, the English society was mainly confined to four principal settlements – namely, Madras (Fort St. George), Calcutta (Fort William), Bombay and Surat. Except Surat, all the remaining three towns were established at new sites and these small settlements were already becoming nuclei of Indian towns where Indian merchants settled for trade and security. The process of urbanization accelerated during British period and further increased in post-independent period especially post-1990s.

Urban Development in Post-Independent India

The five-year plans have been instrumental in bringing out urban development and with the onset of twelfth five-year plan the process of urban development will see new heights. For the first time since Independence, the absolute increase in population is more in urban areas that in rural areas. According to 2011 census, rural population in India is 68.84 per cent and urban population in India is 31.16 per cent. The level of urbanization increased from 27.81 per cent in 2001 Census to 31.16 per cent in 2011 Census. The proportion of rural population declined from 72.19 per cent to 68.84 per cent. The number of rural units (or villages) in India as per 2001 Census is 6, 38,588 and 2011 Census is 6, 40,867 thus marking the increase to 2,279. There has been a spurt in growth of population in urban areas in the country, which could be due to migration, natural increase and inclusion of new areas under 'Urban'.

For the Census of India 2011, the definition of urban area is as follows:

1. All places with a municipality, corporation, cantonment board or notified town area committee, etc.
2. All other places which satisfied the following criteria:
   (i) A minimum population of 5,000;
   (ii) At least 75 per cent of the male main working population engaged in non-agricultural pursuits; and
   (iii) A density of population of at least 400 persons per sq km.

The first category of urban units is known as Statutory Towns. These towns are notified under law by the concerned State/UT Government and have local bodies like municipal corporations, municipalities, municipal committees, etc., irrespective of their demographic characteristics as reckoned on 31 December 2009. The second category of towns (as in item 2 above) is known as Census Town. These were identified on the basis of Census 2001 data.

Urban Agglomeration (UA): An urban agglomeration is a continuous urban spread constituting a town and its adjoining outgrowths (OGs), or two or more physically contiguous towns together with or without outgrowths of such towns. An urban agglomeration must consist of at least a statutory town and its total population, (i.e., all the constituents put together) should not be less than 20,000 as per the 2001 Census. In varying local conditions, there were similar other combinations which have been treated as urban agglomerations satisfying the basic condition of contiguity. Examples: Greater Mumbai UA, Delhi UA, etc.

Out Growths (OG): An Out Growth (OG) is a viable unit such as a village or a hamlet or an enumeration block made up of such village or hamlet and clearly identifiable in terms of its boundaries and location. Some of the examples are railway colony, university campus, port area, military camps, etc., which have come up near a statutory town outside its statutory limits but within the revenue limits of a village or villages contiguous to the town. While determining the outgrowth of a town, it has been ensured that it possesses the urban features in terms of infrastructure and amenities such as pucca roads, electricity, taps, drainage system for disposal of waste water, etc., educational institutions, post offices, medical facilities, banks, etc., and physically contiguous with the core town of the UA. Examples: Central Railway Colony (OG), Triveni Nagar (N.E.C.S.W.) (OG), etc. Each such town together with its outgrowth(s) is treated as an integrated urban area and is designated as an 'urban agglomeration'.

In the 2011 Census, 475 places with 981 OGs have been identified as urban agglomerations as against 384 UAs with 962 OGs in 2001 Census.

Number of UAs/Towns and Out Growths (OGs)

	2011 Census	*2001 Census*
1 Statutory Towns	4,041	3,799
2 Census Towns	3,894	1,362
3 Urban Agglomerations	475	384
4 Out Growths	981	962

At the Census 2011 there are 7,935 towns in the country. The number of towns has increased by 2,774 since last census. Many of these towns are part of UAs and the rest are independent towns. The total number of urban agglomerations/towns, which constitutes the urban frame, is 6,166 in the country (http://censusindia.gov.in/2011).

Population of UAs/Towns

1. The total urban population in the country as per Census 2011 is more than 377 million constituting 31.16 per cent of the total population.
2. *Class I UAs/Towns:* The UAs/towns are grouped on the basis their population in Census. The UAs/towns which have at least 1,00,000 persons as population are categorised as Class I UA/town. At the Census 2011, there are 468 such UAs/Towns. The corresponding number in Census 2001 was 394.
3. Around 264.9 million persons, constituting 70 per cent of the total urban population, live in these Class I UAs/towns. The proportion has increased considerable over the last census. In the remaining classes of towns the growth has been nominal.
4. *Million Plus UAs/Towns:* Out of 468 UAs/towns belonging to Class I category, 53 UAs/towns each has a population of one million or above each. Known as million-plus UAs/cities, these are the major urban centres in the country. Around 160.7 million persons (or 42.6% of the urban population) live in these million-plus UAs/cities. Another 18 new UAs/towns have been added to this list since the last census.
5. *Mega Cities:* Among the million-plus UAs/cities, there are three very large UAs with more than 10 million persons in the country, known as mega cities. These are Greater Mumbai UA (18.4 million), Delhi UA (16.3 million) and Kolkata UA (14.1 million). The largest UA in the country is Greater Mumbai UA followed by Delhi UA. Kolkata UA which held the second rank in Census 2001 has been replaced by Delhi UA. The growth in population in the mega cities has slowed down considerably during the last decade. Greater Mumbai UA, which had witnessed 30.47 per cent growth in population during 1991–2001 has recorded 12.05 per cent during 2001–2011. Similarly Delhi UA (from 52.24% to 26.69% in 2001–2011) and Kolkata UA (from 19.60% to 6.87% in 2001–2011) have also slowed down considerably.

The million-plus cities form the vital core of India's urbanization process and are also the centres of the country's economic, social and cultural activities. The unprecedented and unplanned growth of these cities has led to the emergence of a multitude and complex web of problems – physical, social, political, economic, etc.

Urban Development in Telangana

Urbanization in Telangana and its future implications are examined by P. Padmanabha Rao (1999). Rao says that the concept of encouraging small and medium towns to grow so as to slow down the rate of growth of metropolitan areas is not new. The strategy would be to include growth by developing infrastructural facilities to the hinterland, thereby reversing the rate of growth of the metropolitan cities and increasing the rate of growth of small and medium towns. The region accounts 30.04 per cent of urban population to total population of the region, which is higher than that of state and national average. Except Hyderabad and Rangareddy districts, all other districts have 20 per cent urban population which indicates that the Telangana region has a very poor level of urbanization. The dominance of metropolitan Hyderabad in this region led to the absence of other large towns. The analysis brings out a fact that the region is agricultural in nature. In certain pockets, a rapid transformation is taking place as a result of provision of perennial irrigation. Besides, it is evident that the towns are acting as centres of dissemination of information, technology and other modern developments. The region is benefitted greatly in adopting the new trends and input generated in urban centres.

It is also inferred that the small and medium towns are bringing about a change in rural economy through the trickling-down process. Since small and medium towns are spread evenly in space, any development in them immediately percolates down through the hierarchy, making the rural economy more vibrant. Thus, Rao suggests that a change in paradigm through development from below would be an appropriate capital planning strategy.

Towns, being the focal points of economic, cultural, administrative and other activities of societies, play a leading role in urban and regional development. Urban growth is the most important indicator of the development of a country. Being a complex socio-economic process closely connected with scientific technological revolution, urbanization exercises a growth influence on all aspects of society, reflecting the nature of the economic and regional development.

The concept of encouraging small and medium towns to grow so as to slow down the rate of expansion of metropolitan area is not new. The strategy would be to include growth by developing infrastructural facilities in the hinterland, thereby reversing the rate of growth of metropolitan cities and increasing that of small and medium towns. As the urban population increases, the small and medium towns shrink and become unproductive. If this trend continues for two more decades, such small and medium towns will be neglected resulting in overcrowding of larger cities with increasing pressure on their facilities. It is important to consider the role of these towns as counter magnets to existing large metropolitan centres. If these towns succeed in diverting at least a part of migrations to big cities, there will be some prospect of a more orderly urbanization. But it must be emphasized that the rule of these towns is not in the field of industrialization, but also in the wider spheres of agricultural and rural development.

The slow growth and stagnation and decay of number of small towns are a phenomena which must be studied historically and deserves serious attention from policy makers.

One important observation in study of growth of towns in the Telangana region is related to agriculture and irrigation. They played an important role and had a positive influence in the growth of towns. An increase in agricultural production leads to the migration of people from rural areas to the city. Consequently, the increase in demand of new services and goods due to change in the agricultural technology and income of households stimulate the growth of commercial and agro-servicing activities in small and medium towns.

Telangana region was dominated by small towns up to 1941 with only Hyderabad city in this region. But from 1951 onwards medium size towns started growing much faster and small towns showed a declining trend in their growth as they are either promoting their status or loosing their population to medium sized towns. The high growth of population is associated with mining, manufacturing, transport, a mono-functional and by-functional towns, while slow growth is associated with agricultural and household industrial towns. Most of the small towns are growing at a slower rate while medium towns are growing at a fast rate. It can be seen from the 1991 census that five towns have grown as class I towns with a growth rate 4–6 per cent.

The proportion of urban population to total population in the region was extremely low indicating the socio-economic and cultural backwardness of the region. The vast and varied forest resources are not extensively explored and tapped, which are a potential of this region. The vast and varied forest resources are not extensively explored and tapped, which are potentially most important for the emergence of growth centres. This region thus awaits not only development of means of transportation but also the forest based industrial development.

It can be deduced from the above that the strengthening of the economic base of small and medium towns which act as alternative focal points of development, leads to increasing employment opportunities very essential to encourage the urban informal sector, particularly, tertiary sector in small and medium towns. But these sectors cannot be promoted unless there is at least a modest attempt to promote industrial estates and small scale enterprises that suits the type of economy and specialization of the towns in the hinterland. This may trigger off and accentuate autonomous development of both informal and tertiary sector, which needs support and guided direction for its growth by a positively planned regional development.

This analysis brings out the fact that the region is more of agricultural in nature in certain pockets; a rapid transformation is taking place as a result of provision of perennial irrigation. Besides, it is evident that the towns are acting as centres of dissemination of information, technology and other modern developments. The region is benefited greatly in adopting the new trends and inputs generated in urban centres. It is also inferred that the small and medium towns are bringing about a change in the rural economy through the trickling-down process since small and medium towns spread evenly in space, any development in them immediately percolates down through the hierarchy, making the rural economy more vibrant. Thus, a change in paradigm through development from below would be an appropriate spatial planning strategy in the background environment.

It may be said that urban areas of Andhra Pradesh have well defined social attributes of urbanization, which is the result of religion, different language speaking population, good percentage of male-female literates, migrants, sex ratio, etc. Thus, the second majority population of Muslims is later represented in urban areas of the Andhra Pradesh than the other religious populations. The national language is also represented equally with the neighbouring languages of Andhra Pradesh. Thereby enhancing the socio-cultural milieu. The influence of neighbouring states' language is more than the national language Hindi, in districts bordering the neighbouring states.

Srikrishna Committee has maintained that the level of urbanization is rather low in all regions of Andhra Pradesh – Telangana (22%) and 25 per cent in coastal Andhra and 23 per cent in Rayalaseema. Therefore, Hyderabad district which is fully urbanized has grown at the cost of all the three regions and is now central to the economies of the three regions in Andhra Pradesh.

Cosmopolitanism and Urban Development

It is vital to understand the relationship between cosmopolitanism and urban development. How does cosmopolitanism contribute to urban development? Or does urban development contribute to development of cosmopolitanism. An analysis of these two parameters will reflect that it is both ways, i.e., cosmopolitanism contributes to urban development and so does urban development contribute to the development of cosmopolitanism. Cosmopolitanism creates an ambience and environment for urban development by enhancing social tolerance for diversified cultures.

It has been discussed in the previous chapter that Hyderabad has developed into a cosmopolitan city. It is thus significant to understand whether cosmopolitanism has contributed to urban development. Hyderabad is located on the crossroads of the rivers, Krishna and Godavari in the region of Telangana. Regionally, Hyderabad lies on the convergence of national and state highways and trunk, air and rail routes, which link it with other metropolitan centres and key centres of importance in the country. The well-developed national and regional rail and road networks criss-crossing the city improved the access of Hyderabad to a number of key growth centres within and outside the state. Hyderabad has excellent domestic and international air link to the major metros of India and important international destinations in South-East Asia, Middle East, Europe, North America and other countries. The emergence of new economy industries has catapulted Hyderabad to a prime position in India. The new economy industries and the international airport has placed Hyderabad as a regional hub in this part of the world.

In a fast globalizing world, it is essential for Hyderabad to offer world-class services to attract global investments and urban development. Apart from services, the global investments is possible only in a cosmopolitan ambience. The global companies consider not only the investment climate and economic potential of cities while making investment and location decisions but also the quality of services offered by the cities. In this context, it is imperative that Hyderabad has not only a good investment climate, but also world-class services comparable to other cities. However, the city is experiencing a severe strain on its infrastructure, due to rapid urbanization, unplanned growth and industrial development. The city is deficient in service delivery, and trails other Indian metropolitan cities on most service delivery outcomes. Hyderabad has a low rating in terms of parameters like GDP, literacy rate, drop-out rate, child mortality rate, sewerage, transportation, etc. But yet there is potential for growth as Hyderabad is establishing itself as a technology hub through initiation of various reforms. Its cosmopolitan character can facilitate in urban development. However, past few years of agitation has influenced the development of Hyderabad as a brand to a great extent.

It is vital to note that cosmopolitanism is not merely a philosophy, attitude of universalism, cultural amalgamation but also a catalyst of change and development. With specific reference to Hyderabad, the respondents' views have been sought whether cosmopolitanism has brought about urban development in Hyderabad.

Present-day Cities and Cosmopolitanism

Metropolitan cities have a centripetal effect in the region they exist, as far as migratory patterns are concerned. This invariably alters the demographic composition of the city region. The new entrants into the cities belong to different regions and ethnicities, thereby making them increasingly cosmopolitan. Globalization has only accentuated this process by enabling inter-country migration, thereby making cities more diverse. Critics, however, argue that that it only ensures freer movement of capital and commodities, and not people.

The respondents were asked whether the present-day cities have become increasingly cosmopolitan in nature. Table 4.1 shows that most of the respondents (72.91%) agree to the statement that the present-day cities have become increasingly cosmopolitan in nature. This establishes the critical link between cosmopolitanism and urbanization. However, 26.13 per cent of the sample disagrees with the statement.

Table 4.1 *Present-day Cities and Cosmopolitanism*

Present Day Cities and Cosmopolitanism	*No. of Respondents*	*Percentage*
Yes	2,625	72.91
No	941	26.13
Cannot Say	34	0.94
Total	3,600	100

Cosmopolitanism and the Living Conditions of People in Hyderabad

Cities population grows in two ways – natural growth of the existing population and in-migration into the city. There is exponential growth of the city (both in terms of population and the geographic space it occupies) when the latter eclipses the former. Hyderabad is no exception to this phenomenon, which primarily occurs when the city is the considered as an avenue for employment. Consequently, the provision of urban functions are expanded, which in effect improves the living conditions of the people. However, exponential growth of population also leads to infrastructural stress and strain.

Table 4.2 shows that majority of the respondents (66.55%) believe that cosmopolitanism has improved the living conditions of people in Hyderabad; while 32.30 per cent have negated this.

Table 4.2 *Cosmopolitanism and the Living Conditions of People in Hyderabad*

Cosmopolitanism and the Living Conditions of People in Hyderabad	*No. of Respondents*	*Percentage*
Yes	2,396	66.55
No	1,163	32.30
Cannot Say	41	1.13
Total	3,600	100

Cosmopolitanism and Development

The respondents were asked whether Hyderabad has developed owing to cosmopolitanism. The notion of development for respondents was in terms of physical facilities, like physical and social infrastructure and employment opportunities. This notion was also supported by the instance that multiple cultures are coexisting as part of Hyderabad culture. Table 4.3 shows that majority of the respondents (64.58%) believe that Hyderabad has developed owing to cosmopolitanism. This is refuted by about 34.08 per cent of the respondents.

Table 4.3 *Cosmopolitanism and Development*

Cosmopolitanism and Development	*No. of Respondents*	*Percentage*
Yes	2,325	64.58
No	1,227	34.08
Cannot Say	48	1.33
Total	3,600	100

Cosmopolitanism and Services

The respondents' opinion was taken with regard to improvement in basic facilities and services owing to cosmopolitanism. The facilities and services are – Health Facilities, Roads, Public Transport, Housing, Employment Opportunities, Educational Prospects, Governance and Administration, Purchasing Power, Banking Services, Communication Services. Cosmopolitanism in this context is seen in physical terms and facilities. The attitude favouring cosmopolitanism is instrumental in urban development.

Barring 'Employment Opportunities' (Table 4.8) and 'Governance and Administration' (Table 4.10), nearly (often more than) two-thirds of the respondents feel that the different variables from section Tables 4.4 to 4.13 have improved as a result of Hyderabad becoming a cosmopolitan city. Each of the variable and its analyses is briefly dealt below.

Health Facilities

People believe that health facilities have improved as a result of Hyderabad becoming a cosmopolitan city. A highly substantial part of the sample size, 89.97 per cent agrees to the above said; leaving about 8.6 per cent who refute the claim (Table 4.4). However, there is no denying the fact that there has been a proliferation of hospitals, especially those belonging to the private sector. Hyderabad has become one of the destinations of medical tourism as far as India is concerned.

Table 4.4 *Cosmopolitanism and Health Services*

Cosmopolitanism and Health Services	*No. of Respondents*	*Percentage*
Yes	3,239	89.97
No	310	8.61
Cannot Say	51	1.41
Total	3,600	100

Roads

Central government schemes such as JNNURM (Jawaharlal Nehru National Urban Renewal Mission) in the recent past have improved the conditions of the Indian cities including Hyderabad. It has two sub-missions namely, 'Urban Infrastructure and Governance' and 'Basic Services for the Urban Poor'. The main thrust of the former is on infrastructure projects relating to road network, urban transport, redevelopment of the old city areas, sanitation, sewerage, solid waste management, etc.; while that of the latter is on integrated development of slums through projects for providing shelter and civic amenities to the urban poor in particular.

Table 4.5 *Cosmopolitanism and Roads*

Roads	*No. of Respondents*	*Percentage*
Yes	2,571	71.41
No	1,018	28.27
Cannot Say	11	0.30
Total	3,600	100

The table above shows that most of the respondents (71.41%) feel that roads have improved as a result of Hyderabad becoming a cosmopolitan city; while 28.27 per cent of the respondents oppose this.

Public Transport

Traditionally, a major part of the city (and population) was serviced by bus transport (APSRTC – Andhra Pradesh State Road Transport Corporation). However, since late 1990s (with the advent of IT sector into Hyderabad and a resultant pan-Indian in-migration to the city) Hyderabad was subjected to 'urban sprawl'; hitherto a phenomenon of North American cities, now being increasingly witnessed in developing countries.

With the development of real estate, there is a rapid expansion of the surface area of the city that is not commensurate with its population growth. Simply put, land grows much faster than the population owing to a superior transport network. Hence, a significant loss of prime farmland due to crawling of urban functions, as has happened in Hyderabad. However, this quick geographic expansion reaches a tipping point where the transport network becomes inadequate; necessitating a superior infrastructure (transport) system. Therefore, new modes of transport have been developed. The MMTS (Multi-Modal Transport System), a suburban rail service, was launched in 2003 that takes a considerable load off the bus transport. However, due to its shortcomings and the ever-increasing population (and the area) of the city, the Hyderabad Metro Rail Project has been commissioned. With a cost of over Rupees 14,000 Cr., the first phase of the project is targeted to be operational by 2014.

Table 4.6 *Cosmopolitanism and Public Transport*

Public Transport	*No. of Respondents*	*Percentage*
Yes	2,630	73.05
No	913	25.36
Cannot Say	57	1.58
Total	3,600	100

As far as public transport is concerned, most of the respondents (73.05%) feel it has improved. This is refuted by 25.36 per cent of the sample size (Table 4.6). However, the respondents expressed their displeasure with regard to traffic issues in Hyderabad.

Housing

The apartment culture has become very prominent with reference to housing patterns in Hyderabad. Hyderabad is a city that is much adorned with traditional homes. People opt for both rental and residential housing. But, for the past few years Hyderabad has witnessed a steady rise in property prices. This has made most homes unaffordable for even the middle-income group. Understanding the necessity of low-cost homes in Hyderabad has been a real boost to the Hyderabad housing sector. People are increasingly seeking for affordable homes in Hyderabad that would help them save a considerable amount from their salaries. The rise in number of residential complexes in Hyderabad is one option that is thrown open to the people of Hyderabad. Majority of the respondents (67.67%) feel that housing has improved during the Hyderabad's transition to a cosmopolitan city. About 31.36 per cent of them have disagreed with this (Table 4.7). Their disagreement could be attributed to sky high prices of houses (whether independent or apartment) making it unaffordable for the middle class.

Table 4.7 *Cosmopolitanism and Housing*

Housing	*No. of Respondents*	*Percentage*
Yes	2,434	67.61
No	1,129	31.36
Cannot Say	37	1.02
Total	3,600	100

Employment Opportunities

It is beyond doubt that Hyderabad has seen an increase in the employment opportunities. However, there was shift – from traditionally light manufacturing industries to modern service (predominantly IT sector) industries. When it comes to agriculture or industry, labour is sourced from within (or close to) the city region. Availability of (cheap) labour is a major locational factor. However, the demands of service sector are different. They require a high amount of skill, and any shortage in labour attracts people from all over the country (even internationally). Better pecuniary benefits act as a catalyst, and hence the labour is also more fluid.

Table 4.8 *Cosmopolitanism and Employment Opportunities*

Employment Opportunities	*No. of Respondents*	*Percentage*
Yes	1,780	49.44
No	1,808	50.22
Cannot Say	12	0.33
Total	3,600	100

It is in a similar context India offers a lovely paradox. Though a majority of our GDP (nearly 57%) is composed of service sector, it only employs a minority (barely 10%) of workforce. Majority of Indian working population (over 60%) still is employed in agriculture and allied activities, which barely accounts for 15% of the GDP. Industry is stagnating, both in terms of its contribution to GDP (28%) and workforce employed. Simply put, more opportunities (and income) for lesser population and less opportunities for greater population. This explains in part, as to why the opinion on improvement in employment opportunities is polarized.

Of the total sample size, 49.44 per cent believe that employment opportunities have improved as a result of Hyderabad becoming a cosmopolitan city; while 50.22 per cent refute the claim. The opinion is thus clearly divided among the respondents (Table 4.8).

Educational Prospects

Hyderabad and its contiguous districts saw a rapid expansion of educational institutions in the past decade. Today, as far as engineering colleges are concerned, supply exceeds demand, viz., there are more number of colleges (and seats) than the number of students, leaving thousands of seats vacant every academic year. As early as in 1996, foresighted businessmen and academicians have set up the Indian School of Business that is of international repute. Hyderabad was chosen as one of the locations for both IIIT (Indian Institute of Information Technology) and IIT (Indian Institute of Technology) as well. Prestigious private educational institutes such as BITS (Birla Institute of Technology and Science) have made their foray into the city. As far as Primary and Secondary education is concerned, the density of schools and colleges has substantially increased to meet the demands of the growing population. These developments fairly explain the majority perception of the respondents.

From Table 4.9 it can be inferred that a majority of the respondents, i.e., 72.72 per cent believe that educational prospects have improved, owing to Hyderabad becoming a cosmopolitan city. This is opposed by about 25.47 per cent of the sample size.

Table 4.9 *Cosmopolitanism and Educational Prospects*

Educational Prospects	*No. of Respondents*	*Percentage*
Yes	2,618	72.72
No	917	25.47
Cannot Say	65	1.80
Total	3,600	100

Governance and Administration

In an appraisal of 'Urban Infrastructure and Governance', the steering committee on urbanization, of the Planning Commission (headed by Arun Maira, member of the Planning Commission) feels that numerous schemes of the government say, JNNURM, have been a failure. The report points out several factors for the poor show – poor planning and near absence of peoples participation leading to lack of ownership; acute capacity deficit at municipal level; focus on expenditure-related targets rather than improvements in service-related outcomes; 'one-size-fits-all' approach to reforms; and failure to carry out crucial reforms relating to rationalization of user charges, property tax, land market, etc. Speaking only of JNNURM, more than Rupees 66,000 Cr. of central assistance was given from 2005 for holistic development of 71 cities. But only 60 per cent of the fund has been spent and only 18 per cent of the projects taken up under its sub-mission – UIG (Urban Infrastructure and Governance); and 40 per cent of the projects under the other sub-mission – BSUP (Basic Services to the Urban Poor), have been completed. This completely explains the majority opinion of the sample.

However, the e-governance model (e-seva) that was piloted in Hyderabad (and implemented in the rest of Andhra Pradesh) has set a precedent for good governance. Typically, citizens travel 15 kms, make 5 trips and wait for 1 hour on an average to access a government service. All this underwent a magical transformation with the e-seva model that leveraged information technology. Today, the number of services available at a single point has been increased. This has been branded 'Mee-Seva' ('Mee' in telugu means 'Your') by the Government of Andhra Pradesh. These developments perhaps reflect the views of 30.94 per cent of the sample.

A majority of respondents, i.e., 65.05 per cent feel that governance and administration have not improved as a result of Hyderabad becoming a cosmopolitan city Table 4.10. This is refuted by 30.94 per cent of the sample; while 4 per cent are unsure of either.

Table 4.10 *Cosmopolitanism and Governance and Administration*

Governance and Administration	*No. of Respondents*	*Percentage*
Yes	1,114	30.94
No	2,342	65.05
Cannot Say	144	4
Total	3,600	100

Purchasing Power

What is the purpose of the city and what is the meaning of a world-class city? This question was summarily answered by Jeb Brugmann (an expert on urbanization who teaches at the Cambridge) in his book, 'Welcome to the Urban Revolution – How Cities are Changing the World'. He says, it is a city that enables people to lift themselves out of poverty fast. He feels cities are the best means human civilizations have found to include poor people into the process of economic growth. Hyderabad in this sense is indeed a world-class city. The rising incomes and the numerous employment opportunities it provides have no doubt improved the purchasing power of its population. The per capita income of Hyderabad is at 44,300 rupees, greater than the state's average. However, persistent inflation (food, fuel, real estate, commodities, etc.), has been a problem especially for the urban poor.

Table 4.11 shows that majority of the respondents (64.05%) feel that purchasing power has improved as Hyderabad is turning out to be an increasingly cosmopolitan city. The improvement in purchasing power is owing to multiple reasons including provision of credit cards, discounts, loans and the provision of EMIs. Further, the choices for purchase are highly diversified. This claim is rejected by roughly 35 per cent of the sample.

Table 4.11 *Cosmopolitanism and Purchasing Power*

Purchasing Power	*No. of Respondents*	*Percentage*
Yes	2,306	64.05
No	1,265	35.13
Cannot Say	29	0.80
Total	3,600	100

Banking Services

Hyderabad is the largest contributor to the state's GDP, state tax and other revenues. After Bengaluru, it is India's largest IT exporter that earns large amounts of funds to the country. Availability of (more) money necessitates provisioning of banking services. The growth of Hyderabad as a business hub has greatly improved the density of banking services. Seeing a business opportunity, banks of international repute have established shop in the city. This reflects the majority opinion of the sample too. Most of the respondents (77.38%) feel that banking services have improved owing to Hyderabad's transition to a cosmopolitan city. This is refuted by roughly 22.16 per cent of the sample (Table 4.12).

Table 4.12 *Cosmopolitanism and Banking Services*

Banking Services	*No. of Respondents*	*Percentage*
Yes	2,786	77.38
No	798	22.16
Cannot Say	16	0.44
Total	3,600	100

Communication Services

Improvement (or non-improvement) of communication services more or less mirrors that of erstwhile variable, banking services. Most of the respondents (77.38%) feel that communication services have improved; and roughly 21.27 per cent of them negate this (Table 4.13).

Table 4.13 *Cosmopolitanism and Communication Services*

Communication Services	*No. of Respondents*	*Percentage*
Yes	2,786	77.38
No	766	21.27
Cannot Say	48	1.33
Total	3,600	100

Globalization and Cosmopolitanism

The respondents' opinion was sought whether globalization has contributed in development of cosmopolitanism in Hyderabad. Globalization refers to a process by which the world is said to become a single space. In this process, social life is increasingly affected by international influences. Perhaps the most powerful form of globalization is economic. On the contrary it is argued by writers such as R. Robertson that the cultural and social characteristics of globalization are ignored as the economic dimension is overstated. Irrespective of the dimension (be it political and trade ties or shared music and clothing styles), a majority of the respondents, i.e., 2,279 accounting to 63.30 per cent of the sample believe that globalization has contributed in development of cosmopolitanism in Hyderabad (Table 4.14).

This is opposed by roughly one-third, i.e., 33.72 per cent of the sample. Political scientists have periodically claimed that nationalism has declined and been replaced by internationalism. The collapse of communism (fall of Soviet Union) and the rise of globalization encouraged many sociologists to assume that nationalism (implied regionalism) as an ideology would mean nothing in increasingly globalized, multicultural societies. On the contrary, the break up of USSR saw a resurgence of nationalist identities.

Globalization has in some cases accentuated tension among groups, contributing to the growth of right-wing extremism and not cosmopolitanism.

Table 4.14 *Globalization and Cosmopolitanism*

Globalization and Cosmopolitanism	*No. of Respondents*	*Percentage*
Yes	2,279	63.30
No	1,214	33.72
Cannot Say	107	2.97
Total	3,600	100

Cosmopolitanism and Multicultural Groups Living Together

The respondents were asked whether cosmopolitanism helps in living with people who are culturally different from each other. Exposure to (and hence knowledge of) diverse cultural groups may result in increased accommodation (exchanges) between various groups, and a consequential improvement in the levels of tolerance. In this process, with time, a melting-pot culture might evolve, wherein individual groups lose their identity to a group identity. Consequently, there is greater integration among groups. This partly explains the majority opinion of the respondents in Tables 4.15 and 4.20 also.

However, on the other hand, few groups might sense a threat of losing their identity, and hence reinforce the same by taking fundamentalist positions. It has been argued that the ethnic complexity of the modern urban society tends to reduce trust, produces a fear of outsiders, and thus creates a propensity to adopt nationalist or regionalist ideologies. Social diversity undermines community, and the erosion of common values and shared sentiments undermines trust. This gets manifested in the various forms of friction between classes and ethnicities, especially in urban areas.

These diametrically opposite processes explain the divide in the perception of the respondents.

Table 4.15 indicates that 2,068 respondents, accounting for 57.44 per cent of the total sample believe that cosmopolitanism helps in living with people who are culturally different from each other. About 41.02 per cent of the respondents think otherwise. This opinion could be possibly due to the incidents and agitations for separate state of Telangana in Hyderabad in the last few years.

Table 4.15 *Cosmopolitanism and Multicultural Groups Living Together*

Cosmopolitanism and Multicultural Groups Living Together	*No. of Respondents*	*Percentage*
Yes	2,068	57.44
No	1,477	41.02
Cannot Say	55	1.52
Total	3,600	100

Cosmopolitanism and Togetherness

Table 4.16 indicates that a discernable majority of respondents accounting for 79.69 per cent of the sample believe that cosmopolitanism enhances togetherness among people who are culturally diverse. This is a contributing factor for urban development. Roughly 19.94 per cent, nearly the remainder of the sample, however, rejects this notion.

Table 4.16 *Cosmopolitanism and Togetherness*

Cosmopolitanism and Togetherness	*No. of Respondents*	*Percentage*
Yes	2,869	79.69
No	718	19.94
Cannot Say	13	0.36
Total	3,600	100

Cities are a meeting point of different cultures. If there is no accommodation of these cultures, peaceful existence of urban citizens becomes increasingly difficult.

Cosmopolitanism and Social Mobility

The respondents were asked whether cosmopolitanism helps in social mobility. It is the movement or transition from one social position to another between different levels of social hierarchy.

P.A. Sorokin defines mobility as a process by which individuals move from one social class to another. Implicit in the concept of mobility is the recognition of graduation in a society, which is done in terms of power, prestige and privileges, i.e., hierarchical structure in the society. Study of social mobility needs to concern itself with the movements of individuals as well the consequences of these movements for the social groups and the total structure that encompass these individual moves.

Table 4.17 *Cosmopolitanism and Social Mobility*

Cosmopolitanism and Social Mobility	*No. of Respondents*	*Percentage*
Yes	2,283	63.41
No	1,199	33.30
Cannot Say	118	3.27
Total	3,600	100

While recent ethnographic research has complicated our understanding of the 'cosmopolitan', assumptions persist that those who are cosmopolitan must be metropolitan, mobile, consumers.

Majority of the respondents (63.41%) feel that cosmopolitanism increases the prospects of social mobility, the movement of individuals between different levels of social hierarchy. The caste rigidities are not strong in the urban set, and the class hierarchies which are present in cities are not rigid and thus support social mobility. Around 33.30 per cent of the sample refutes this idea; while about 3.27 per cent are unsure of either (Table 4.17).

Tables 4.2, 4.8 and 4.11 have demonstrated the link between cosmopolitanism and better living conditions, improved – employment opportunities and purchasing power. These indicators have a direct influence on the social mobility of the population. Hence, the majority opinion as far as cosmopolitanism and social mobility are concerned, is in tandem with its causal factors.

Cosmopolitanism and Conflicts

Cosmopolitanism brings diverse groups together and thus brings exposure to multiple cultures and ethnicities. However, how this exposure influences in reducing or inducing conflicts is debatable. The respondents' opinions were sought on relationship between cosmopolitanism and conflicts. Interestingly, majority of the respondents, 2246, accounting for 62.38 per cent of the sample feel that cosmopolitanism reduces conflicts by enhancing intercultural contact and interaction between people Table 4.18. However, 36.58 per cent of the sample feels that cosmopolitanism enhances conflicts between people with diversified values and practices.

Table 4.18 *Cosmopolitanism and Conflicts*

Cosmopolitanism and Conflicts	*No. of Respondents*	*Percentage*
Cosmopolitanism enhances conflicts between people with diversified values and practices	1,317	36.58
Cosmopolitanism reduces conflicts between people with diversified values and practices	2,246	62.38
Cannot Say	37	1.02
Total	3,600	100

Cosmopolitanism and Transnational Identities

Table 4.19 shows that majority of the respondents (72.88%) feel that cosmopolitanism has created transnational identities. On the contrary, a little over quarter, i.e., 26.08 per cent of the respondents feel that it has not done so.

However, it is problematic to infer from globalization that multiculturalism will help create transnational identities that will be free from nationalist conflict. Attraction of nationalist identity might increase with globalization, because a national (or a regional) identity offers some psychological stability. Common beliefs, values, social ends have a cementing action among people sharing the same identity.

Table 4.19 *Cosmopolitanism and Transnational Identities*

Cosmopolitanism and Transnational Identities	*No. of Respondents*	*Percentage*
Yes	2,624	72.88
No	939	26.08
Cannot Say	37	1.02
Total	3,600	100

Cosmopolitanism and separatism and segregation

The respondents' opinions were sought whether cosmopolitanism helps in solving problems associated with separatism and segregation. Cosmopolitanism has long been concerned with how to respond to a world where different cultures live, as Kant described it, 'unavoidably side by side'. Cosmopolitanism implies diversity, plurality and seeks to expand the realm of moral inclusion to include all of humanity. The cosmopolitan challenge is to acknowledge and embrace the reality that individuals have multiple belongings and divided loyalties and that they coexist with other individuals of different cultures with similarly divided loyalties and complex identities.

Separatism is the advocacy of a state of cultural, ethnic, tribal, religious, racial, governmental or gender separation from the larger group. While it often refers to full political secession, separatist groups may seek nothing more than greater autonomy. Some groups refer to their organizing as independence, self-determination, partition or decolonization movements instead of, or in addition to, autonomist, separatist or secession movements. While some critics may equate separatism and religious segregation, racial segregation or sexual segregation, separatists argue that separation by choice is not the same as government-enforced segregation and may serve useful purposes.

Groups may have one or more motivations for separation, including (Spencer, 1998: 2–4) emotional resentment of rival communities, protection from ethnic cleansing and genocide, justified resistance by victims of oppression, including denigration of their language, culture or religion, propaganda by those who hope to gain politically from intergroup conflict and hatred the economic and political dominance of one group that does not share power and privilege in an egalitarian fashion, economic motivations: seeking to end economic exploitation by more powerful group or, conversely, to escape economic redistribution from a richer to a poorer group, preservation of threatened religious, language or other cultural tradition, destabilization from one separatist movement giving rise to others, geopolitical power vacuum from break-up of larger states or empires, continuing fragmentation as more and more states break up, feeling that the perceived nation was added to the larger state by illegitimate means the perception that the state can no longer support one's own group or has betrayed their interests.

Table 4.20 shows that the majority of the respondents (55.72%) feel that cosmopolitanism helps in resolving the problems associated with separatism and segregation. Nearly 41.72 per cent of the sample feels otherwise. In some cities, pockets of serenity can be found where people of many races find themselves mingling and enjoying each other's presence. Yale sociologist Elijah Anderson, author of *The Cosmopolitan Canopy: Race and Civility in Everyday Life,* has studied these public spaces and shares what they reveal about us and our hope as a society.

Table 4.20 *Cosmopolitanism and Separatism and Segregation*

Cosmopolitanism and Separatism and Segregation	*No. of Respondents*	*Percentage*
Yes	2,006	55.72
No	1,502	41.72
Cannot Say	92	2.55
Total	3,600	100

Cosmopolitanism and Equal Rights and Obligations

There is a need for the creation a kind of cosmopolitan democracy where political and social institutional arrangements exist on a multiple of levels, both above and below the state. It is argued that such overlapping and interconnecting institutions and structure of governance promotes interculturalism between individuals and societies. Cosmopolitans also argue that institutions, and in particular the social and political institutions of states, should be based on a kind of civic nationalism or what Habermas has termed 'constitutional patriotism'. It is argued that the promotion of the rule of law, equal rights, the practice of democracy and a civic identity allows people of diverse cultures and differing ethnic, religious or national identities to form a common bond and to coexist within the framework of common law and equal rights.

Table 4.21 *Cosmopolitanism and Equal Rights and Obligations*

Cosmopolitanism and Equal Rights and Obligations	*No. of Respondents*	*Percentage*
Yes	2,230	61.94
No	1,264	35.11
Cannot Say	106	2.94
Total	3,600	100

The respondents were asked whether cosmopolitanism confers equal rights and obligations to all irrespective of cultural and ethnic differences. Table 4.21 shows that majority of the respondents (61.94%) are of the notion that cosmopolitanism confers equal rights and obligations to all irrespective of cultural and ethnic differences. This is opposed by 35.11 per cent of the total sample size.

Cosmopolitanism and Economically Well-to-do Class

It has been generally debated that cosmopolitanism is appreciated by economically well-to-do class. The nebulous core shared by all cosmopolitan views is the idea that all human beings, regardless of their political affiliation, do (or at least can) belong to a single community, and that, this community should be cultivated. Different versions of cosmopolitanism envision this community in different ways, some focusing on political institutions, others on moral norms or relationships, and still others focusing on shared markets or forms of cultural expression. The philosophical interest in cosmopolitanism lies in its challenge to commonly recognized attachments to fellow-citizens, the local state, parochially shared cultures, and the like.

Table 4.22 shows that most of the respondents (2,258 respondents), accounting to nearly 62.72 per cent of the sample feels that cosmopolitanism is appreciated by economically well-to-do class. On the contrary, about 36.30 per cent of the sample feels that this is not the case.

Table 4.22 *Cosmopolitanism and Economically Well-to-do Class*

Cosmopolitanism and Economically Well-to-do Class	*No. of Respondents*	*Percentage*
Yes	2,258	62.72
No	1,307	36.30
Cannot Say	35	0.97
Total	3,600	100

Relationship between Cosmopolitanism and Urban Development

A majority of 2,573 respondents, making up to 71.47 per cent of the sample see a relationship between cosmopolitanism and urban development (Table 4.23).

Table 4.23 *Relationship Between Cosmopolitanism and Urban Development*

Relationship Between Cosmopolitanism and Urban Development	*No. of Respondents*	*Percentage*
Yes	2,573	71.47
No	1,007	27.97
Cannot Say	20	0.55
Total	3,600	100

However, a little over 1,000 respondents, accounting for nearly 27.97 per cent of the sample do not see a link between the two. Not all cities are cosmopolitan and cosmopolitanism is no prerequisite for urban development per se. However, it does create an ambience and environment for urban development. The Indian Census classifies cities into various classes based on population and the general discourse of classification, divides cities into various tiers. Urbanization in India is skewed; the four metropolitan cities of Delhi, Mumbai, Kolkata and Chennai alone, account for over 25 per cent of India's urban population. The cities of Hyderabad and Bangalore have gained national prominence in the past two decades. It is these set of cities that are (viewed) cosmopolitan as they attract people from all corners of India (and internationally). Hence, the opinion of respondents on cosmopolitanism and urban development is divided; though majority affirms a link between both the processes.

Conclusion

The present chapter deals with cosmopolitanism and urban development. With the help of several parameters (like health facilities, road, public transport, housing, employment opportunities, educational prospects, governance and administration, purchasing power, banking services and communication services), the opinions of the respondents on relation between cosmopolitanism and urban development has been established. It is significant to conclude that in understanding the association between cosmopolitanism and urban development, the notion of cosmopolitanism is analysed in terms of physical and social infrastructure and provision of various services to urban citizens. With specific reference to Hyderabad, the respondents have clearly established that cosmopolitanism in Hyderabad has contributed to its urban development. The succeeding chapter is on regionalism and urban development.

5 Regionalism and Urban Development

A region is a unit having concern for its homogeneity and identity. However, it has got different meaning for different scholars. A geographer tries to emphasize on geographical area, an anthropologist a cultural area, while for a sociologist it is composed of a constellation of communities characterized by 'homogeneity of economic and social structure'. Nonetheless, for a political scientist, it is a political sub-system with components of its own and interactions among these components laying a boundary within the national system.

A region becomes significant in a nation only when it becomes a unit dominated by a widely prevalent sentiment of 'togetherness', a sense of particularistic and separate identity. When the particularistic attitude of the region claims recognition of its cultural identity, it is better understood as 'regionalization' or regional movement. Thus, Professor Haqqi writes, '... Whatever the context or parameter, "region" may be said to connote an area, at least sufficiently large in size, which is differentiated and/or distinguishable from others by a variety of factors (or at least a combination of some of them) such as language, culture, religion or caste/creed, socio-economic life, political background, historical background, geographical continuity and certainly, group consciousness and of being neglected, deprived and/or discriminated by the "majority" and/or those in authority' (Haqqi, 1984).

Regionalism is a multidimensional phenomenon a feeling or sentiment backed by objective factors like language, culture, economic development, etc. It is a manifestation of emotional, psychological and sub-national socio-cultural forces confined to a particular region within a larger political set-up. It has often been described as a psychic phenomenon where a particular part faces the psyche of relative deprivation. It is also regarded as a quest for self-identity and self-fulfilment on the part of an area (Narain, 1976). Hedwig Hintze (1924) observes regionalism as a counter-movement to any exaggerated or aggressive form of centralization. Philip Mason speaks of 'linguistic and regional separatism', while Professor A.D. Pant (1984) explains regionalism through the concept of 'maldevelopment syndrome'. As a whole, at the root of regionalism there may be economic causes or certain ethnic factors such as cultural, traditional or linguistic peculiarities.

Economic Component of Regionalism

Regionalism has distinct economic overtones. Nothing makes a docile and passive community more aggressive and revoltist than the feeling of relative economic deprivation, discrimination and neglect. The colonial rulers created provinces to subserve their own economic ends and not for the economic benefit of natives with the result that what India inherited from the Britishers was not only areas with political disparity but also states suffering from grave economic imbalance and unevenness. Not only states were unequal in terms of industrial development, even the so-called industrialized states had depressed and underdeveloped pockets, thereby causing intrastate sectoral inequality.

Since each state is dependent upon the centre for financing of plans, the less it receives, the more vocal, if not violent it becomes in denouncing the centre. Charges of discrimination and unfairness are openly traded among recipient states. What actually is the plight of the states is ably brought out by Raghavachar who said, 'If the States have to depend on the Centre for 52 per cent of their total expenditure on revenue and capital account, and if out of this nearly 70 per cent is provided by discretionary plan grants and Central loans, and only 30 per cent by tax-sharing and statutory grants-in-aid, one can understand the extent of centralization'. Each state clamours for more funds and its denial leads to violent protests. Thus, it is the economic imbalance which is the main casual factor of regional consciousness in India. As Kousar Azam states, 'economic regionalism which could have helped integrate the various regions of the country, resulted only in further imbalance. Politically, it reduced planning into a process of power adjustment between the various states and added one more factor to the dynamics of group-conflict. The entrance of planned money in politics was in a sense, the beginning of planned political corruption'.

Thus, the desire to share the economic development encourages regional feelings and aspirations. As Pant has observed, 'Regionalism is the response of unequal sharing of the benefits of developmental activity. It is a protest against the stabilization and monopolization of advantages through policies aiming at institutionalization of existing stratification system ...' It may result from a process of cumulative de-equalization, in which any nascent inequality is intensified over time through cumulative causation channels' (Morris-Jones, 1967).

The demand for equitable sharing of economic development and distributive justice may take the shape of political protests, movements and agitations. The scramble for the location of steel plants, petroleum refinery and other industrial complexes followed by a threat of secession in case of non-fulfilment of these demands, is symptomatic of a symbiotic relationship that obtains between the Indian Union and its constituent units. As population increases, demands increase and they outrun resources. Charges of unfair distribution are freely levelled and tension between migrants and sons of the soil increases. It conduces to the creation and emergence of a number of chauvinist groups professing aggressive nativism. As Harrison Selig has pointed out:

> As population mounts, densely populated regions cry lebensraum at their neighbours. Bihari labourers flock to jobs in the mining and industrial towns, bordering Bengal, and overcrowded Bengal protests in return that the towns should be the preserves of its own jobless. The tea plantation of Assam became a battleground between rival groups of Assamese and Bengali unemployed. Tamilnadu demands the border plantation land of Malayalam speaking Travancore to protect Tamil coolies from Malayalee

> competition. With each year that more and more people made more in more group-consciousness by scarcity compete even more feverishly for limited economic spoils, the hope for ultimate escape from India's vicious circle grows more remote. (Selig, 1960)

Regional imbalances are producing both prosperity and poverty among regions. Within the regions they are also giving rise to the birth of two classes – rich and poor. Take, for example, the case of Punjab. The Punjab economy recorded a very high rate of growth during the sixties as a result of the green revolution. It also resulted in uneven development in different region of the state. The fruits of the green revolution have been grabbed by the just 20 per cent of Jat rich farmers who own more than 60 per cent of the total land. It is the prosperous peasants who sought commanding positions in the Akali Dal as they are keen to match their economic muscle with political power. On the contrary, the number of landless had doubled, and that of the marginal peasants has increased three times in ten years. With capital intensive agriculture the ratio of landless workers in the total agricultural workforce rose from 17.3 per cent in 1961 to 32 per cent in 1971. According to Bhalla, 24 per cent of the small peasants and 31 per cent of marginal peasants live below the poverty line (Bhalla and Alagh, 1982).

Thus, the green revolution has increased prosperity of the land-owning class and enhanced frustration among the large army of the landless and marginal farmers. The prosperous class also became frustrated when they found themselves trapped in the nexus of capitalist market economy. It is their frustration which contributes to the development of alienation among them. True, it is not the sole cause, but it is certainly an important one. Let us briefly discuss about Telangana regional movement which is very important to understand the regionalism in Hyderabad.

Telangana Regional Movement

To understand the interplay of sub-regional forces in India Professor Bhawani Singh in the article "Regionalism and Politics of Separatism in India" gives the instance of Telangana. He says located in the south central belt of India, the area once belonged to the Nizam of Hyderabad. Having undergone a long period of misrule, the area was scarcely developed and its subsequent union with the Telugu-speaking areas of former Madras Presidency created the first fissures in a unilingual state and Telangana became a prominent expression of sub-regional impulses and ethos of a people who after a long period of subjugation, witnessed the dawn of freedom only to be disappointed by the lack of developmental prospects in a united state of Andhra Pradesh. Earlier, after the Police Action in Hyderabad, the Telangana region became a part B state in the Indian Union. It was a multilingual state with the majority of people speaking Telugu but a larger number of people also spoke Hindi, Urdu, Marathi and Kannada also. But in 1956, after the states reorganization, this area was merged with the state of Andhra Pradesh and this was to create developmental strains and tensions. The reason is that people of Andhra Pradesh who belonged to the Telangana region were under the overlordship of the Nizam of Hyderabad. Between the British India and the Princely India there was a great developmental lag and this gave a natural advantage to more educated people belonging to the Andhra region. The result according to Bhawani Singh of this union was that those people who belonged to the Andhra state began cornering all plum jobs at the cost of all the natives of Telangana and they were compelled to raise an agitation which in effect meant that erstwhile people of Madras were to leave the Telangana region and its jobs must belong only to the sons of the soil. The demand grew more intense as time went on and eventually voices were raised for the separation of Telangana from the greater Andhra Pradesh. This was to be a fitting finale to the sub-regional consciousness of the people of this region. G. Ram Reddy and B.A.V. Sharma have very rightly said 'Nothing can better illustrate the general process of regionalism with its sub-regional manifestation in contemporary Indian polity than Telangana. If regionalism in India is to be designed as a process of interaction of the pan-Indian and peripheral forces, Telangana, since its admission to the Indian federal polity, has remained an expression of sub-regionalism' (Reddy and Sharma, 1979).

The state of Andhra Pradesh came into existence on 1 October 1953 by bifurcating the old Madras state, which consisted of eleven districts and Kurnool was its capital. It was fairly viable state but the State Reorganization Commission recommended the merger of Telugu-speaking Telangana into Andhra to create the present bigger state of Andhra Pradesh. Swami Ramananda Tirtha, the veteran freedom fighter belonging to the Congress championed the cause of an integrated Vishalandhra which was also supported by the Communist Party. The leader of Andhra Mahasabha, Pitamala Madapati Hanumantha Rao, though from Telangana, supported the cause of an integrated Andhra Pradesh. Since these people wielded considerable political clout in New Delhi, the creation of Visalandhra became a foregone conclusion and this demand was conceded.

It is interesting to remember that the States Reorganization Commission initially did not propose a merger of Telangana and Andhra Pradesh and had then suggested the formation of a separate state of Telangana composed of nine districts. This state could merge with Andhra after five years in case its legislature decided, by a two-thirds majority, to join a bigger state. Since this was not conceded by the central government and Telangana was merged with Andhra on 1 November 1956, it lead to a lot of heart burning and protest. The result was a Gentleman's Agreement between the leadership of both regions and the institutionalization of assurances for equitable sharing of resources. It was also decided that the financial surplus from Telangana would be used for the benefit and development of Telangana region. Representation in public services would be in proportion to the population in two regions. It was also agreed that the people of Telangana would have 40 per cent reservation in state cabinet and if the chief minister is from the Andhra region, in that case there would also be a deputy chief minister from Telangana region. A Telangana Regional Committee was formed to look after the economic, social and political interests of the people of Telangana region.

However, none of these assurances were honoured. Both Gentlemans' Agreement and the Telangana Region Committee were bypassed and ignored. These agreements were honoured more in the breach than in the observance. This gave birth to a regional leadership in the Congress and it caused factionalist struggle. This factionalist politics ultimately resulted in the demand for a separate state of Telangana in 1969.

It is obvious that the demand for a separate state was rooted in the developmental disparity between the two regions. The inadequate and equitable distribution of economic resources, the diversion of Telangana's surplus to Andhra region and the bypassing of solemn assurances led to the demand of the formation of a separate state of Telangana, but the central government was adamant in keeping a united and bigger Andhra and this led to the petering out of any zeal among the separatist for carving out a new state out of the existing Andhra Pradesh. As time went on, the leadership began veering round to the view that the bigger state of Andhra with its vast and untapped natural resources would prove to be a great boom to the people of the state than a segmented Andhra. Today, the Telugu-speaking people constitute the one of the largest segments of population in India and the state sends forty two members to the Lok Sabha. Obviously, it sends a very large representation to the union parliament and this increases its bargaining capacity vis-à-vis the central government. Owing to this reason, the demand for bifurcation today is not very strong and the people have more or less reconciled themselves to the position of living in a bigger unilingual state of Andhra Pradesh. This does not mean that the Telangana subregional sentiment is dead. Only, it is not so strong, open and vocal now, as it was before.

In an article 'The Movement for Telangana: Myth and Reality' Rama S. Melkote and others (Melkote et al., 2010) are of the opinion that subsequent to the announcement by Home Minister P. Chidambaram on 9 December 2009 about initiating the process for a separate Telangana state, a number of wrong notions are being peddled about the history, politics, development of Andhra Pradesh and its people. They present few myths and subsequent reality pertaining to them which are discussed below and have been liberally quoted from the article.

(1) Myth about Potti Sriramulu and present-day Andhra Pradesh: Potti Sriramulu struggled for the separation of Telugu-speaking areas from Madras Presidency to form an Andhra State. More specifically, went on a fast 1952 for a separate Andhra state with Madras as its capital. This proposal of T. Prakasam was rejected outright by C. Rajagopalachari, the then chief minister of Madras Presidency. While the proposal for linguistic states was accepted by the Calcutta Congress Committee in 1934, the proposal for the formation of a linguistic state of Telugus was approved by the Madras assembly in 1937. It was only after the death of Potti Sriramulu that the movement for a separate Andhra

intensified. Andhra state was formed in 1953 with Kurnool as its capital and T. Prakasam as its chief minister. The political evolution of Hyderabad state under Nizam's rule took a different direction. Telugu, Urdu, Marathi and Kannada-speaking areas and people were part of Hyderabad, a princely state. It went through political turmoil when the Nizam refused to merge with the Indian Union at the time of independence in 1947. The Razakars, the armed militia of the Majlis, violently opposed the merger. At this time Telangana also witnessed an armed peasant struggle led by the Communist Party, against feudal oppression.

In September 1948, the Indian army undertook what is known as 'Police Action' putting an end to the Nizam's rule and merged the Hyderabad state with the Indian union. The 'Police Action' also suppressed the peasant struggle. It must be noted that Muslims were a part of the struggle against the Razakars. After the merger, the Congress won in the first elections in Hyderabad state held in 1952 and Burgula Ramakrishna Rao became its first chief minister. Rao's government brought progressive land legislation in the form of Hyderabad Tenancy Act that gave protection to tenants. By 1956, there was substantial progress in land reforms in Telangana.

(2) Merger was against the Wishes of the Telangana People: When Telangana was merged with Andhra state in 1956, there was much resentment against the influx of people from other states, including Andhra region. These migrants began to occupy most civil services posts. From 1948–52, many from Andhra state got jobs in Telangana as English education and experience in British administrative procedures gave them an edge over the local people. They also obtained false *mulki* (nativity) certificates to settle down and bought vast stretches of land. In 1952, the Hyderabad state witnessed a major student agitation, known as the Mulki agitation. It began in Warangal but soon spread to all the other areas, forcing the Hyderabad government to appoint a committee to look into violations of Mulki Rules. The demand for Visalandhra that gained momentum at this time was described by Nehru as inspired by a desire for imperialist occupation of land (*Indian Express,* 17 October 1953).

The first States Reorganization Commission (SRC) also did not recommend the merger. Consisting of three members, Justice Fazal Ali (chairman), Hridaynath Kunzru and K.M. Panikkar, it recommended that Telangana could remain a separate state for five years, i.e., till 1961. At the end of this period, if two-thirds majority of elected representatives agree to the merger of the two regions, the merger could take place. There was opposition to the merger by a section of the Congress. The then chief minister, B.R.K. Rao too expressed apprehensions about the merger as Telangana and Andhra were two different cultural formations. Telangana was cosmopolitan with a composite culture of mingling different linguistic groups and had developed a distinct identity of its own.

It was in this background of widespread resentment and apprehensions of Telangana people that the debate on Visalandhra took place. Telangana was merged with Andhra state to form Andhra Pradesh, much against the wishes of the people. The fears of Telangana people were sought to be allayed through the 'Gentlemen's Agreement' which stipulated that: (a) Opportunities for employment in the public services, admissions to educational institutions for Telangana students to the extent of 1/3 of the total admissions in the entire state. Or admissions to Telangana colleges should be restricted entirely to Telangana students. This was to protect the educational and employment opportunities of Telangana people against the onslaught of more educated and opportunity-seeking Telugus from the coastal Andhra region. (b) After the proportional sharing of expenditures by both the regions, the balance revenues would be spent on the development of Telangana. This was to ensure that the resources of Telangana would be spent within the region that they would not be diverted. (c) A Regional Council would be established to ensure all-round development of Telangana. It is untrue to say that Telangana people or B. Ramakrishna Rao favoured a united Andhra; it is precisely because of their fears that the Gentleman's Agreement was formulated. Development was the promise given at the time of founding Andhra Pradesh to the people of Telangana. This has not been translated into reality till date.

(3) Telangana was an independent, viable; revenue-surplus state at the time of merger while Andhra state was not: Andhra had a financially difficult existence during 1953–56. Telangana, as Hyderabad state was popularly known, enjoyed a comparative

revenue-surplus. Andhra state had low per capita revenue. Comparatively, Telangana had higher land and excise revenues keeping it in a financially comfortable situation. The SRC argued that Telangana would be a stable and viable unit with an area of 45,000 sq km, a population of 1.13 crore and an annual revenue of Rs 17 crore. It had such a surplus on its revenue account that it was sufficient to finance irrigation projects. Considering the lag in education and employment levels, the commission felt that a merger with coastal Andhra would result in diversion of resources, employment and educational opportunities for the Telangana people. Telangana was neither poor nor backward as it indeed had rich resources. However, it lagged behind due to the absence of English educational facilities and employment opportunities under the Nizam. If the merger had not happened, under their own government, the Telangana people would have attained similar educational and employment standards that people from coastal Andhra had. Melkote and others assert that there should be no doubt that Telangana would prosper as a smaller state.

(4) Telangana was promised opportunities and resources, but never received its due share: Telangana has not received its due share in investment allocations, and the surpluses from the region (the difference between what ought to have been spent and what has actually been spent) have been diverted to other regions. The accumulated surplus based on the estimates of the Lalit Committee (1969) – given the task of determining the surplus due to Telangana for the period is November 1956 to 31 March 1968 – exceeded Rs 100 crore in 1969 itself and its present value would be Rs 2,300 crore (Rao, 2005). The revenue from Telangana region (excluding Hyderabad) has formed more than half of Andhra Pradesh's total income in recent times (2003–04 to 2006–07). Seventy-five per cent of the total sales tax revenues and 66 per cent of total excise revenue comes from the Telangana region. Revenue from coal comes entirely from Telangana and at least 44 per cent of income from forest resources comes from this region. Thus, it is evident that Telangana contributes a higher share of revenue to Andhra Pradesh, but the expenditure on the region and its people is far less (Rao and Shastry, 2009). The regional committee that was

supposed to ensure all-round development of Telangana was abolished in 1973. The reports of the Bhargava Committee (1969) set up by the central government under Indira Gandhi to assess the revenue surpluses of Telangana to investigate into the actual expenditures on Telangana have never been made public.

(5) Telangana is growing under its own steam, but at a huge cost: Growth is taking place in Telangana. This is also established by Andhra Pradesh Human Development Report, 2007. The districts of Karimnagar and Warangal have recorded fairly good agricultural growth. But the growth has been achieved at a high cost. Unlike coastal Andhra, especially Krishna and two districts of Godavari and Guntur which have canal irrigation, in large parts of Telangana, 70 per cent of irrigation is through groundwater and deep tube wells (Subramanyam, 2003). The numerous promised but incomplete (e.g., Ichchampalli, Dummugudem, Srisailam Left Canal), unfilled (e.g., Sriramsaagar) or abandoned (e.g., Devanuru) irrigation projects have meant that individual farmers have to make a much greater investment in agriculture. Farming has become risky in Telangana, as indicated in the large number of suicides by farmers. Telangana accounts for as many as two-thirds of the total number of suicides reported in the state between 1998 and 2006. In recent times, Telangana has been allocated a higher share in expenditure on irrigation (55%) than its share in population (41%). However, compared to coastal Andhra, the unit cost of irrigation is much higher in Telangana (as it is situated on the Deccan plateau) as lifting of water requires huge investments in pumping machinery and power. The promise of 'development' was always made to Telangana people whenever they rose up against the unequal treatment that was meted out to them. The Gentlemen's Agreement (1956), and the Six-point Formula (1973) and the Regional Development Board (2006) given at different phases of Telangana movement all promised development.

Rama Melkote and others are of the opinion that many promises have remained unfulfilled, some of which are the following:

- Regional Councils, Mulki Rules, Subcommittees for the development of backward regions.

- President's Order on Public Employment (or, more accurately, The Andhra Pradesh Public Employment (Organization of Local Cadres and Regulation of Direct Recruitment) 1975 issued on the basis of a six-point formula to undo the injustice caused in the matter of Telangana recruitment following the Telangana agitation in 1969.
- Government Order 610 (1985) – issued to repatriate all the non-locals appointed in Telangana to their respective native zones and appoint local candidates in the resulting vacancies.
- Girglani Commission's recommendations (2004) – set up to determine the deviations from the presidential order.
- Grievances, remedial measures, and safeguards (Summary of Final Report of One Man Commission, (SPF), Sri J.M. Girglani, Hyderabad 2004 (http://www.telangana.org/Papers/article16.asp). Strangely, from 1973, what the Telangana people were arguing as a matter of right to self-respect got converted into an issue of 'developing backward areas'. Within this paradigm, a uniform approach for promoting accelerated development of backward areas became the strategy of the State. With this move, the state successfully nullified the special status for Telangana region accorded earlier due to the historically specific conditions of merger. Telangana got equated with all other backward regions of the state. It became easy to project it as an issue of development and backwardness without any reference to questions of justice and above all to its self-respect.

Regionalism and Urban Development

The regional movements especially if separatist in nature cause economic losses which influences the rate of urban development. For instance, The Federation of Andhra Pradesh Chamber of Commerce and Industries (Fapcci), a representative body of trade and commerce in Andhra Pradesh, reported in August 2012 that more than 60 companies have decided to set up facilities in other states due to ongoing agitation and political uncertainty causing loss to State and impacting the economy. Bandhs and agitation in support of separate statehood of Telangana, conservatively result in financial loss of about Rs 200 crore a day. Companies are not willing to set up base in Hyderabad or other attractive locations in the State, and are instead going to Pune, Bengaluru, Chennai and Gurgaon. Telangana strike, lead to loss of 20,000 manufacturing and 40,000 services jobs (http://www.thehindubusinessline.com). The industry and trade has lost around Rs 1,800 crore in terms of production in Telangana region due to agitations and bandhs for the past 12 days as part of *sakal janula samme* and will lose another Rs 1,000 crore due to the two-day industry shutdown. (http://ibnlive.in.com/news/dated 26 September 2011)

Regionalism and Sense of Identity

Regionalism is an ideology based on the belief that people with a common characteristic, such as language or ethnicity constitute a separate and a distinctive (political) community. The community attempts to preserve this social distinctiveness for various motives (most often, for rewards). It is in this process that identities get reinforced and typified. Perhaps, this could be one of the explanations in support of the majority opinion of the sample.

On the question of whether regionalism is associated with any sense of identity (for example a state, a nation, a religious group or a linguistic group), most of the respondents (79.55%) have responded in the affirmative (Table 5.1). Around 18.75 per cent of the respondents however, think otherwise.

Table 5.1 *Regionalism and Sense of Identity*

Regionalism and Sense of Identity	*No. of Respondents*	*Percentage*
Yes	2,864	79.55
No	675	18.75
Cannot Say	61	1.69
Total	3,600	100

Feelings Associated with Regionalism

A majority of respondents, (2,129), accounting 59.13 per cent of the sample possess both positive and negative feelings associated with regionalism Table 5.2. This is followed by negative feelings that accounts for a quarter, i.e., 25.19 per cent of the sample and then, a positive imagery to about 13.25 per cent of the total sample size.

Table 5.2 *Feelings Associated with Regionalism*

Feelings Associated with Regionalism	*No. of Respondents*	*Percentage*
Positive	477	13.25
Negative	907	25.19
Both Positive and Negative	2,129	59.13
Cannot Say	87	2.41
Total	3,600	100

Cultural Differences and Development of Regionalism

The respondents were asked if the cultural differences were responsible for development of regionalism. Table 5.3 shows that most of the respondents (83.63%) feel that cultural differences are responsible for development of regionalism. This is, however, negated by about 16 per cent of the sample.

Table 5.3 *Cultural Differences and Development of Regionalism*

Cultural Differences and Development of Regionalism	*No. of Respondents*	*Percentage*
Yes	3,011	83.63
No	562	15.61
Cannot Say	27	0.75
Total	3,600	100

The functionalist view argues that people need a sense of belonging which gives them strength to sustain themselves in times of pressure, and this is provided by a cultural (ethnic) group. Though this makes the in-group stronger, it undermines the notion of community in the society alongside trust. Trust and a community feeling in culturally diverse societies is difficult to achieve because of the differences of interest, of social beliefs and values, and of social ends. In such societies, social (ethnic) groups will employ strategies of social closure to secure advantages over outsiders who are perceived as competitors. Hence, regionalist feelings are strongly manifested. This fairly explains the majority opinion of respondents.

Cultural Identities and Regionalism

When asked whether cultural identities are vital in regionalism, 2,098 respondents, making up majority of 58.27 percent of the sample, replied in the affirmative (Table 5.4). This was refuted by 35.91 percent of the sample; while 5.8 percent of them remained unsure of either.

Table 5.4 *Cultural Identities and Regionalism*

Cultural identities and Regionalism	*No. of Respondents*	*Percentage*
Yes	2,098	58.27
No	1,293	35.91
Cannot Say	209	5.80
Total	3,600	100

Political Identities and Regionalism

When it came to political identities, a larger number of respondents (as against those who believe cultural identities are vital in regionalism) accounting for 67.97 per cent of the sample size, replied in the affirmative (Table 5.5). At the risk of generalization, it can be said that regionalism is (relatively) more about politics than culture. Regionalism is based on the demand that governments should share the same cultural identity as the governed. The aspirations of the group are legitimated and institutionalized through political means. Hence, it can be argued that political identities play a major role in regionalism.

However, 29.83 per cent of the respondents feel political identities do not play a vital role in regionalism.

Table 5.5 *Political Identities and Regionalism*

Political Identities and Regionalism	*No. of Respondents*	*Percentage*
Yes	2,447	67.97
No	1,074	29.83
Cannot Say	79	2.19
Total	3,600	100

Relationship between Regionalism and Migration

About 63.02 per cent of the respondents see a relationship between regionalism and migration. This is contested by 29.22 per cent of respondents, while 7.75 per cent have not given any opinion (Table 5.6).

Though migration has existed since ages, the character of migration is changing rapidly with globalization. The partial liberalization of the labour market and the greying of populations of the industrialized societies are some of the major causes effecting change in the trends of migration. Societies, especially cities, that act as engines of economic growth are becoming more culturally diverse; alongside exponential growth of their population.

This creates a classic case of supply exceeding demand. More labour chasing fewer opportunities. The new entrants into the cities create pressure on the job market by competing with the local population. Since migrant workforce is more willing to work on lower wages, they allegedly hurt the prospects of the local populace. This results in greater friction among groups and consequent social (ethnic) tension. The above said argument explains in part the findings of Table 5.7 and 5.8.

Table 5.6 *Relationship between Regionalism and Migration*

Regionalism and Migration	*No. of Respondents*	*Percentage*
Yes	2,269	63.02
No	1,052	29.22
Cannot Say	279	7.75
Total	3,600	100

In-migration and Regionalism

When questioned, if reduction in in-migration helps solve the problems related to regionalism, most of the respondents (69.27%) responded in the affirmative (Table 5.7). They believe that it will solve the problems related to regionalism. The reduction in in-migration according to respondents, would contain the migrants from competing with the local population and thus reduce the frustration. This, however, was contested by 22.63 per cent of the sample size. About 8.08 per cent of the respondents were indifferent to the question.

Table 5.7 *In-migration and Regionalism*

In-migration and Regionalism	*No. of Respondents*	*Percentage*
Yes	2,494	69.27
No	815	22.63
Cannot Say	291	8.08
Total	3,600	100

Out-migration and Regionalism

Table 5.8 below shows that majority of the respondents (69.66%) feel that an increased rate of out-migration reduces the feelings of regionalism. This is refuted by 28.63 per cent of the sample. In fact, in-migration and out-migration leads to cultural interaction and exchanges among various cultures. This, there fore, increases the possibilities of enhanced exposure to various cultural traits and practices.

Table 5.8 *Out-migration and regionalism*

Out-migration and Regionalism	*No. of Respondents*	*Percentage*
Yes	2,508	69.66
No	1,031	28.63
Cannot Say	61	1.69
Total	3,600	100

Reasons for Regionalism

About three-fourths of the sample size, i.e., (75.22%) believes that the most important cause for regionalism is economic (Table 5.9). When we analysed migration, a similar trend was reflected – a majority of respondents felt that economic causes was mainly responsible for migration. Relative deprivation is considered to be the root cause of regionalism. This deprivation is glaringly manifested in the economic sphere; acting as a fuel in accentuating regionalist feelings.

As reasons could be multiple, the respondents were allowed to pick more than one choice. Second comes cultural, accounting for 35.58 per cent of the sample. According to few theorists, India's cultural and linguistic diversity is the major contributor to regionalism. They argue that language and culture becomes the core of an individual's identity, which when politicized take a virulent turn.

This is followed by political (30.55% of the sample), psychological (26.63% of the sample), and social (about 25.08% of the sample). Other reasons accounted for about 8.22 per cent of the sample, while geographical reasons took the last position (3.30% of the sample). The lack of political power and political assertion, relative deprivation, greater utility of the opportunities by the non-local residents are critical factors in regionalism.

Table 5.9 *Reasons for Regionalism*

Reasons for Regionalism	*No. of Respondents*	*Percentage*
Economic	2,708	75.22
Social	903	25.08
Political	1,100	30.55
Cultural	1,281	35.58
Psychological	959	26.63
Geographical	119	3.30
Any Other	296	8.22
Total	7,366*	100

* Respondents have given more than one response

Lack of Employment and Regionalism

The respondents were asked whether lack of employment opportunities contribute to regionalism. An overwhelming number of respondents, 3,166 of them, accounting to 87.94 per cent of the sample, feel that lack of employment opportunities contribute to regionalism. This has been rejected by about 10.30 per cent of the sample (Table 5.10).

Table 5.10 *Lack of Employment and Regionalism*

Lack of Employment and Regionalism	*No. of Respondents*	*Percentage*
Yes	3,166	87.94
No	371	10.30
Cannot Say	63	1.75
Total	3,600	100

Maldevelopment and Feelings of Regionalism

The respondents were asked whether maldevelopment has contributed to the development of feelings of regionalism. Table 5.11 below shows that most of the respondents (79.83%) are of the notion that maldevelopment contributed to the development of feelings of regionalism. While 18.13 per cent are opposed to this, about 2.02 per cent of the sample remained indifferent.

Table 5.11 *Maldevelopment and Feelings of Regionalism*

Maldevelopment and Feelings of Regionalism	*No. of Respondents*	*Percentage*
Yes	2,874	79.83
No	653	18.13
Cannot Say	73	2.02
Total	3,600	100

Masses Support for Regional Formations

When asked whether masses support regional formations because their expectation of material security, political security and advancement is not met, the opinion is more or less divided equally. The local residents, who have been deprived continuously, usually support regional formations to not only assert their regional identities but also to press for overall development. About 51.02 per cent of the sample has disagreed while 48.16 per cent of them agreed to the statement question (Table 5.12).

Table 5.12 *Masses Support for Regional Formations*

Masses Support Regional Formations	*No. of Respondents*	*Percentage*
Yes	1,734	48.16
No	1,837	51.02
Cannot Say	29	0.80
Total	3,600	100

Regionalism and Disintegration

About two-thirds of the sample size agree (and strongly agree) on the notion that regionalism leads to disintegration of a country. However, nearly one-third of the respondents disagrees (and strongly disagrees) to this notion. Of the individual responses, 'strongly agree' is the most opted response, accounting to 44.94 per cent of the sample; followed by 'disagree' (about 31.08% of the sample), 'agree' (21.19% of the sample), 'strongly disagree (barely accounting for 1.4% of the total sample size) (Table 5.13).

Though Indian society was divided owing to regional diversity, this did not pose a threat in the run up to our independence as the whole country was united in fighting against a common enemy – the British. Simply put, feelings of nationalism eclipsed regionalism during the brief period of our freedom struggle. So was the case world over, where nationalism became associated with the movements for self-determination against imperialism, especially in the Third World.

However, post-independence, the contradictions began to manifest themselves in the numerous regionalist movements across the country. Regionalism has broadly the following dimensions – that of supra-state (North-South or the Aryan-Dravidian divide), inter-state (numerous riparian disputes), intra-state (Telangana, Vidarbha or the Gorkhaland aspirations). While none of these pose any threat to the integration of the country, the secessionist movements (Naga, Khalistan) did affect India's unity. This explains the majority opinion of the sample; and in part clarifies the findings in Table 5.13.

Table 5.13 *Regionalism and Disintegration*

Regionalism and Disintegration	*No. of Respondents*	*Percentage*
Strongly Agree	1,618	44.94
Agree	763	21.19
Disagree	1,119	31.08
Strongly Disagree	52	1.44
Cannot Say	48	1.33
Total	3,600	100

Regionalism and Relative Deprivation

The respondents were asked whether regionalism is the result of feeling of deprivation on the part of a people of an area. Nearly two-thirds, i.e., 65.05 per cent of the respondents feel that regionalism is result of feeling of deprivation on the part of people, followed by about 18.08 per cent of the sample who are unsure whether deprivation plays a role or not (Table 5.14). A minority of 16.86 per cent of the respondents feel that deprivation plays no role in accentuating regionalism.

Table 5.14 *Regionalism and Relative Deprivation*

Regionalism and Relative Deprivation	*No. of Respondents*	*Percentage*
Yes	2,342	65.05
No	607	16.86
Cannot Say	651	18.08
Total	3,600	100

Political Elite and Regional Deprivation

Table 5.15 shows that 2,752 of the 3,600 respondents, accounting to about 76.44 per cent of the sample, feel that political elite exploit situations of regional deprivation and unrest and convert them into movements to forge and strengthen their individual and factional support bases.

There is a difference between a group that claims ethnic distinctiveness and the one which has distinctiveness imposed upon it by some politically superior group in a context of political struggle. Ethnicity may, therefore, become the basis either for separatism (say a regional movement) or for political subordination. The latter reflects the majority opinion of the respondents. It can also be argued that respondents have a negative imagery of the politically dominant.

This view is, however, countered by about 23.08 per cent of the sample size.

Table 5.15 *Political Elite and Regional Deprivation*

Political Elite and Regional Deprivation	*No. of Respondents*	*Percentage*
Yes	2,752	76.44
No	831	23.08
Cannot Say	17	0.47
Total	3,600	100

Caste and Regionalism

Indian social organization can be said to have these important foundations – Ashrama system, Varna system, Joint family system and Caste system. Caste is a segmental division of society. Caste divides the whole society into separate groups in which the status, social duties and rights are different. Each caste had its own rules and regulations and if a member breaks, he is expelled from the caste. The moral allegiance to caste came first and then community. In the urban, industrialized societies, this has lost its rigidity – in rural India it still persists.

A majority (66.91% of the sample) feel that caste does not play a role in the context of regionalism. While 21.94 per cent feel it plays a role, about 11.13 per cent are unsure of either (Table 5.16).

Table 5.16 *Caste and Regionalism*

Caste	*No. of Respondents*	*Percentage*
Yes	790	21.94
No	2,409	66.91
Cannot Say	401	11.13
Total	3,600	100

Religion and Regionalism

Similar to caste, majority of the respondents (69.69%) feel that religion does not play a role in the context of regionalism. At least in the Indian context, it seems to be right since we see people of different religions are dispersed across regions. However, 27.33 per cent of the sample contests this argument (Table 5.17).

Table 5.17 *Religion and Regionalism*

Religion	*No. of Respondents*	*Percentage*
Yes	984	27.33
No	2,509	69.69
Cannot Say	73	2.02
Total	3,600	100

Sharing of Waters and Regionalism

A substantial majority of respondents, accounting to 81.88 per cent of the sample feel inequitable sharing of waters plays a major role in the context of regionalism. This has been negated by roughly 17.22 per cent of the sample (Table 5.18).

Sharing of waters has been a sensitive issue in our country. The linguistic reorganization of states has cut states across geographic boundaries. This has arbitrarily divided features such as hills or river basins across states, thereby affecting its geographic personality. Consequently, numerous riparian disputes have arisen among various states (and less often, among regions within a state itself).

Table 5.18 *Sharing of Waters and Regionalism*

Sharing of Waters and Regionalism	*No. of Respondents*	*Percentage*
Yes	2,948	81.88
No	620	17.22
Cannot Say	32	0.88
Total	3,600	100

Language and Regionalism

Though India is lingual mosaic, the linguistic reorganization of states after independence has polarized identities. An overwhelming

87.44 per cent of the respondents feel that language plays a major role in the context of regionalism, especially in shaping the regional identities. In India we see several dialects too. Further even if the language is same, accents vary according to region. Thus, it would not be an exaggeration to state that apart from geographical difference, language is one of the most significant factors for regionalism. This is opposed by a minority of the sample accounting to 8.66 per cent of the sample (Table 5.19).

According to the latest census (available data), there are 1,652 mother tongues in India. Of these, the census lists 216 mother tongues with a total number of speakers 10,000 or more at an all-India level, grouped into 114 languages of which 22 mentioned in the Constitution (Eighth Schedule). These are called Scheduled languages. Also, as many languages, so many identities. Any (perceived) threat to one's language has resulted in strong reactions. The anti-Hindi agitation in Tamil Nadu is a case in point. It is not language alone, even the dialect of a region has given way to regionalist sentiment. A classic example would be of the Telangana region.

Table 5.19 *Language and Regionalism*

Language and Regionalism	*No. of Respondents*	*Percentage*
Yes	3,148	87.44
No	312	8.66
Cannot Say	140	3.88
Total	3,600	100

Economic Imbalances and Regionalism

Nearly 85 per cent agree (46.33% strongly agree and 38.55% agree) that economic imbalances are responsible for regionalism. This is corroborated by numerous studies so far, which held economic, (viz., regional) imbalances accentuate regionalism. When uneven development creates profound regional imbalances, the peripheral (marginalized or excluded) regions engage in regionalist movements to secure more equal distribution of economic rewards. This fairly explains the findings of Table 5.20.

However, a minority of 7 per cent of the respondents disagrees (6.08% disagree and 0.91% strongly disagree) to this; and about 8.11 per cent could not make a choice between the two.

Table 5.20 *Economic Imbalances and Regionalism*

Economic Imbalances – Regionalism	*No. of Respondents*	*Percentage*
Strongly Agree	1,668	46.33
Agree	1,388	38.55
Disagree	219	6.08
Strongly Disagree	33	0.91
Cannot Say	292	8.11
Total	3,600	100

Demands for New States: Unequal Distribution of Development Benefits

Table 5.21 below indicates that most of the respondents, accounting for 86.30 per cent of the sample feel that most of the demands for constituting new states are based on unequal distribution of development benefits. This is rejected by about 13.19 per cent of the sample.

Table 5.21 *Demands for New States: Unequal Distribution of Development Benefits*

New States: Unequal Distribution of Development Benefits	*No. of Respondents*	*Percentage*
Yes	3,107	86.30
No	475	13.19
Cannot Say	18	0.5
Total	3,600	100

Regionalism and Threat to Unity of the Country

Table 5.22 indicates that majority of the respondents (62.38%) see regionalism as a very serious threat to the development, progress and unity of the country. These set of respondents see regionalism as a separatist force which breaks down the existing social structures and systems. This percentage is much higher than those whose feelings are negatively associated with regionalism (25.19% in Table 5.2). There is considerable opposition to this view that accounts to 35.41

per cent of the sample. They are of the opinion that regionalism is important to press the need for equitable development.

Table 5.22 *Regionalism and Threat to Unity of the Country*

Regionalism and Unity of the Country	*No. of Respondents*	*Percentage*
Yes	2,246	62.38
No	1,275	35.41
Cannot Say	79	2.19
Total	3,600	100

Regionalism and Sense of Brotherhood

Approximately three-fourths of the sample (75.72%) feels that regionalism encourages people to develop a sense of brotherhood and commonness on the basis of common language, religion or historical background. Commonly held values and beliefs and shared interests could be a major cause for this perception. However, 23.33 per cent of the respondents think otherwise (Table 5.23).

Table 5.23 *Regionalism and Sense of Brotherhood*

Regionalism and Sense of Brotherhood	*No. of Respondents*	*Percentage*
Yes	2,726	75.72
No	840	23.33
Cannot Say	34	0.94
Total	3,600	100

Feeling of Regionalism and Neglect of a Particular Region

Table 5.24 clearly indicates that most of the respondents (71.58%) of the sample feel that regionalism probably develops due to the continuous neglect of a particular area or region by the ruling authorities. Regional development imbalance is a major cause of feeling of being neglected. There is a combination of both economic and psychological factors. A considerable number of respondents, 26.80 per cent of the sample have disagreed with the above said.

Table 5.24 *Feeling of Regionalism and Neglect of a Particular Region*

Regionalism – Neglect of Region	*No. of Respondents*	*Percentage*
Yes	2,577	71.58
No	965	26.80
Cannot Say	58	1.61
Total	3,600	100

Regionalism and Political Awareness of Backward People

Table 5.25 below indicates that majority of the respondents (61.47%) feel that regionalism develops as a result of increasing political awareness of backward people who have been discriminated against. Regionalism locates the political legitimacy of the state in self-government by people belonging to the same region, viz., they (excluded lot) believe that the government should share the same cultural identity as the governed. Also, as far as India is concerned, the system of universal adult suffrage has put everyone (all the communities) on an equal footing; in effect boosting the aspirations for self-governance. The need for self-governance, (viz., autonomy) explains the findings in Table 5.25.

However 37.47 per cent of the respondents do not believe that regionalism develops as a result of increasing political awareness of backward people who have been discriminated against.

Table 5.25 *Regionalism and Political Awareness of Backward People*

Regionalism – Political Awareness	*No. of Respondents*	*Percentage*
Yes	2,213	61.47
No	1349	37.47
Cannot Say	38	1.05
Total	3,600	100

Political Leaders and the Feeling of Regionalism

Table 5.26 shows that most of the respondents (80.94%) feel that often some political leaders encourage the feeling of regionalism to maintain their hold over a particular area or group of people. This is vindicated by the fact that 82.68 per cent of the candidates got elected to the Lok Sabha in 2009 general elections, by securing not even 50 per cent of the total votes polled in their constituencies. Critics of the electoral system have blamed this on the 'first past the post' system, which they say encourages candidates to focus on securing votes of a (small) segment of the electorate. In order to do this, they accentuate or reinforce social divisions based on narrower considerations that lead to divisive tendencies and social conflict However, a minority of 10.83 per cent of the respondents deny this argument.

Table 5.26 *Political Leaders and the Feeling of Regionalism*

Political Leaders – Regionalism	*No. of Respondents*	*Percentage*
Yes	2,914	80.94
No	390	10.83
Cannot Say	296	8.22
Total	3,600	100

Demand by States to Greater Autonomy from the Centre

The majority of the respondents (55.86%) in Table 5.27 feel that regionalism often led to the demand by states to greater autonomy from the Centre. Jammu and Kashmir is a case in point. This has been opposed by a considerable 38.36 per cent of the respondents; while 5.77 per cent of the sample was indifferent.

Table 5.27 *Demand by States to Greater Autonomy from the Centre*

Demand by States to Greater Autonomy from the Centre	*No. of Respondents*	*Percentage*
Yes	2011	55.86
No	1,381	38.36
Cannot Say	208	5.77
Total	3,600	100

People's Awareness and Feeling of Regionalism

The respondents were asked whether people have become aware in the backward areas that they are being discriminated against has promoted feeling of regionalism. Most of the respondents (72.88%)

feel that people from backward regions have become conscious that their being discriminated against has perpetuated a feeling of regionalism (Table 5.28). A considerable 25.94 per cent of the sample, however, thinks otherwise, that people are not yet self-aware.

Table 5.28 *People's Awareness and Feeling of Regionalism*

People Awareness and Feeling of Regionalism	*No. of Respondents*	*Percentage*
Yes	2,624	72.88
No	934	25.94
Cannot Say	21	0.58
Total	3,600	100

Promotion of Even Development to Resolve Problems in Regionalism

An overwhelming majority of respondents have strongly agreed (66.27%) and agreed (21.77%) that promoting even development of the neglected areas will resolve the problems associated with regionalism and thus accelerate urban development. This statement is a corollary to the findings of Tables 5.20, 5.21, and 5.24.

Table 5.29 *Promotion of Even Development in Resolving Regionalism Problems*

Promotion of Even Development Regionalism	*No. of Respondents*	*Percentage*
Strongly Agree	2,386	66.27
Agree	784	21.77
Disagree	297	8.25
Strongly Disagree	69	1.91
Cannot Say	64	1.77
Total	3,600	100

Special care alone, to the neglected area is not the solution. It is important to shorten the gulf ('accumulated gap') between the developed and the underdeveloped regions, as both the regions prosper. However, about 10 per cent of the sample do not think so, (viz., they disagree or strongly disagree to the statement)

System of National Education and Regionalism

When asked whether introduction of a system of national education would help people to overcome regional feelings and develop an attachment towards the nation, 36.41 per cent of the respondents have agreed while 23.91 per cent of the sample strongly agreed to the statement (Table 5.30).

However, 25.77 per cent of the respondents strongly disagree; while 19.91 per cent of the sample has disagreed with the statement. These set of respondents feel that a unified system of national education will not be helpful in mitigating regional feelings. In line with Benedict Anderson's views of a nation as an 'imagined community', critics of nationalism argue that nationalism is an artificial, parasitic ideology; because it is often impossible to identify a single characteristic common to all the members of a society who claim to belong to a common nation. This is more so the case with a cultural mosaic such as India. In this view, nationalism is a myth created by intellectuals, who are the exponents of romantic notions of national language and identity. Therefore, any system of national education, according to the respondents of this opinion, can only be of cosmetic than real value.

Table 5.30 *System of National Education and Regionalism*

System of National Education and Regionalism	*No. of Respondents*	*Percentage*
Strongly Agree	861	23.91
Agree	1,311	36.41
Disagree	393	19.91
Strongly Disagree	928	25.77
Cannot Say	107	2.97
Total	3,600	100

Relationship between Regionalism and Urban Development

A little over three-fourths, i.e., 76.19 per cent of the sample sees a relationship between regionalism and urban development, i.e., if the problems associated with regionalism go beyond control then development in urban areas is hampered. This has been negated by about 21.44 per cent of the respondents (Table 5.31).

Table 5.31 *Relationship between Regionalism and Urban Development*

Relationship between Regionalism and Urban Development	*No. of Respondents*	*Percentage*
Yes	2,743	76.19
No	772	21.44
Cannot Say	85	2.36
Total	3,600	100

Conclusion

The present chapter deals with regionalism and urban development. Regionalism is strongly associated with sense of identity and has both positive and negative feelings. The cultural differences are vital in regionalism. The economic factors are most significant in feelings of regionalism. The lack of employment opportunities contribute to regionalism. Caste and religion are not very significant in feelings of regionalism. Promoting even development in all regions will help in resolving the problems related with regionalism. Sharing of waters is an important factor in development of regionalism. Most significantly it has been established that regionalism and urban development are related in the sense that the negative feeling associated with regionalism will hamper economic development. The following chapter is the last chapter which discusses the findings and presents the conclusions of the study.

6 Findings and Conclusions

The previous chapters dealt with various facets and aspects of cosmopolitanism, regionalism and urban development with specific context to Hyderabad. The post-globalization phase has brought several changes in all the spheres of human life. It has accelerated the mobility across continents, thus facilitating interaction with multiple economies and cultures. With specific reference to Hyderabad, the post-1990 phase not only brought the IT revolution but also many cultures to Hyderabad, consolidating Hyderabad's status as a cosmopolitan city. This is, however, not to suggest that cosmopolitanism in Hyderabad is a recent phenomenon.

Simultaneous to globalization, it is being witnessed that the regional and ethnic identities are becoming prominent world over. The people's movements to assert the regional and ethnic identities are assuming importance. It is, however, again not to suggest that regional feelings, identities and regionalism like cosmopolitanism is a recent phenomenon. The interplay between cosmopolitanism and regionalism in post-industrial societies, however, requires to be understood when both the processes are becoming highly significant even if in different perspectives.

Cosmopolitanism

The historical context of the philosophical resurgence of cosmopolitanism during the Enlightenment is made up of many factors: The increasing rise of capitalism and world-wide trade and its theoretical reflections; the reality of ever expanding empires whose reach extended across the globe; the voyages around the world and the 'discoveries' facilitated through these; the emergence of a notion of human rights and a philosophical focus on human reason. Under the influence of the American Revolution, and especially during the first years of the French Revolution, cosmopolitanism received its strongest impulse. The 1789 declaration of 'human' rights had grown out of cosmopolitan modes of thinking and reinforced them in turn.

In the eighteenth century, the terms 'cosmopolitanism' and 'world citizenship' were often used not as labels for determinative philosophical theories, but rather to indicate an attitude of open-mindedness and impartiality. A cosmopolitan was someone who was not subservient to a particular religious or political authority, someone who was not biased by particular loyalties or cultural prejudice. Furthermore, the term was sometimes used to indicate a person who led an urbane lifestyle, or who was fond of travelling, cherished a network of international contacts, or felt at home everywhere. In this sense the Encyclopédie mentioned that 'cosmopolitan' was often used to signify a 'man of no fixed abode, or a man who is nowhere a stranger'. Though philosophical authors such as Montesquieu, Voltaire, Diderot, Addison, Hume, and Jefferson identified themselves as cosmopolitans in one or more of these senses, these usages are not of much philosophical interest.

Especially in the second half of the century, however, the term was increasingly also used to indicate particular philosophical convictions. Rousseau complains that cosmopolitans 'boast that they love everyone (tout le monde, which also means "the whole world"), to have the right to love no one' (Geneva Manuscript version of The Social Contract, 158). Johann Georg Schlosser, in the critical poem *Der Kosmopolit* writes, 'It is better to be proud of one's nation than to have none', obviously assuming that cosmopolitanism implies the latter.

Yet most eighteenth-century defenders of cosmopolitanism did not recognize their own view in these critical descriptions. They understood cosmopolitanism not as a form of ultra-individualism, but rather, as implying the positive moral ideal of a universal human community, and they did not regard this ideal as inimical to more particular attachments such as patriotism. According to Immanuel Kant, all rational beings are members in a single moral community. They are analogous to citizens in the political (republican) sense in that they share the characteristics of freedom, equality, and independence, and that they give themselves the law. Their common laws, however, are the laws of morality, grounded in reason. Moral cosmopolitans regarded all humans as 'brothers' (though with obvious gender bias) – an analogy with which they aimed to indicate the fundamental equality of rank of all humans, which precluded slavery, colonial exploitation, feudal hierarchy, and tutelage of various sorts.

Some cosmopolitans developed their view into a political theory about international relations. The most radical of eighteenth-century political cosmopolitans was Anacharsis Cloots who advocated the abolition of all existing states and the establishment of a single world state under which all human individuals would be directly subsumed. His arguments drew first of all on the general structure of social contract theory. If it is in the general interest for everyone to submit to the authority of a state that enforces laws that provide security, then this argument applies worldwide and justifies the establishment of a world-wide 'republic of united individuals', not a plurality of states that find themselves in the state of nature vis-à-vis each other. Second, he argues that sovereignty should reside with the people, and that the concept of sovereignty itself, because it involves indivisibility, implies that there can be but one sovereign body in the world, namely, the human race as a whole

The most common cosmopolitanism – moral cosmopolitanism – does not always call itself such. But just as ancient cosmopolitanism was fundamentally a 'moral' commitment to helping human beings as such, much contemporary moral philosophy insists on the duty to aid foreigners who are starving or otherwise suffering, or at least on the duty to respect and promote basic human rights and justice. One can here distinguish between strict and moderate forms of cosmopolitanism.

Moral cosmopolitanism has sometimes led to political cosmopolitanism. Again, we can draw useful distinctions among the political cosmopolitans. Some advocate a centralized World State, some favour a federal system with a comprehensive global body of limited power, some would prefer more limited international political institutions that focus on particular concerns, (e.g., war crimes, environmental preservation), and some defend a different alternative altogether. Perhaps the most common invocations of the label 'cosmopolitan' in recent philosophical literature have been in the disputes over cultural cosmopolitanism. Especially, with disputes over multiculturalism in educational curricula and with resurgent nationalisms, cultural claims and counter-claims have received much attention. The cosmopolitan position in both of these kinds of disputes rejects exclusive attachments to parochial culture. So on the one hand, the cosmopolitan encourages cultural diversity and appreciates a multicultural mélange, and on the other hand, the cosmopolitan rejects a strong nationalism. Economic cosmopolitanism is perhaps less often defended among philosophers and more often among economists, (e.g., Hayek, Friedman) and certain politicians, especially in the richer countries of this world. It is the view that one ought to cultivate a single global economic market with free trade and minimal political involvement. It tends to be criticized rather than advanced by philosophical cosmopolitans, as many of them regard it as at least a partial cause of the problem of vast international economic inequality. These debates about the desirability of a fully globalized market have intensified in recent years, as a result of the end of the Cold War and the increasing reach of the market economy.

As *Stanford Encyclopedia of Philosophy* mentions the more serious and philosophically interesting challenges to cosmopolitanism come in two main forms. The first calls into question the possibility of realizing the cosmopolitan ideal, while the second queries its desirability. With reference to *political cosmopolitan* it is often argued that it is impossible to change the current system of states and to form a World State or a global federation of states. This claim is hard to maintain, however, in the face of the existence of the United Nations, the existence of states with more than a billion people of heterogeneous backgrounds, and the experience with the United States and the European Union. So in order to be taken seriously, the objection must instead be that it is impossible to form a good state or federation of that magnitude, i.e., that it is impossible to realize or even approximate the cosmopolitan ideal in a way that makes it worth pursuing and that does not carry prohibitive risks. Here, political cosmopolitans disagree among themselves. On one end of the spectrum we find those who argue in favour of a strong World State, on the other end we find the defenders of a loose and voluntary federation, or a different system altogether.

Some authors argue that the (partial or whole) surrender of state sovereignty required by the cosmopolitan scheme is an undue violation of the principle of the autonomy of states or the principle of democratic self-determination of their citizens.

Various arguments have been used to show that *economic cosmopolitanism* is not a viable option. Marx and later Marxists have argued that capitalism is self-destructive in the long run, because the exploitation, alienation, and poverty that it inflicts on the proletariat will provoke a world-wide revolution that will bring about the end of capitalism. In the twentieth century, when nationalist tendencies proved to be stronger (or in any case more easily mobilized) than international solidarity, and when the position of workers was strengthened to the point of making them unwilling to risk a revolution, this forced the Left to reconsider this view.

Critics of the economic cosmopolitan ideal have also started to emphasize another way in which capitalism bears the seeds of its own destruction within itself, namely, insofar as it is said to lead to a global environmental disaster that might spell the end of the human species, or in any event the end of capitalism as we know it. The effects of excessive consumption (in some parts of the world) and the exploitation of nature would make the earth inhospitable to future human generations. Even if one does not think that these first two problems are so serious as to make economic cosmopolitanism unviable, they can still make it seem undesirable in the eyes of those who are concerned with poverty and environmental destruction.

Moreover, there are several other concerns that lead critics to regard economic cosmopolitanism as undesirable. First among these is the lack of effective democratic control by the vast majority of the world's population, as large multinationals are able to impose demands on states that are in a weak economic position and their populations, demands that they cannot reasonably refuse to meet, although this does not mean that they meet them fully voluntarily. These concerns, for example, labour conditions or the use of raw materials in so-called Third World countries.

Second, economic cosmopolitans are accused of failing to pay attention to a number of probable side effects of a global free market. In particular, they are criticized for neglecting or downplaying issues such as (a) the presupposition of large-scale migration or reschooling when jobs disappear in one area (the loss of ties to friends and family, language, culture, etc., and the monetary costs of moving or retooling), (b) the lack of a guarantee that there will be a sufficient supply of living-wage jobs for all world citizens (especially given increasing automation), and (c) the problem of the detrimental effects of income disparities. They are similarly accused of failing to take seriously the fact that there might be circumstances under which it would be profitable for some states to be protectionist or wage war, such as wars about markets or raw materials and energy (e.g., oil).

Another version of the criticism of economic cosmopolitanism is, it targets the psychological assumptions of moral cosmopolitanism. Here it is said that human beings must have stronger attachments toward members of their own state or nation, and that attempts to disperse attachments to fellow-citizens in order to honour a moral community with human beings as such will cripple our sensibilities. If this is a viability claim and not simply a desirability claim, then it must be supposed that moral cosmopolitanism would literally leave large numbers of people unable to function. So, it is claimed that people need a particular sense of national identity in order to be agents, and that a particular sense of national identity requires attachment to particular others perceived to have a similar identity. This argument seems plausible if it is assumed that cosmopolitanism requires the same attitudes towards all other human beings, but moderate cosmopolitanism does not make that assumption. Rather, the moderate cosmopolitan has to insist only that there is some favourable, motivating attitude toward all human beings as such; this leaves room for some special attitudes towards fellow-citizens. Of course, the strict moral cosmopolitan will go further and will deny that fellow-citizens deserve any special attitudes, and it might be thought that this denial is what flouts the limits of human psychology. But this does not seem to be true as an empirical generalization. The cosmopolitan does not need to deny that some people do happen to have the need for national allegiance, so long as it is true that not all people do; and insofar as some people do, the strict cosmopolitan will say that perhaps it does not need to be that way and that cosmopolitan education might lead to a different result. The historical record gives even the strict cosmopolitan some cause for cheer, as human psychology and the forms of political organization have proven to be quite plastic.

Ulrich Beck speaks about three hostile forces to cosmopolitanism: first of all *nationalism*, second, *globalism* and third, *democratic authoritarianism*.

In sum, a range of interesting and difficult philosophical issues is raised by the disputes between cosmopolitans of various stripes and their critics. As the world becomes a smaller place through increased social, political, and economic contacts, these disputes and the issues they raise will only become more pressing.

The notion of cosmopolitanism in modern times is strongly associated with the material and physical facilities and infrastructure and is not merely confined to philosophy of accepting the world as home and not being a stranger anywhere in the world.

Regionalism

A region is a nucleus of social aggregation for a variety of purposes. A particular territory is set apart, over a period of time, when different variables operate in different degrees. These variables may be geography, topography, religion, language, usages and customs, socio-economic and political stages of development, common historical traditions and experiences, a common way of living, and, more than anything else, a widely prevalent sentiment of 'togetherness'. This togetherness leads to development of regionalism. At the core of regionalism is a profound sense of identity, which is as real, and as dear, to a people than their feeling of identity with a state or a nation or a religious group, or a linguistic group. These are cultural realities and one cannot wish them away.

An aggressive regionalism may develop from varying apprehensions and threats, real or perceived. To start, there may be economic competitions leading to fears about possible shrinking of job market. This is especially true on the part of working class and the lower middle class. We may cite the example of Telangana people's apprehensions against the Andhra-migrant. Then there may be status-threats posed by the migrants to the social status of the middle classes as was the case of Maharashtrian's fears against the South Indians in Bombay (now Mumbai). There may be political fears of some social classes to the threat of migrants to their long term interests.

Further, regionalism develops if the native population is likely to be immobile relative to other groups in the population, in other words, if the rate of in-migration is higher than that of out-migration.

Regionalism, and the concept of 'Sons-of-soil' raises certain basic questions with regard to relationship between the claims of individual citizens to equal access and the collective claims of ethnic groups to equality. This concept implies that the people belonging to a particular territory have a special and the first, if not exclusive, claim to all the welfare-facilities within the territory. This implies a sort of ownership by a specific group of territory it occupies. This also implies a special collective territorial right of an ethnic group. It means that the indigenous has a first claim on everything and the newcomers (migrants are outsiders) are entitled to benefits only after these have been adequately distributed to the indigenous population.

Regionalism in the Indian context, as perhaps elsewhere also, is a nebulous concept. It has both a positive and a negative dimension. Speaking in positive terms, it embodies a quest for self-fulfilment on the part of the people of an area. It is worthwhile to emphasize that the positive thrust of regionalism has, more often than not, been ignored by political analysis of the Indian situation. Every regional movement, thus, becomes suspect and is taken as an earnest of the balkanization of the country. Regionalism reflects a psyche of relative deprivation on the part of a people. More often than not, it is also believed, whether correctly or not, that deprivation is deliberately infected by the powers that be and this leads to acuteness of feeling on the part of those who carry the psyche of deprivation. The belief is easily cultivated in a milieu characterized by politics of scarcity as in India. The redeeming feature, however, is that to the extent the psyche of deprivation is the consequence of specific grievance, its growth could be halted and even the process reversed if the grievances are remedied.

Regionalism is a multidimensional phenomenon in terms of its components – geographical, historic-cultural, economic, politico-administrative and psychic. Indeed, economic component is the crux of regionalism. It is common knowledge that India is underdeveloped economically in spite of the many achievements registered since independence. The resources are scarce and demands disproportionately heavy and ever growing on account of continued population explosion. There is, thus, acute competition among individuals, groups and regions within a state.

Area of Study: Hyderabad

Hyderabad is one of the fastest growing cosmopolitan cities with people of different cultural and ethnic communities coming and living together. Since city life generates its own lifestyle and value system, at an apparent level the regional and cultural diversities seem to sink. However, at a latent level, regional identities are of tremendous significance. When the ethnicity of the regional groups is hit by globalization, regional identities are threatened and they become rigid and thus start the process of questioning cosmopolitanism.

In its historic evolution and development, Hyderabad city has experienced many changes since its foundation as the capital of the medieval kingdom of Golconda in the 16th century to its present status as the metropolis of a modern state. Each historic phase of development has significantly influenced its physical, social, economic and cultural growth. Hyderabad, under the influence of Deccan, Irani and native culture, synthesized and evolved its very own *Hyderabadi Tehzeeb*. It truly represented the assimilation (yet uniqueness) of diverse cultures which inhabited Hyderabad. More than four hundred years later HITEC City (Hyderabad) today presents a different picture. Whether it is its structural and spatial expansion, infrastructural development or its socio-cultural ethos, contemporary Hyderabad has evolved phenomenally and for many natives, beyond recognition. There is a need to understand the cultural journey of Hyderabad.

The city of Hyderabad was founded by Muhammad Quli Qutub Shah, the fifth ruler of the kingdom of Golconda, in AD 1591 on the south bank of the river Musi which is a major tributary of the river Krishna. Hyderabad (Bhagyanagar), the city of luck symbolizes spectrum of obsessions – love, pearls, cuisine, *pan,* Irani *chai*, beautiful monsoons and many more. The icing, however, is the *nawabi* style and splendorous *Ganga-Jamuna Tehzeeb.* Hyderabad culture is knitted through its history and thus to understand the various facets of *Hyderabadi Tehzeeb* it is worthwhile to walk down the memory lane of Qutub Shahis and Asaf Jahis, the dynasties which laid down the foundation of modern Hyderabad.

Cosmopolitanism in Hyderabad

Hyderabad was known originally as Bhagyanagar, a city Sultan Muhammad Quli of the Qutub Shahi dynasty had founded and named after his beloved Bhagmati or Bhagyamati in 1590. Once she entered the royal household and embraced Islam, she was rechristened Hydermahal and as a natural consequence, the city got its second name, Hyderabad. Hyderabad is one of metropolitan and cosmopolitan city of India. It is also described as a *panchanami sangam,* a place where five linguistic and cultural patterns met – Telugu, Marathi, Kannada, Tamil and Urdu have mingled and enriched a city famous for its Nawabi traditions of graciousness. Introducing a sixth culture stream to the sangam has been that of combination of French and British. However, the contemporary Hyderabad is a meeting point of several cultural strings.

Hyderabad and Secunderabad, the twin cities fused into one, is a city where north meets south, Islam meets Hinduism and consent meets cosmopolitanism. All the cultures that reigned left indelible marks and resulted in a unique cultural amalgam, a social blend to which modernism has added its might. Major industries, educational institutions and important research and training centres are located in this city that is the pride of Deccan which enjoys a central location in India. A mild climate and world values of courtesy and politeness are the attractions of the cosmopolitan city of Hyderabad.

Cosmopolitanism in Hyderabad can be witnessed in its food habits. Hyderabadis love to eat out and this is apparent from the number of restaurants and eating-joints that dot the landscape all across the city. They cater to a wide range of tastes offering everything from spicy Andhra cuisine to exotic Thai, and one can serve the delicious Hyderabadi Biryani and a fragrant cup of Irani Chai from any corner stall.

Hyderabad has witnessed several socio-economic and cultural changes in the past three decades, especially in the post-IT phase with establishment of HITEC City and several multinational companies coming to India. The process of globalization resulted in exchange of goods and services and enhanced the movement of people across countries and continents. The lifestyle of people in Hyderabad and its culture has undergone significant transformation. The respondents' opinion was asked on socio-cultural changes in Hyderabad.

The socio-economic changes are reflected in changes in family patterns (both structurally and functionally), caste-class nexus, changing occupational structure and forms of employment, the purchasing power and preferences, usage of consumer goods, etc. Culturally Hyderabad has witnessed increasing night life, highly diversified food preferences, westernized dressing patterns, changes in means of recreation, etc. While administering the schedule some respondents were of the opinion that Hyderabadi (some also said Deccani) tehzeeb has changed drastically.

The major findings and conclusions with reference to cosmopolitanism in Hyderabad are:

Most of the respondents (83.72%) feel that Hyderabad has witnessed socio-economic and cultural changes in the last one decade and most (70.97%) of the sample is of the opinion that Hyderabad has become more culturally diversified and heterogeneous during this period.

The respondents' opinion was sought whether Hyderabad has emerged as one of the fastest growing cosmopolitan cities. The analysis showed that most of the respondents have expressed their agreement. Most of the respondents (53.36%) strongly agree and 34.41 per cent agree with the notion that Hyderabad has emerged as one of the fastest growing cosmopolitan cities in India.

The respondents views were sought on variables and cultural traits such as dressing patterns and eating habits; lifestyles; folkways and mores as expressed through norms and values; traditions, customs; the other variables being – education, occupation, means of recreation and sociability. Most of the respondents (94.55%) felt that dressing patterns have undergone changes. There are 80.27 per cent of the respondents who are of the opinion that the eating habits have been altered. There are 83.44 per cent of the respondents who felt that there has been a noticeable change in lifestyles. Most of the respondents (75.11%) are of the notion that norms and values have changed. A little over two-thirds of the respondents (68.86%) believe that there has been a change in traditions and customs; while 27.08 per cent opine that the traditions and customs have not undergone changes. One of the respondent said Irani chai has not changed and neither have Charminar and Hyderabadi Nawabi style. About 72 per cent of the respondents feel that there has been a change in the type of occupations as far as Hyderabad is concerned. Over three-fourths of the respondents' (76.27%) have noticed changes in sociability, while about 20.47 per cent think otherwise. Most of the respondents (79.22%) have felt changes in education as against 16.66 per cent who have not.

Most of the respondents (70.38%) attribute these changes, (viz., the variables dressing patterns and eating habits; lifestyles, folkways and mores as expressed through norms and, Values; traditions, customs; the other variables being – education, occupation, means of recreation and sociability) to Hyderabad becoming a cosmopolitan city.

A majority of 1,631 respondents, accounting for 45.30 per cent of the respondents have felt that different cultures do not peacefully coexist in Hyderabad. This view can be possibly attributed to the conditions prevailing in Hyderabad for the past 3–4 years. The respondents expressed their unhappiness over frequent bandhs and agitations and communal riots which affected some parts of Hyderabad to a great extent. Despite the distrurbances and agitations most of the respondents (83.16%) believe that Hyderabad has developed a cosmopolitan outlook.

Cosmopolitanism and Urban Development

Hyderabad has developed into a cosmopolitan city. It is thus significant to understand whether cosmopolitanism has contributed to urban development. The emergence of new economy industries has catapulted Hyderabad to a prime position in India. The new economy industries and the international airport have placed Hyderabad as a regional hub in this part of the world.

In a fast globalizing world, it is essential for Hyderabad to offer world-class services to attract global investments and urban development. Apart from services, global investments are possible only in a cosmopolitan ambience. The city is experiencing a severe strain on its infrastructure, due to rapid urbanization, unplanned growth and industrial development. The city is deficient in service delivery and trails other Indian metropolitan cities on most service delivery outcomes. Hyderabad has a low rating in terms of parameters like GDP, literacy rate, drop-out rate, child mortality rate, sewerage, transportation, etc. But yet there is potential for growth, as Hyderabad is establishing itself as a technology hub through initiation of various reforms. Its cosmopolitan character can facilitate in urban development. However, past few years of agitation has influenced Hyderabad brand to a great extent.

It is vital to note that cosmopolitanism is not merely a philosophy, attitude of universalism and cultural amalgamation but also a catalyst for change and development. With specific reference to Hyderabad, the respondents views have been sought – whether cosmopolitanism has brought about urban development or not.

The major findings and conclusions with reference to cosmopolitanism and urban development in Hyderabad are:

Majority of the respondents (66.55%) believe that cosmopolitanism has improved the living conditions of people in Hyderabad; while 32.30 per cent have negated this. Further, majority of the respondents (64.58%) believe that Hyderabad has developed owing to cosmopolitanism. This is refuted by about 34.08 per cent of the respondents.

The respondents' opinion was taken with regard to improvement in basic facilities and services owing to cosmopolitanism. The facilities and services are – health facilities, roads, public transport, housing, employment opportunities, educational prospects, governance and administration, purchasing power, banking services, and communication services. People believe that health facilities have improved as a result of Hyderabad becoming a cosmopolitan city. A highly substantial part of the sample size, 89.97 per cent, agrees to the above said. Most of the respondents (71.41%) feel that roads have improved as a result of Hyderabad becoming a cosmopolitan city; while 28.27 per cent of the respondents oppose this.

As far as public transport is concerned, most of the respondents (73.05%) feel it has improved. This is refuted by 25.36 per cent of the sample size. Majority of the respondents (67.67%) feel that housing has improved during the Hyderabad's transition to a cosmopolitan city. About 31.36 per cent of them have disagreed with this. Of the total sample size, 49.44 per cent believe that employment opportunities have improved as a result of Hyderabad becoming a cosmopolitan city; while 50.22 per cent refute the claim. A majority of the respondents, i.e., 72.72 per cent believe that educational prospects have improved, owing to Hyderabad becoming a cosmopolitan city. A majority of respondents, i.e., 65.05 per cent feel that governance and administration have not improved as a result of Hyderabad becoming a cosmopolitan city. This is refuted by 30.94 per cent of the sample; while 4 per cent are unsure of either.

About 64 per cent of the respondents feel that purchasing power has improved as Hyderabad is turning out to be an increasingly cosmopolitan city. About 77.38 per cent of the respondents feel that banking services have improved owing to Hyderabad's transition to a cosmopolitan city. A majority of the respondents, i.e., 2,279 accounting for 63.30 per cent of the sample believe that globalization has contributed in development of cosmopolitanism in Hyderabad. A discernable majority of respondents accounting for 79.69 per cent of the sample believe that cosmopolitanism enhances togetherness among people who are culturally diverse. This is a contributing factor for urban development. About 63.41 per cent of the respondents feel that cosmopolitanism increases the prospects of social mobility. Interestingly, majority of the respondents (2,246), accounting for 62.38 per cent of the sample feel that cosmopolitanism reduces conflicts by enhancing intercultural contact and interaction between people. The majority of the respondents (55.72%) feel that cosmopolitanism helps in resolving the problems associated with separatism and segregation.

A majority of 2,573 respondents, making up to 71.47 per cent of the sample see a relationship between cosmopolitanism and urban development.

Regionalism and Urban Development

Regionalism is a multidimensional phenomenon a feeling or sentiment backed by objective factors like language, culture, economic development, etc. It is a manifestation of emotional, psychological and sub-national socio-cultural forces confined to a particular region within a larger political set-up. Regional imbalances are producing both prosperity and poverty among regions. Within the regions they are also giving rise to the birth of two classes – rich and poor. The regional movements especially if separatist in nature cause economic losses which influences the rate of urban development.

On the question of whether regionalism is associated with any sense of identity (for example a state, a nation, a religious group or a linguistic group), most of the respondents (79.55%) have responded in the affirmative. A majority of respondents (2,129), accounting 59.13 per cent of the sample possess both positive and negative feelings associated with regionalism. This is followed by negative feelings that accounts for a quarter, i.e., 25.19 per cent of the sample and then, a positive imagery of about 13.25 per cent of the total sample size.

A highly substantial majority of the respondents (83.63%) feel that cultural differences are responsible for development of regionalism. About 63.02 per cent of the sample size sees a relationship between regionalism and migration. This is contested by 29.22 per cent of respondents, while 7.75 per cent have not given any opinion. When questioned, if reduction in in-migration help solve the problems related to regionalism, about 69.27 per cent of the sample size responded in the affirmative. They believe that it will solve the problems related to regionalism.

About three-fourths of the sample size, i.e., 75.22 per cent believes that the most important cause for regionalism is economic. When we analysed migration, a similar trend was reflected; a majority of respondents felt that economic causes were majorly responsible for migration. Relative deprivation is considered to be the root cause of regionalism. This deprivation is glaringly manifested in the economic sphere; acting as a fuel in accentuating regionalist feelings. Second comes cultural accounting for 35.58 per cent of the sample. According to few theorists, India's cultural and linguistic diversity is the major contributor to regionalism. They argue that language and culture becomes the core of an individual's identity, which when politicized take a virulent turn. This is followed by political (30.55% of the sample), psychological (26.63% of the sample), and social (about 25.08% of the sample). Other reasons accounted for about 8.22 per cent of the sample, while geographical reasons took the last position (3.30% of the sample).

An overwhelming number of respondents, 3,166 of them, accounting for 87.94 per cent of the sample, feel that lack of employment opportunities contribute to negative effects of regionalism. A majority of respondents, 79.83 per cent of the sample are of the notion that maldevelopment contributed to the development of negative feelings of regionalism. About two-thirds of the sample size agree (and strongly agree) on the notion that regionalism leads to disintegration of a country. However, nearly one-third of the respondents disagree (and strongly disagree) to this notion. Of the individual responses, 'strongly agree' is the most opted response, accounting for 44.94 per cent of the sample; followed by 'disagree' (about 31.08% of the sample), 'agree' (21.19% of the sample), 'strongly disagree' (barely accounting for 1.4% of the total sample size).

Regionalism is the result of feeling of deprivation on the part of a people of an area.

Nearly two-thirds, i.e., 65.05 per cent of the respondents feel that regionalism is the result of feeling of deprivation on the part of a people. A majority (66.91% of the sample) feel that caste does not play a role in the context of regionalism. A substantial majority of respondents, accounting for 81.88 per cent of the sample feel inequitable sharing of waters plays a major role in the context of regionalism. An overwhelming 87.44 per cent of the respondents feel that language plays a major role in the context of regionalism. Nearly 85 per cent agree (and strongly agree) that economic imbalances are responsible for regionalism. This is corroborated by numerous studies so far, which held economic, (viz., regional) imbalances accentuate regionalism. When uneven development creates profound regional imbalances, the peripheral (marginalized or excluded) regions engage in regionalist movements to secure more equal distribution of economic rewards. A substantial number of respondents, accounting for 86.30 per cent of the sample feel that most of the demands for constituting new states are based on unequal distribution of development benefits. Around 62.38 per cent of the respondents see regionalism as a very serious threat to the development, progress and unity of the country. Approximately three-fourths of the sample feels that regionalism encourages people to develop a sense of brotherhood and commonness on the basis of common language, religion or historical background. An overwhelming majority of respondents have 'strongly agreed' (66.27%) and 'agreed' (21.77%) that promoting even development of the neglected areas will resolve the problems associated with regionalism and thus accelerate urban development. A little over three-fourths, i.e., 76.19 per cent of the sample sees a relationship between regionalism and urban development, i.e., if the problems associated with regionalism go beyond control then development in urban areas is hampered.

Significant Relationships

The present study discussed certain significant relationships between variables like age and cosmopolitanism; caste and cosmopolitanism; language and regionalism; income and cosmopolitanism; educational qualifications and regionalism; nature of employment and regionalism.

Age and Cosmopolitanism

Null Hypothesis: There is no significant difference between age and feelings towards cosmopolitanism.

Table 6.1 *Age and Cosmopolitanism*

Age Composition (in years)	*Total No. of Respondents*	*No. of Respondents*	*Total*
Below 20 Years	49	40	89
21–30 years	209	201	410
31–40 years	1,437	1,021	2,458
41–50 years	1,823	941	2,764
51–60 years	57	41	98
61–70 years	18	9	27
71–80 years	7	2	9
Total	3,600	2,255	5,855

$\chi^2 = 58.67$, Significant at 0.01 and 0.05 levels of significance.

Calculated value of χ^2 is greater than the table value. Therefore, null hypothesis is rejected, i.e., there is significant difference between age and feelings towards cosmopolitanism.

Caste and Cosmopolitanism

Null Hypothesis: There is no significant difference between caste and feelings towards cosmopolitanism.

Table 6.2 *Caste and Cosmopolitanism*

Caste	*Total No. of Respondents*	*No. of Respondents*	*Total*
SC	932	530	1,462
ST	509	418	927
BC	966	812	1,778
OC	1,126	937	2,063
Any Other	67	29	96
Total	3,600	2,726	6,326

$\chi^2 = 45.25$, Significant at 0.01 and 0.05 levels of significance.

Calculated value of χ^2 is greater than the table value. Therefore, null hypothesis is rejected, i.e., there is significant difference between caste and feelings towards cosmopolitanism.

Language and Regionalism

Null Hypothesis: There is no significant difference between language and feelings towards regionalism (regional identity).

Table 6.3 *Language and Regionalism*

Language	*Total No. of Respondents*	*No. of Respondents*	*Total*
Telugu	1,398	1,324	2,722
Urdu	1,034	989	2,023
Hindi	597	201	798
Any Other	571	321	892
Total	3,600	2,835	6,435

χ^2= 181.17, Significant at 0.01 and 0.05 levels of significance.

Calculated value of χ^2 is greater than the table value. Therefore, null hypothesis is rejected, i.e., there is significant difference between language and feelings towards regionalism (regional identity).

Income and Cosmopolitanism

Null Hypothesis: There is no significant difference between different income levels and favourability towards cosmopolitanism.

Table 6.4 *Income and Cosmopolitanism*

Income (Per month)	*Total No. of Respondents*	*No. of Respondents*	*Total*
Less than Rs 10,000	77	12	89
Rs. 10,001 to Rs 20, 000	485	218	703
Rs. 21,001 to Rs 30,000	1,736	1,241	2,977
Rs. 31,001 to Rs 40,000	1,081	956	2,037
More than Rs 40,000	221	203	424
Total	3,600	2,630	6,230

χ^2= 90.72, Significant at 0.01 and 0.05 levels of significance.

Calculated value of χ^2 is greater than the table value. Therefore, null hypothesis is rejected, i.e., there is significant difference between different income levels and favourability towards cosmopolitanism.

Educational Qualifications and Regionalism

Null Hypothesis: There is no significant difference between educational qualifications and feelings towards regionalism.

Table 6.5 *Educational Qualifications and Regionalism*

Educational Qualifications	*Total No. of Respondents*	*No. of Respondents*	*Total*
Illiterate	8	7	15
Literate	213	202	415
Primary School	37	21	58
Secondary school	125	112	237
Intermediate	105	99	204
Degree	319	186	505
PG	1,969	1,398	3,367
Professional Education	736	701	1,437
M.Phil	12	10	22
Ph.D	58	33	91
Any other	18	12	30
Total	3,600	2,781	6,381

χ^2= 42.09, Significant at 0.01 and 0.05 levels of significance.

Calculated value of χ^2 is greater than the table value. Therefore, null hypothesis is rejected, i.e., there is significant difference between educational qualifications and feelings towards regionalism.

Nature of Employment and Regionalism

Null Hypothesis: There is no significant difference between nature of employment (Govt/private) and feelings towards regionalism.

Table 6.6 *Nature of Employment and Regionalism*

Nature of Employment	*Total No. of Respondents*	*No. of Respondents*	*Total*
Private Employment	1,662	1,024	2,686
Govt. Employment	1,938	1,739	3,677
Total	3,600	2,763	6,363

χ^2= 53.11, Significant at 0.01 and 0.05 levels of significance.

Calculated value of χ^2 is greater than the table value. Therefore, null hypothesis is rejected, i.e., there is significant difference between nature of employment (Govt/private) and feelings towards regionalism.

Policy Implications

The research very clearly proves that regionalism has both positive and negative effects. The negative effects of regionalism can be curtailed only by balanced regional development. As the forces of globalization are becoming prominent, simultaneously cosmopolitanism and regionalism are reflected very prominently in day-to-day living. For instance when globalization is affecting the regional identities there is greater assertion for the same. On the other hand, globalization has increased greatly in migration and out-migration and thus greater exposure to multiple cultures and lifestyles and in turn, leading to cosmopolitanism. Interestingly, the study also proves that both forces of cosmopolitanism and regionalism are strongly associated with urban development. In this background the clear policy implications of the research study are:

- An integrated effort by the state and civil society for balanced regional development.
- The regional conflicts to be controlled sternly since it halts urban development.
- To create and enhance skills, better employment and educational opportunities, health facilities and build up a strong and sustainable infrastructure for urban development. If all are developing equally, the negatives of regionalism will be wiped out and positives of cosmopolitanism will be increased.
- The post-industrial cities are service and growth centres encouraging cosmopolitan outlook since the focus is on economic growth. There is need to provide all infrastructural (physical and social) support for further growth and sustainable development.
- There is a greater need to have 'glocal' appeal in all our policies (think globally and act locally). Focus should be on capacity building measures and effective urban governance.
- To strengthen the secular outlook and social tolerance towards diversities.

Conclusion

The present study began with the premise that the globalization of economies, migration, culture and communications, combined with a worldwide reassertion of diverse cultural affiliations, are producing intense pressures on the coexistence of different national, ethnic, religious, racial, and linguistic groups who share the same cities. This has its implications on the development process of urban areas. In cities throughout the world, social tensions and open conflict over region, culture and identity are overwhelming all other aspects of normal urban life. The post-industrial cities suffer different degrees of social disintegration and physical destruction, sometimes so severe that the future possibilities for peace, security and sustained urban development cannot be foreseen. The present study aimed to understand how cosmopolitanism is related with regionalism. Further, it also attempted to understand how negatives of extreme regionalism lead to regional conflicts.

In the present globalized cities the forces of cosmopolitanism and regionalism operate simultaneously. At least, with reference to Hyderabad it has been proven true. In both the forces urban economy and development are critical factors. This means that for present-day urban development, both are required but definitely in a balanced share. If cosmopolitanism fosters universality and social tolerance, regionalism consolidates brotherhood. All these ingredients are vital for creating ambience for urban development.

It is significant to state that the cosmopolitanism helps in reducing or exaggerating regional conflicts. Moreover, the notions of cosmopolitanism and regionalism are strongly associated with the process of urban development.

References

Alam, S.M. and W. Khan (1972). *Metropolitan Hyderabad and its Region: A Strategy for Development*, Bombay: Asia Publishing House, pp. 5–6.

Albrow, Martin (1996). *The Global Age*, Cambridge: Polity Press.

Alikhan, Raza (1986). *Hyderabad: A City in History*, Hyderabad: Allen.

—— (1991). *Hyderabad 400 Years (1591–1991)*, Australia: Allen and Unwin.

Amin, Ash (2004). 'Multi-Ethnicity and the Idea of Europe', *Theory, Culture and Society*, 21(2): 1–24.

Anderson, A. (1998). 'Cosmopolitanism, Universalism, and the Divided Legacies of Modernity', in P. Cheah and B. Robbins (eds), *Cosmopolitics: Thinking and Feeling Beyond the Nation*, Minneapolis and London: University of Minnesota Press, pp. 265–89.

—— (2001). *The Powers of Distance: Cosmopolitanism and the Cultivation of Detachment*, Princeton, NJ: Princeton University Press.

Anderson, Benedict (1991). *Imagined Communities: Reflections on the Origin and Spread of Nationalism*, London: Verso.

Appadurai, A. (1993). 'Patriotism and its Futures', *Public Culture*, 5(3): 411–29.

—— (2000). 'Grassroots Globalization and the Research Imagination', *Public Culture*, 12(1): 1–19.

Appiah, K. (2006). *The Ethics of Identity*, Princeton, NJ: Princeton University Press.

Archibugi, D. (2000). 'Cosmopolitical Democracy', *New Left Review*, 4: 137–50.

—— (2004). 'Cosmopolitan Guidelines for Humanitarian Intervention', *Alternatives*, 29: 1–21.

Archibugi, D. and D. Held (1995). 'Editors' Introduction', in D. Archibugi and D. Held (eds.), *Cosmopolitan Democracy: An Agenda for a New World Order*, Cambridge: Polity.

Arendt, Hannah (1968). *Men in Dark Times*, New York: Harcourt Brace.

—— (1986). *The Origins of Totalitarianism*, London: André Deutsch.

Arjomand, Saïd Amir (2004). 'Social Theory and the Changing World: Mass Democracy, Development, Modernization and Globalization', *International Sociology*, 19(3): 321–53.

Banagiri, Vanaja (2007). *Butterflies and Barbed Wires*, Delhi: Rupa.

Barber, B. (1996). 'Constitutional Faith', in J. Cohen (ed.), *For Love of Country*, Boston, MA: Beacon Press.

Barry, B. (1999). 'Statism and Nationalism: A Cosmopolitan Critique', in I. Shapiro and L. Brilmayer (eds), *Nomos Global Justice*, New York: New York University Press.

Bauman, Zygmunt (1997). 'The Making and Unmaking of Strangers', *Thesis Eleven*, 43: 1–16.

—— (2003). *Liquid Love: On the Frailty of Human Bonds*, Cambridge: Polity Press.

Beck, U. (1992). *Risk Society: Towards a New Modernisation*, London: Sage.

—— (1998). 'Cosmopolitan Manifesto', *New Statesman*, 20 March.

—— (1999). *What is Globalization?* Cambridge: Polity Press.

—— (2000a). 'The Cosmopolitan Perspective: Sociology of the Second Age of Modernity', *British Journal of Sociology*, 51(1): 79–106.

—— (2000b). *World Risk Society*, Cambridge: Polity Press.

—— (2001). 'Cosmopolitan Social Science: Redefining "Power" for the Global Age', Lecture for the New School of Social Research, April.

—— (2002a). 'The Cosmopolitan Society and its Enemies', *Theory, Culture and Society*, 19(1–2): 17–44.

—— (2002b). 'Rooted Cosmopolitanism', in U. Beck and N. Sznaider (eds), *Global America? The Cultural Consequences of Globalization*, Frankfurt/M: Suhrkamp (forthcoming).

—— (2002c). 'The Terrorist Threat: World Risk Society Revisited', *Theory, Culture and Society*, 19(4): 39–55.

—— (2003a). 'Understanding the Real Europe', *Dissent*, 50 (Summer): 32–38.

—— (2003b). 'Toward a New Critical Theory with a Cosmopolitan Intent', *Constellations*, 10(4): 453–68.

—— (2004). 'Cosmopolitical Realism: On the Distinction between Cosmopolitanism in Philosophy and the Social Sciences', *Global Networks*, 4(2): 131–56.

—— (2006). *Cosmopolitan Vision*, Cambridge: Polity Press.

Beck, U. and E. Beck-Gernsheim (2002). *Individualization*, London: Sage.

Beggs, J.J., J.S. Hurlbert and V.A. Hains (1996). 'Community Attachment in a Rural Setting: A Refinement and Empirical Test of the Systemic Model', *Rural Sociology*, 61(3): 407–26.

Bendix, Reinhardt and Benett Berger (1959). 'Images of Society and Problems of Concept Formation in Sociology', in L. Gross (ed.), *Symposium on Sociological Theory*, New York: Harper and Row.

Benhabib, Seyla (2002). 'In Search of Europe's Borders', *Dissent*, 49 (Fall): 33–39.

—— (2004). *The Claims of Culture: Equality and Diversity in the Global Era*, Princeton, NJ: Princeton University Press.

Berger, Peter, Brigitte Berger and Hansfried Kellner (1974). *The Homeless Mind: Modernization and Consciousness*, New York: Vintage Books.

Berges, Sandrine (2005). 'Loneliness and Belonging: Is Stoic Cosmopolitanism Still Defensible?', *Res Publica*, 11(1): 3–25.

Bernstorff, D. (1979). 'Region and Nation: The Telangana Movement's Dual Identity', in David Taylor and Malcolm Yapp (eds.), *Political Identity in South Asia*, London: Curzon, p. 140.

Bhalla, G.S. and Y.K. Alagh (1982). 'Green Revolution and Small Peasants: A Study of Income Distribution in Punjab Agriculture', *Economic and Political Weekly*, 7, 2 May: 876.

Bhattacharya, B. (2006). *Urban Development in India*, New Delhi: Concept Publishers.

Bhaunani, A.P.A. (January 1917). 'A Short History and the Foundation and Growth of the City of Hyderabad and Some of its Buildings', *The Journal of the Hyderabad Archeological Society*.

Billig, M. (1995). *Banal Nationalism*, London: Sage.

Bhushan, M. Bharath and N. Venugopal (eds.) (2009). *Telangana: The State of Affairs*, Hyderabad: AdEd Value Ventures.

Bourne, L.S. (1975). *Urban System: Strategies for Regulation*, Oxford: Clarendon.

Brass, Paul (1994). *The Politics of India Since Independence*, Second Edition, Cambridge: Cambridge University Press.

Brennan, T. (2001). 'Cosmopolitanism and Internationalism', *New Left Review*, 2(7): 75–84.

Burnett, J. (2007). 'Britain's "Civilising Project": Community Cohesion and Core Values', *Policy and Politics*, 35(2): 353–57.

Cabral, A. (1979). *Unity and Struggle: Speeches and Writings*, trans. M. Wolfers, New York: Monthly Review.

Calhoun, Craig (1999). 'Nationalism, Political Community and the Representation of Society. Or, Why Feeling at Home is Not a Substitute for Public Space', *European Journal of Social Theory*, 2(2): 217–31.

—— (2002). 'Imagining Solidarity: Cosmopolitanism, Constitutional Patriotism, and the Public Sphere', *Public Culture*, 14(1): 147–71.

—— (2003). '"Belonging" in the Cosmopolitan Imaginary', *Ethnicities*, 3(4): 531–68.

Campbell, L.B. (2005). 'The Political Economy of Environmental Regionalism in Asia', in T.J. Pempel (ed.), *Remapping East Asia: The Construction of a Region*, Ithaca, NY: Cornell University Press, pp. 216–35.

Carter, A. (2001). *The Political Theory of Global Citizenship*, London and New York: Routledge.

Castells, M. (1997). *The Power of Identity*, Oxford: Blackwell.

Cheah, P. and B. Robbins (eds) (1996 and 1998). *Cosmopolitics: Thinking and Feeling Beyond the Nation*, Minneapolis and London: University of Minnesota Press.

Cheah, P. (2006a). 'Cosmopolitanism', *Theory, Culture and Society*, 23(2–3): 486–96.

—— (2006b). *Inhuman Conditions: On Cosmopolitanism and Human Rights*, Cambridge: Harvard University Press.

Chernilo, D. (2006a). 'Methodological Nationalism and its Critique', in G. Delanty and K. Kumar (eds), *The Sage Handbook of Nations and Nationalism*, London: Sage.

—— (2006b). 'Social Theory's Methodological Nationalism', *European Journal of Social Theory*, 9(1): 5–22.

—— (2007). *A Social Theory of the Nation–State*, London: Routledge.

—— (2008). 'Classical Sociology and the Nation–State', *Journal of Classical Sociology*, 8(1): 27–43.

Clifford, J. (1998). 'Mixed Feelings', in P. Cheah and B. Robbins (eds), *Cosmopolitics: Thinking and Feeling Beyond the Nation*, Minneapolis and London: University of Minnesota Press, pp. 362–70.

Cohen, Robin and Robert Fine (2002). 'Four Moments of Cosmopolitanism', in R. Cohen and S. Vortevec (eds), *Conceiving Cosmopolitanism*, Oxford: Oxford University Press, pp. 137–64.

Cohen, Jean (2004). 'Whose Sovereignty? Empire versus International Law', *Ethics and International Affairs*, 18(3): 1–24.

Coleman, James S. (1990). *Foundations of Social Theory*, London: The Belknap Press of Harvard University Press.

Dahrendorf, R. (1999). 'Whatever Happened to Liberty?', *New Statesman*, 6 September: 25–27.

Dalrymple, William (2004). *White Mughals: Love and Betrayal in Eighteenth-Century India*, New Delhi: Penguin.

Dallmayr, F. (1996). *Beyond Orientalism: Essays on Cross-Cultural Encounter*, New York: State University of New York Press.

Das Gupta, Jyotirindra (1997). 'Nation, Region and Welfare: Ethnicity, Regionalism and Development Politics in South Asia', *Annals AAPSS*, September, p. 132.

Dave, Robert (1958). 'Regionalism in Maharashtra', *Janta*, 13, 23 March.

Delanty, G. (2000). *Citizenship in a Global Age: Society, Culture, Politics*, Buckingham: Open University Press.

—— (2003). 'The Making of a Post-Western Europe: A Civilizational Analysis', *Thesis Eleven*, 72: 8–24.

—— (2005). 'The Idea of a Cosmopolitan Europe', *International Review of Sociology*, 15(3): 405–21.

—— (2006a). 'The Cosmopolitan Imagination: Critical Cosmopolitanism and Social Theory', Special Issue on Cosmopolitan Sociology, *British Journal of Sociology*, 57(1): 25–47.

—— (ed.) (2006b). *Europe and Asia Beyond East and West*, London: Routledge.

—— (2006c). 'Cosmopolitanism and Nationalism', in G. Delanty and C. Rumford, *Rethinking Europe: Social Theory and the Implications of Europeanization*, London: Routledge.

Derrida, Jacques (1997). *Cosmopolites de Tous les Pays, Encore un Effort!* Paris: Galilée.

Deutsch, E. (ed.) (1991). *Culture and Modernity: East-West Philosophic Perspectives*, Honolulu: Hawaii University Press.

Dharwadker, V. (2001). 'Introduction: Cosmopolitanism in its Time and Place', in V. Dharwadker (ed.), *Cosmopolitan Geographies: New Locations in Literature and Culture*, New York and London: Routledge, pp. 1–13.

Diderot, D. and J.L.R. d'Alembert (1751–65). *Encyclopédie ou Dictionnaire raisonné des Sciences, des Arts, et des Métiers*, Paris: Briasson, David, Le Breton, Durand.

Dirlik, A. and X. Zhang (eds) (2000). *Postmodernism and China*, Durham, NC: Duke University Press.

Donnelly, Jacques (1989). *Universal Human Rights in Theory and Practice*, London: Cornell University Press.

Dryzek, J. (2006). *Deliberative Global Politics: Discourse and Democracy in a Divided World*, Cambridge: Polity Press.

Durkheim, Emile (1915). *Germany Above All*, Paris: Collin.

—— (1964a). *The Division of Labour in Society*, New York: The Free Press.

—— (1964b). *The Rules of Sociological Method*, New York: The Free Press.

—— (1973). 'Individualism and the Intellectuals', in R. Bellah (ed.), *On Morality and Society*, Chicago: University of Chicago Press.

—— (1992). *Professional Ethics and Civic Morals*, London and New York: Routledge and Kegan Paul.

Durkheim, E. and M. Mauss (1998). 'Between Sociology and Anthropology, I: Note on the Notion of Civilization', in J. Rundell and S. Mennell (eds.), *Classical Readings in Culture and Civilization*, London: Routledge.

Eagleton, T. (2000). *The Idea of Culture*, Oxford: Blackwell.

Edwards, R.R. (2001). '"The Metropol and the Mayster-toun": Cosmopolitanism and Late Medieval Literature', in V. Dharwadker (ed.), *Cosmopolitan Geographies: New Locations in Literature and Culture*, New York and London: Routledge, pp. 33–62.

Elias, N. (1991). *The Society of Individuals*, Oxford: Basil Blackwell.

—— (1994). *The Established and Outsiders*, London: Sage.

Emmet, Dorothy (1994). *The Role of the Unrealisable: A Study in Regulative Ideals*, New York: St. Martin's Press.

Falk, Richard (1994). 'The Making of Global Citizenship', in Bart van Steenbergen (ed.), *The Condition of Citizenship*, London: Sage, pp. 127–40.

Fanon, F. (1963). *The Wretched of the Earth*, trans. C. Farrington, New York: Grove Press.

Featherstone, Mike (2002). 'Cosmopolis: An Introduction', *Theory, Culture and Society*, 19(1–2): 1–16.

Fichte, J.G. (1978). *Reden an die deutsche Nation*, Hamburg: Felix Meiner.

Fine, Robert (2001). *Political Investigations: Hegel, Marx, Arendt*, London: Routledge.

—— (2002). *Democracy and the Rule of Law*, New Jersey: The Blackburn Press.

—— (2003). 'Taking the "Ism" Out of Cosmopolitanism: An Essay in Reconstruction', *European Journal of Social Theory*, 6(4): 451–70.

—— (2006). 'Cosmopolitanism and Violence: Difficulties of Judgement', *British Journal of Sociology*, 57(1): 49–67.

Fine, Robert and Daniel Chernilo (2004). 'Between Past and Future: The Equivocations of the New Cosmopolitanism', *Studies in Law, Politics, and Society*, 31: 25–44.

Fishkin, J.S. and R.C. Luskin (2005). 'Experimenting with a Democratic Ideal: Deliberative Polling and Public Opinion', *Acta Politica*, 40: 284–98.

Flanagan, S.C. (1982). 'Changing Values in Advanced Industrial Societies', *Comparative Political Studies*, 14: 403–44.

Flikschuh, Katrin (2004). 'The Limits of Liberal Cosmopolitanism', *Res Publica*, 10(2): 175–92.

Forrester, Duncan B. (1970). 'Sub-regionalism in India', *Pacific Affairs*, 43(1): 5–21.

Francis, Christina (2012). 'Twin Cities, Four Identities', *Hyderabad Times*, 22 September.

Frank, A.G. (1998). *Re-Orient: Global Economy in the Asian Age*, Berkeley: University of California Press.

Freitag, Michel (2002). 'The Dissolution of Society within the "Social"', *European Journal of Social Theory*, 5(2): 175–98.

Frisby, David and Derek Sayer (1986). *Society*, London: Ellis Horwood and Tavistock.

Frost, M. (1996). *Ethics in International Relations: A Constitutive Theory*, Cambridge: Cambridge University Press.

Gadamer, G.H. (1975). *Truth and Method*, London: Sheed and Ward.

Gangas, Spiros (2004). 'Axiological and Normative Dimensions in George Simmel's Philosophy and Sociology: A Dialectical Interpretation', *History of the Human Sciences*, 17(4): 17–44.

Gaonkar, D.P. (ed.) (2001). *Alternative Modernities*, Durham, NC: Duke University Press.

Giddens, Anthony (1991). *Modernity and Self-Identity: Self and Society in the Late Modern Age*, Stanford, CA: Stanford University Press.

—— (1994). *Beyond Left and Right*, Cambridge: Polity Press.

—— (2002). *Runaway World: How Globalisation is Reshaping Our Lives*, London: Profile Books.

Gilroy, P. (1993). *The Black Atlantic: Modernity and Double Consciousness*, London and New York: Verso.

Gohman, V.M., M. Lappote, I.M. Mayergoiz and Y.G. Mashbits (1976). 'The Economic-Geographical Aspects of World Urbanization and its Specific Features in the Developing Countries', cf. S.M. Alam and V.V. Pokshishevsky (eds.), *Urbanization in Developing Countries*, Hyderabad: Osmania University Press, p. 29.

Golmohamad, Muna (2004). 'World Citizenship, Identity and the Notion of an Integrated Self', *Studies in Philosophy and Education*, 23: 131–48.

Gouldner, Alvin W. (1957). 'Cosmopolitans and Locals: Toward an Analysis of Latent Social Roles I', *Administrative Science Quarterly*, 2(3): 281–306.

—— (1958). 'Cosmopolitans and Locals: Toward an Analysis of Latent Social Roles II', *Administrative Science Quarterly*, 2(4): 444–80.

Gubert, R. (1999). *Territorial Belonging between Ecology and Culture*, Trento: University of Trento Press.

—— (2000). 'Territorial Belonging', in E.F. Borgotta and R.J.V. Montgomery (eds.), *Encyclopedia of Sociology*, Vol. 5, New York: Macmillan, pp. 3128–37.

Guha, Ramachandra (1989). *The Unquiet Woods: Ecological Change and Peasant Resistance in the Himalayas*, New Delhi: Oxford University Press.

Guibernau, M. (2004). *Catalan Nationalism: Francoism, Transition and Democracy*, London: Routledge.

Guruswamy, Mohan (2008). There was Once a Hyderabad. http://www.india-seminar.com

Gutman, Amy (2002). 'Civic Minimalism, Cosmopolitanism, and Patriotism', in Stephen Macedo and Yael Tamir (eds), *Moral and Political Education*, New York: New York University Press, pp. 23–57.

Habermas, Jürgen (1997). 'Kant's Idea of Perpetual Peace, with the Benefit of Two Hundred Years Hindsight', in James Bohman and

Matthias Lutz-Bachmann (eds), *Perpetual Peace: Essays on Kant's Cosmopolitan Ideal*, Cambridge, MA: MIT Press.

—— (1998a). *Postmetaphysical Thinking*, Cambridge: Polity Press.

—— (1998b). *The Inclusion of the Other: Studies in Political Theory*, Cambridge, MA: MIT Press.

—— (1999). 'Bestiality and Humanity: A War on the Borders between Legality and Morality', *Constellations*, 6(3): 263–72.

—— (2001). *Postnational Constellation: Political Essays*, Cambridge: Polity.

—— (2003). 'Toward a Cosmopolitan Europe', *Journal of Democracy*, 14(4): 86–100.

Hacohen, M.H. (1999). 'Karl Popper, Jewish Identity and Central European Culture', *Journal of Modern History*, 71: 105–49.

Hannerz, Ulf (1990). 'Cosmopolitans and Locals in World Culture', in Mike Featherstone (ed.), *Global Culture: Nationalism, Globalization and Modernity*, London: Sage.

—— (1996). *Transnational Connections: Culture, People, Places*, London: Routledge.

Haqqi, S.A.H. (1984). 'Regionalism in Indian Politics', in *Working Papers* (Forty-third All-India Political Science Conference), 18–20 October, p. 31.

Haragopal, G. (1987). 'Dimensions of Regionalism, Nationality Question in Andhra Pradesh', Seminar Proceedings on Nationality Question in India, Pune: TDSS.

Hardgrave, Robert L. (August 1965). 'The Riots in Tamil Nadu', *Asian Survey*, 5(8): 402.

Harrington, Austin (2005). 'Introduction to Georg Simmel's Essay "Europe and America in World History"', *European Journal of Social Theory*, 8(1): 63–72.

Harris, Lee (2003). 'The Cosmopolitan Illusion', *Policy Review*, 118: 45–60.

Hayden, P. (2005). *Cosmopolitan Global Ethics*, Aldershot: Ashgate.

Heater, Derek (1999). *What is Citizenship?* Cambridge: Polity Press.

—— (2000). 'Does Cosmopolitan Thinking have a Future?', *Review of International Studies*, 26 (5): 179–97.

—— (2002). *World Citizenship: Cosmopolitan Thinking and its Opponents*, London and New York: Continuum.

Held, David (1995a). *Cosmopolitan Democracy*, Cambridge: Polity Press.

—— (1995b). *Democracy and the Global Order: From the Modern State to Cosmopolitan Governance*, Stanford, CA: Stanford University Press.

—— (2003). 'Cosmopolitanism: Taming Globalization', in David Held and Anthony McGrew (eds.), *The Global Transformations Reader: An Introduction to the Globalization Debate*, Cambridge: Polity Press, pp. 514–29.

Held, David, A.G. McGrew, D. Goldblatt and J. Perraton (1999). *Global Transformations*, Cambridge: Polity Press.

Herrmann, R.K., T. Risse and M.B. Brewer (eds) (2004). *Transnational Identities: Becoming European in the EU*, New York: Rowman and Littlefield.

Hill, Lisa (2000). 'The Two Republicae of the Roman Stoics: Can a Cosmopolite be a Patriot?', *Citizenship Studies*, 4(1): 65–79.

Hintze, Hedwig (1924). 'Regionalism', *Encyclopaedia of Social Sciences*, Vol. XIII, New York: Macmillan, pp. 208–18.

Honneth, Axel (2004). 'Organized Self-Realization: Some Paradoxes of Individualization', *European Journal of Social Theory*, 7(4): 463–78.

http://www.ghmc.gov.in

http://hyderabad-india-online.com

http://www.hyderabadmetrorail.in/home.html

http://www.india-seminar.com/2008/

http://www.hyderabad.co.uk

http://www.census2011.co.in/census/district/122-hyderabad.html

http://www.apind.gov.in/library/district/hyderabad

http://www.hyd.co.in/government/

http://censusindia.gov.in/2011

Humayun, Afrin (2012). 'Gods of Small and Big Things', *Hyderabad Times*, 22 September.

Hutchinson, J. (2005). *Nations as Zones of Conflict*, London: Sage.

Ignatieff, Michael (2000). 'Human Rights as Politics and Human Rights as Idolatry', The Tanner Lectures, Princeton University.

Inglehart, R. (1977). *The Silent Revolution: Changing Values and Political Styles among Western Publics*, Princeton, NJ: Princeton University Press.

—— (1990). *Culture Shift in Advanced Industrial Society*, Princeton, NJ: Princeton University Press.

—— (1997). *Modernization and Postmodernization: Cultural, Economic, and Political Change in 43 Societies*, Princeton, NJ: Princeton University Press.

Inglehart, R. and W.E. Baker (2000). 'Modernization, Cultural Change and the Persistence of Traditional Values', *American Sociological Review*, 65(1): 19–51.

Inglehart, R. and C. Welzel (2005). 'Exploring the Unknown: Predicting the Responses of Publics Not Yet Surveyed', *International Review of Sociology*, 15(1): 173–201.

Irschick, Eugene F. (1969). *Politics and Social Conflict in South India: The Non-Brahmin Movement and Tamil Separation*, Bombay: Oxford University Press.

Jaisi, Sidq (2004). *The Nocturnal Court: The Life of a Prince of Hyderabad*, trans. Narendra Luther, Oxford: Oxford University Press

Joas, Hans (2003). *War and Modernity*, Cambridge: Polity.

Jones, D.M. (2001). *The Image of China in Western, Social and Political Thought*, Basingstoke: Palgrave.

Joshi, Ram (December 1970). 'The Shiv Sena: A Movement in Search of Legitimacy', *Asian Survey*, 10(11): 908.

Kada, Vedasri (2012). 'Of Minarets, Towers, Spires and High Rises', *Hyderabad Times*, 22 September.

Kant, Immanuel (1968a). *Critique of Pure Reason*, London: Macmillan.

—— (1968b). 'Idee zu einer allgemeinen Geschichte in weltbürgerlicher Absicht', in W. Weischedel (ed.), *Werkausgabe*, Vol. XI, Frankfurt am Main: Suhrkamp.

—— (1968c). 'Kritik der Urteilskraft', in W. Weischedel (ed.), *Werkausgabe*, Vol. X, Frankfurt am Main: Suhrkamp.

—— (1968d). 'Die Metaphysik der Sitten', in W. Weischedel (ed.), *Werkausgabe*, Vol. VIII, Frankfurt am Main: Suhrkamp.

—— (1968e). 'Zum ewigen Frieden. Ein philosophischer Entwurf', in W. Weischedel (ed.), *Werkausgabe*, Vol. XI, Frankfurt am Main: Suhrkamp.

—— (1973). *Critique of Pure Reason*, London: The Macmillan Press.

—— (1991 and 1999). *Political Writings*, Cambridge: Cambridge University Press.

Kanter, Rosabeth Moss (1995). *World Class: Thriving Locally in the Global Economy*, London: Simon and Schuster.

Kateb, George (1999). 'Can Cultures be Judged? Two Defenses of Cultural Pluralism in Isaiah Berlin's Work', *Social Research*, 66(4): 1009–38.

Kaufmann, J.C. (1994). *Schmutzige Wäsche*, Konstanz: Universitätsverlag.

Keane, John (2003). *Global Civil Society?* Cambridge: Cambridge University Press.

Keating, M. (1988). *State and Regional Nationalism: Territorial Politics and the European State*, Hemel Hempstead: Harvester Wheatsheaf.

Kendall, G.I., Woodward & Z. Skrbis (2008). 'The Sociology of Cosmopolitanism: Globalization Identity Culture and Govt. London: Palgrave, Macmillan.

Khan, Rasheedudin (1970). 'Political and Socio-Cultural Determinants of Federalism', in K.R. Bombwall (ed.), *National Power and State Autonomy*, New Delhi: Meenakshi, p. 110.

Kiuchi, S. and T. Ishimizu (1963). 'Some Aspects of Urbanization and Metropolitanization in Japan', Papers and Proceedings of the Regional Science Association, Tokyo, Vol. 1, September, p. 280.

Kleingeld, Pauline (1999). 'Six Varieties of Cosmopolitanism in Late Eighteenth-Century Germany', *Journal of the History of Ideas*, 60: 505–24.

Kleingeld, Pauline and Eric Brown (2011). 'Cosmopolitanism', in Edward N. Zalta (ed.), *The Stanford Encyclopedia of Philosophy*, Spring 2011 Edition, http://plato.stanford.edu/archives/spr2011/entries/cosmopolitanism

Knutsen, O. (1989). 'The Priorities of Materialist and Post-Materialist Values in the Nordic Countries: A Five-Nation Comparison', *Scandinavian Political Studies*, 12: 221–43.

—— (1990). 'Materialist and Postmaterialist Values and Social Structures in the Nordic Countries', *Comparative Politics*, 22: 85–104.

Kohli, Atul (1988). 'The NTR Phenomenon in Andhra Pradesh: Political Change in a South Indian State', in G. Delanty and K. Kumar (eds.), *The Sage Handbook of Nations and Nationalism*, London: Sage.

Krebs, D. (1992). 'Werte in den alten und neuen Bundesländern', in J. Zinnecker (ed.), *Im Spiegel der Wissenschaften*, Opladen: Leske und Budrich, pp. 35–48.

Kristeva, Julia (1991). *Strangers to Ourselves*, London: Harvester Wheatsheaf.

Kurasawa, F. (2004). 'Cosmopolitanism from Below: Alternative Globalization and the Creation of a Solidarity without Bounds', *European Journal of Sociology*, XLV(2): 233–55.

Kymlicka, W. and B. He (eds.) (2005). *Multiculturalism in Asia*, Oxford: Oxford University Press.

Larraín, Jorge (1979). *The Concept of Ideology*, London: Hutchinson.

Lasch, Christopher (1995). *The Revolt of the Elites and the Betrayal of Democracy*, London: W.W. Norton.

Lash, S. (2002). 'Foreword: Individualization in a Non-linear Mode', in U. Beck and E. Beck-Gernsheim, *Individualization*, London: Sage.

Latif, Bilkis (2008). The Soul of Hyderabad. http://www.india-seminar.com

Latour, B. (2001). *Das Parlament der Dinge: Naturpolitik*, Frankfurt/M.: Suhrkamp.

—— (2002). 'Is Remodernization Occurring – and, if so, How to Prove It?', *Theory, Culture and Society* (forthcoming).

Lavenex, S. (2004). 'EU External Governance in "Wider Europe"', *Journal of European Public Policy*, 11(4): 680–700.

Lawson, S. (2003). *Europe and Asia-Pacific: Culture, Identity, and Representations of a Region*, London: Routledge.

Leonard, Karen (2007). *Locating Home: India's Hyderabadis Abroad*, Stanford: Stanford University Press.

Levy, D. and N. Sznaider (2001). *Erinnerung im globalen Zeitalter: Der Holocaust*, Frankfurt/M.: Suhrkamp.

Levandowski, Susan (1980). *Migration and Ethnicity in Urban India*, New Delhi: Manohar, p. 204.

Lukes, Steven (1973). *Emile Durkheim: His Life and Work*, London: Penguin.

Luther, Narendra (2008). Bridging Two Cultures. http://www.india-seminar.com

MacIntyre, Alasdair (1981). *After Virtue: A Study in Moral Theory*, London: Duckworth.

—— (1995). 'Is Patriotism a Virtue?', in Ronald Beiner (ed.), *Theorizing Citizenship*, Albany: State University of New York Press, pp. 209–28.

Majeed, Akhtar (1978). 'Maldevelopment and Sub-regional Tensions', *Indian Journal of Politics*, December, p. 206.

—— (1984). *Regionalism: Developmental Tensions in India*, New Delhi: Cosmo Publications.

Markandey, Kalpana (1986). *Regional Urban Centres: Structure and Interaction*, New Delhi: Inter-India Publications.

Marx, Karl and Friedrich Engels (1932). *The German Ideology*, London: Lawrence & Wishart.

—— (1976). 'Manifesto of the Communist Party', in K. Marx and F. Engels, *Collected Works*, Vol. 6, London: Lawrence & Wishart.

Marx, Karl (1973). *Grundrisse*, London: Penguin.

—— (1978). *The Marx-Engels Reader*, R. Tucker (ed.), London: W.W. Norton.

Mazlish, Bruce (2005a). 'Roudometof: A Dialogue', *Current Sociology*, 53(1): 137–41.

—— (2005b). 'The Global and the Local', *Current Sociology*, 53(1): 93–111.

Mazzini, G. (1961). *The Duties of Man and Other Essays*, trans. T. Jones, London: J.M. Dent.

McCrone, D. (2001). *Understanding Scotland: The Sociology of a Stateless Nation*, London: Routledge.

McCutcheon, A.L. (1987). *Latent Class Analysis: Quantitative Applications in the Social Sciences Series*, London: Sage.

McDonald, Kevin (2004). 'Oneself as Another: From Social Movement to Experience Movement', *Current Sociology*, 52(4): 575–93.

Meadow, R.H. (1973). 'A Chronology for the Indo-Iranian Borderlands and Southern Baluchistan 4000–2000 B.C.', in D.P. Agrawal and A. Ghosh (eds.), *Radio-carbon and Indian Archaeology*, Bombay: Tata Institute of Fundamental Research, pp. 190–91.

Mehta, Pratap Bhanu (2000). 'Cosmopolitanism and the Circle of Reason', *Political Theory*, 28(5): 619–39.

Mehta, A. (1961). 'The Future of Indian Cities: National Issues and Goals', cf. R. Turner (ed.), *India's Urban Future*, California: University of California, p. 417.

Meinecke, F. (1917). *Weltbürgertum und Nationalstaat: Studien zur Genesis des deutschen Nationalstaates*, Munich: R. Oldenbourg.

—— (1970). *Cosmopolitanism and the National State*, Princeton, NJ: Princeton University Press.

Meisner, M. (1967). *Li Ta-chao and the Origins of Chinese Marxism*, Cambridge, MA: Harvard University Press.

Melkote, Rama S., E. Revathi, K. Lalita, K. Sajaya and A. Suneetha (2010). 'The Movement for Telangana: Myth and Reality', *Economic and Political Weekly*, XLV(2).

Merton, Robert K. (1968). *Social Theory and Social Structure*, New York: The Free Press.

Meyer, John W., John Bol, George M. Thomas and Francisco O. Ramirez (1997). 'World Society and the Nation–State', *The American Journal of Sociology*, 103(1): 144–81.

Milward, A. (1993). *The European Rescue of the Nation–State*, London: Routledge.

Mishra, Lokenath (December 1955). Debates on the Report of the State's Re-organization Commission, Vol. 1, Col. 647, New Delhi: Lok Sabha Secretariat.

Miyoshi, M. and H. Harootunian (eds) (1989). *Postmodernism and Asia*, Durham, NC: Duke University Press.

Mol, A. and J. Law (1994). 'Regions, Networks and Fluids: Anaemia and Social Topology', *Social Studies of Science*, 24: 641–71.

Morris-Jones, W.H. (1967). 'Language and Religion within the Indian Union', in Philip Mason (ed.), *India and Ceylone: Unity and Diversity*, Bombay: Oxford University Press, pp. 51–52.

Narain, Iqbal (1976). 'Cultural Pluralism, National Integration and Democracy', *Asian Survey*, 16(10): 907.

Nash, K. (2003). 'Cosmopolitan Political Community: Why Does it Feel So Right?', *Constellations*, 10(4): 506–18.

Nederveen Pieterse, J. (2006). 'Emancipatory Cosmopolitanism: Towards an Agenda', *Development and Change*, 37(6): 1247–57.

Nehru, Jawaharlal (1946). *The Discovery of India*, New York: Doubleday.

Nietzsche, F. (1910). *Human, All-Too-Human*, London: Foulis.

Nussbaum, Martha C. (1996). *For Love of Country: Debating the Limits of Patriotism*, Boston, MA: Beacon Press.

—— (2002). 'Education for Citizenship in an Era of Global Connection', *Studies in Philosophy and Education*, 21: 289–303.

—— (2003). 'Genocide in Gujarat: The International Community Looks Away', *Dissent*, 50 (Summer): 15–23.

Olofsson, A. and S. Öhman (2006). 'General Beliefs and Environmental Concern: Transatlantic Comparisons', *Environment and Behavior*, 38(6): 768–90.

Onuma, Y. (2007). 'A Transcivilisational Perspective on Global Issues in the Twenty-First Century', in J. Helen (ed.), *Civil Society, Religion and Global Governance*, New York: Routledge.

Ong, A. (1999). *Flexible Citizenship: The Cultural Logics of Transnationality*, Durham: Duke University Press.

Oommen, T.K. (2004). 'Socio-Political Transition in the Indian Republic and the European Union', *European Journal of Social Theory*, 7(4): 519–37.

Outhwaite, W. (2008). *European Society*, Cambridge: Polity Press.

—— (2006). *The Future of Society*, Oxford: Blackwell.

Pagden, Anthony (2000). 'Stoicism, Cosmopolitanism and the Legacy of European Imperialism', *Constellations*, 7(1): 3–22.

Palonen, Kari (2001). 'Was Max Weber a "Nationalist"? A Study in the Rhetoric of Conceptual Change', *Max Weber Studies*, 2(1): 196–214.

Pant, A.D. (1984). 'Introduction', in Akhtar Majeed (ed.), *Regionalism: Developmental Trends in India*, New Delhi: Cosmo Publications, p. 23.

Park, R.E. (1928). *The Marginal Man*, Chicago, IL: University of Chicago Press.

Parsons, T. (1937). *The Structure of Social Action*, New York: McGraw-Hill.

—— (1971). *The System of Modern Societies*, Englewood Cliffs, NJ: Prentice Hall.

Pasupulate, Karthik (2012). 'Hum Aiseich Hai', *Hyderabad Times*, 22 September.

Pels, Dick (2000). *The Intellectual as Stranger: Studies in Spokespersonship*, London: Routledge.

Pichler. F. (2008). 'How real is cosmopolitanism in Europe?' Sociology 42(6); 1107–26.

Pieterse, J. (2006). 'Emancipatory Cosmopolitanism: Towards an Agenda', *Development and Change*, 37(6): 1247–57.

Piggot, Stuart (1961). *Prehistoric India to 1000 B.C.*, New York: Penguin Press, p. 22.

Poggi, Gianfranco (2000). *Durkheim*, Oxford: Oxford University Press.

Pollock, S. (2002). 'Cosmopolitan and Vernacular in History', in C.A. Breckenridge et al. (eds.), *Cosmopolitanism*, Durham, NC: Duke University Press, pp. 15–53.

Pollock, S., H.K. Bhabha, C.A. Breckenridge and D. Chakrabarty (2000). 'Cosmopolitanisms', *Public Culture*, 12(3): 577–90.

Pollini, G. (2005a). 'Socio-Territorial Belonging in a Changing Society', *International Review of Sociology*, 15(3): 493–96.

—— (2005b). 'Elements of a Theory of Place Attachment and Socio-Territorial Belonging', *International Review of Sociology*, 15(3): 497–515.

Prasad, Dharmendra (1986). *Social and Cultural Geography of Hyderabad City: A Historical Perspective*, New Delhi: Inter Alia Publications.

Preston, P. and J. Gilson (eds) (2001). *The European Union and East Asia*, Cheltenham: Edward Elgar.

Rabinow, P. (1996). *The Anthropology of Reason*, Princeton, NJ: Princeton University Press, p. 56.

Raj, Sheela (1987). *Medievalism to Modernism: Socio-Economic and Cultural History of Hyderabad – 1869–1911*, Bombay: Popular Prakashan.

Ramchandran, Priya (2012). 'Hyderabad in a Cup', *Hyderabad Times*, 22 September.

Randeria, S. (1999). 'Jenseits von Soziologie und soziokultureller Anthropologie', *Soziale Welt*, 50(4): 373–82.

Rao, C.H. Hanumantha (2005). 'Budgetary Surpluses of Telangana', in *Essays on Development Strategy*, Hyderabad: Academic Foundation.

—— (2010). *Regional Disparities, Smaller States and Statehood for Telangana*, New Delhi: Academic Foundation, p. 125.

Rao, P. Padmanabha (1999). Urbanisation in Telangana and its Future Implications in Rao, Ram Mohan and S. Simhadri (eds) (1999) Indian Cities towards next Millennium. Jaipur: Rawat Publications.

Rao, Ram Mohan and S. Simhadri (eds) (1999). *Indian Cities: Towards Next Millennium*, Jaipur: Rawat Publications.

Rao, Narayana K.V. (1973). *The Emergence of Andhra Pradesh*, Bombay: Popular Prakashan.

Rao, S. Kishan and Rahul Shastry (2009). 'Telangana Surplus Revenue Issue: Imbalances in Expenditure/Resource Allocation Pattern', in *Andhra Pradesh Economy: Dynamics of Transformation with a Focus on Regional Disparities*, Hyderabad: National Academy of Development.

Ravi, S., M. Rutten and G. Beng-Lan (eds) (2004). *Asia in Europe: Europe in Asia*, Leiden: International Institute for Asian Studies.

Reddy, G. Ram and B.A.V. Sharma (1979). *Regionalism in India: A Study of Telangana*, New Delhi: Concept Publishing Company.

Report of the State's Re-organization Commission (1955). Delhi: Publication Division, p. 255.

Richardson, H.W. (1972). 'Optimally in City Size, System of Cities and Urban Policy: A Sceptic's View', *Urban Studies*, 9(1): 38.

Robertson, R. (1992). *Globalization: Social Theory and Global Culture*, London: Sage.

Robbins, B. (1998). 'Comparative Cosmopolitanisms', in P. Cheah and B. Robbins (eds.), *Cosmopolitics: Thinking and Feeling Beyond the Nation*, Minneapolis and London: University of Minnesota Press, pp. 246–64.

Robinson, D. (2005). 'The Search for Community Cohesion: Key Themes and Dominant Concepts of the Public Policy Agenda', *Urban Studies*, 42(8): 1411–28.

Rosenberg, J. (2000). *The Follies of Globalization Theory*, London: Verso.

Rosenfeld, Sophia A. (2002). 'Citizens of Nowhere in Particular: Cosmopolitanism, Writing, and Political Engagement in Eighteenth-Century Europe', *National Identities*, 4(1): 25–43.

Roudometof, V. (1999). 'Nationalism, Globalisation, Eastern Orthodoxy: Unthinking the "Clash of Civilizations" in South-Eastern Europe', *European Journal of Social Theory*, 2(2): 233–47.

—— (2003). 'Glocalization, Space and Modernity', *The European Legacy*, 8(1): 37–60.

—— (2005a). 'Transnationalism, Cosmopolitanism and Globalization', *Current Sociology*, 53(1): 113–35.

—— (2005b). 'Response: The Moral Conundrums of the Global Age', *Current Sociology*, 53(1): 143–47.

Rousseau, J.J. ([1766] 1997). 'Discourse on the Origin and the Foundations of Inequality among Men', in V. Gourevitch (ed. and trans.), *The Discourses and Other Political Writings*, Cambridge: Cambridge University Press.

Roy, N.C., Usha Mehta and S.P. Aiyar (eds) (1965). *The Growth of Linguistic States in Indian Federalism*, Bombay: Allied Publishers, p. 215.

Rumford, C. (ed.) (2006). *Cosmopolitanism and Europe*, Liverpool: Liverpool University Press.

Sarma, Rani (2008). *The Deodis of Hyderabad: A Lost Heritage*, Delhi: Rupa.

Sassen, S. (1991). *The Global City: New York, London, Tokyo*, Princeton, NJ: Princeton University Press.

—— (1998). *Globalization and its Discontents*, New York: New Press.

—— (2000). 'New Frontiers Facing Urban Sociology at the Millennium', *British Journal of Sociology*, 51(1): 143–60.

Scheffler, S. (1999). 'Conceptions of Cosmopolitanism', *Utilitas*, 11(3).

Schermerhorn, R.A. (1978). *Ethnic Plurality in India Arizona*, Arizona: University of Arizona Press, p. 15.

Schrader-Klebert, Karin (1968). 'Der Begriff der Gesellschaft als regulative Idee', *Soziale Welt*, 19: 97–118.

Schlereth, Thomas J. (1977). *The Cosmopolitan Ideal in Enlightenment Thought*, Notre Dame, IN: University of Notre Dame Press.

Schluchter, Wolfgang (1996). *Paradoxes of Modernity: Culture and Conduct in the Theory of Max Weber*, Stanford, CA: Stanford University Press.

Schmitt, C. (1996). *The Concept of the Political*, Chicago: University of Chicago Press.

Schütz, Alfred (1944). 'The Stranger: An Essay in Social Psychology', *The American Journal of Sociology*, 49(6): 499–507.

Schwartz, B. (1985). *The World of Thought in Ancient China*, Cambridge, MA: Harvard University Press.

Selig, Harrison (1960). *India: The Most Dangerous Decades*, Madras: Oxford University Press, p. 9.

Sennett, Richard (1998). *The Corrosion of Character*, New York: Norton.

Shah, N. (2006). 'Cosmopolitanizing and Decosmopolitanizing Globalization: Metaphorical Re-description and Transformations of Political Community', *Globalizations*, 3(3): 393–411.

Shaw, M. (2000). 'Historical Sociology and the Global Transformation', in R. Parlan (ed.), *Global Political Economy*, London and New York: Routledge, pp. 229–41.

Sharma, Jyotirmayi (2008). Shahar baaki hai Mohabbat ke nishaan baki hai. http://www.india-seminar.com

Sherwani, H.K. (1967). *Muhammad Quli Qutub Shah: Founder of Hyderabad*, Bombay: Asia Publishing House.

Shriram, Maheshwari (1973). 'Regionalism in India: Political and Administrative Response', *Indian Journal of Public Administration*, October-December, 442.

Simmel, G. (1909). 'The Problem of Sociology', *American Journal of Sociology*, 15(3): 289–320.

—— (1949). 'The Sociology of Sociability', *American Journal of Sociology*, 55(3): 254–61.

—— (1950). 'The Stranger', in K.H. Wolff (ed.), *The Sociology of Georg Simmel*, New York: The Free Press, pp. 402–08.

—— (1994). 'The Problem of Sociology', in D. Frisby (ed.), *Georg Simmel: Critical Assessments*, Vol. 1, London: Routledge.

—— (2004). *The Philosophy of Money*, London: Routledge.

Skrbis, Z., G. Kendall and I. Woodward (2001). 'Locating Cosmopolitanism: Between Humanist Ideas and Grounded Social Category', *Theory, Culture and Society*, 21(6): 115–36.

Smelser, Neil (1997). *Problematics of Sociology*, Berkeley: University of California Press.

Smith, Anthony (2003). 'Towards a Global Culture?', in David Held and Anthony McGrew (eds), *The Global Transformations Reader: An Introduction to the Globalization Debate*, Cambridge: Polity Press, pp. 278–86.

Somerville, John (1981). 'Patriotism and War', *Ethics*, 91(4): 568–78.

Spencer, Metta (ed.) (1998). *Separatism: Democracy and Disintegration*, Lanham, MD: Rowan & Littlefield, pp. 2–4.

Srinivas. M.N. (1962). Caste in Modern Indian and other Essays. London: Asia Publishing House.

Stedile, J.P. (2004). 'Brazil's Landless Battalions: The Sem Terra Movement', in T. Mertes (ed.), *A Movement of Movements: Is Another World Really Possible?* New York: Verso.

Stevenson, N. (2002). *Cultural Citizenship: Cosmopolitan Questions*, Buckingham: Open University Press.

Stohr, Walter B. (1974). 'Inter Urban Systems and Regional Economic Development', Commission on College Geography, Resource Paper No. 26, Washington, DC: Association of American Geographers, p. 21.

Strange, S. (1996). *The Retreat of the State*, Cambridge: Cambridge University Press.

Subramanyam, S. (2003). 'Regional Disparities: Causes and Remedies', in C.H. Hanumantha Rao and S. Mahendra Dev (eds.), *Andhra Pradesh Development Economic Reforms and Challenges Ahead*, Hyderabad: Centre for Economic and Social Studies.

Sumner, William Graham (1979). *Folkways*, New York: Arno Press.

Swedberg, Richard (2003). 'The Changing Picture of Max Weber's Sociology', *Annual Review of Sociology*, 29: 283–306.

Szerszynski, Bronislaw and John Urry (2002). 'Cultures of Cosmopolitanism', *Sociological Review*, 50(4): 461–81.

Tan, K.C. (2004). *Justice without Borders: Cosmopolitanism, Nationalism and Patriotism*, Cambridge: Cambridge University Press.

Therborn, G. (1995). 'Route to/through Modernity', in M. Featherstone, S. Lash and R. Robertson (eds), *Global Modernities*, London: Sage, pp. 724–39.

—— (2000). 'At the Birth of Second Century Sociology: Times of Reflexivity, Spaces, and Nodes of Knowledge', *British Journal of Sociology*, 51(1): 37–57.

—— (2006). 'Post-Western Europe and the Plural Asias', in G. Delanty (ed.), *Europe and Asia Beyond East and West*, London: Routledge, pp. 24–44.

Thompson, W.R. (1965). 'Urban Economic Growth and Development in a National System of Cities', cf. P.M. Hauser and L.F. Schnore, *The Study of Urbanization*, New York: John Wiley, p. 139.

Toulmin, Stephen (1990). *Cosmopolis: The Hidden Agenda of Modernity*, Chicago: The University of Chicago Press.

Tomlinson, J. (1999). *Globalisation and Culture*, Cambridge: Polity Press.

Turner, B.S. (2000). 'Liberal Citizenship and Cosmopolitan Virtue', in A. Vandenberg (ed.), *Citizenship and Democracy in a Global Era*, London: Macmillan.

—— (2002). 'Cosmopolitan Virtue, Globalization and Patriotism', *Theory, Culture and Society*, 19(1–2): 45–63.

—— (2006). 'Classical Sociology and Cosmopolitanism: A Critical Defence of the Social', *British Journal of Sociology*, 57(1): 133–55.

Turner, Charles (1992). *Modernity and Politics in the Work of Max Weber*, London: Routledge.

Urry, John (2000). *Sociology Beyond Societies*, London: Routledge.

Varshney, Ashutosh (2003). *Ethnic Conflict and Civic Life*, New Haven: Yale University Press.

Vedantam, T. (1971). A Monograph on Muharram in Hyderabad City, Census of India.

Vertovec, Steven and Robin Cohen (2003). *Conceiving Cosmopolitanism: Theory, Context and Practice*, Oxford: Oxford University Press.

Wagner, Peter (2001). *A History and Theory of the Social Sciences*, London: Sage.

Waldron, J. (1995). 'Minority Cultures and the Cosmopolitan Alternative', in W. Kymlicka (ed.), *The Rights of Minority Cultures*, Oxford: Oxford University Press, pp. 93–119.

Wallace, W. (1999). 'The Sharing of Sovereignty: The European Paradox', *Political Studies*, 47(3): 503–21.

Walzer, Michael (1983). *Spheres of Justice: A Defense of Plurality and Equality*, New York: Basic Books.

Weber, Max (1949). *The Methodology of the Social Sciences*, New York: The Free Press.

—— (2001). *The Protestant Ethic and the Spirit of Capitalism*, London: Routledge.

Weiner, Myron (1978). *Sons of the Soil: Migration and Ethnic Conflict in India*, Bombay: Oxford University Press, p. 285.

Wheeler, Nicholas J. (2003). *Saving Strangers: Humanitarian Intervention in International Society*, Oxford: Oxford University Press.

Wrong, Dennis (1961). 'The Oversocialized Conception of Man', *The American Sociological Review*, 26: 184–93.

Yu-lan, Fung (1973). *A History of Chinese Philosophy*, Vol. 2, 7th Edition, Princeton, NJ: Princeton University Press.

Zhang, W. (ed.) (1998). *Dialogue between the Dalai Lama and Han Chinese*, Washington: Foundation for China in the 21st Century.

Zubrzycki, John (2006). *The Last Nizam: An Indian Prince in the Australian Outback*, Australia: Pan Macmillan.

Index